THE COMMON EU MARITIME TRANSPORT POLICY

The Common EU Maritime Transport Policy

Policy Europeanisation in the 1990s

ATHANASIOS A. PALLIS

Ashgate

Published by
Ashgate Publishing Limited
Gower House
Croft Road
Aldershot
Hampshire GU11 3HR
England

Ashgate Publishing Company
131 Main Street
Burlington, VT 05401-5600 USA

Ashgate website: http://www.ashgate.com

British Library Cataloguing in Publication Data
Pallis, Athanasios A.
   The common EU maritime transport policy : policy
   Europeanisation in the 1990s. - (Transport and mobility
   series)
   1.European Union 2.Shipping - Government policy - European
   Union countries 3.Shipping - Government policy - European
   Union countries - History
   I.Title
   387.5'094'09049

Library of Congress Control Number: 2001096480

ISBN 0 7546 1913 3

Printed in Great Britain by Antony Rowe Ltd, Chippenham, Wiltshire.

Contents

List of Figures and Tables

Figures

Tables

Foreword

Sectoral studies of policy development have in recent years proved very illuminating and informative about decision-making in the European Union. This study of maritime transport policy in the 1990s is among the best.

Maritime transport has traditionally been an area where international regulation has been the dominant shaper of policy. On the face of it, therefore, maritime transport is an unpromising candidate for the Europeanisation of policy-making. This study chronicles meticulously the stages by which the European Community (later the EU) has moved into the maritime transport policy field and has persuaded the key political actors of the merits of expanding the European policy dimension. The result is full of implications for European integration theory, lending strong support to 'new institutionalist' perspectives.

Alan Butt Philip
Jean Monnet Reader in European Integration
School of Management, University of Bath

Preface

This book sets out to investigate the factors that have determined the progress and development of the Common EU Maritime Transport Policy (CMTP) in the 1990s. The focus is on two policy areas that have been central stage throughout these years: the establishment of European Union (EU) policies on safe seas and shortsea shipping respectively.

In essence a study of policy Europeanisation, the volume concentrates on both the economic environment of maritime transport and the interaction of policy makers and organised interests during the EU policy-making process. The emphasis is on the ways that these factors account for why, when, and how, the specific common EU policy is developed.

The outcome is an explanatory model that focuses on the distinctive institutional dynamism of the EU without, however, being reductionist insofar as the other policy actors or the economic context are concerned. This model takes into account the vital role of the EU decision-making institutions within the policy-making process and, consequently, the advancement and content of EU level policies. Moreover, it stresses the critical mediation of the extant institutional framework on the activities of all the involved policy actors.

The contextual economic internationalisation and the ineffectual policy responses of the non-EU policy-making levels have provided the stimulus for discussing EU policy developments. But the progress of the CMTP is detailed by a dialectic relationship between national governments, interest groups, the EU institutions, and their ideas. Within this relationship the EU institutions play a decisive role. An internal EU policy arena with its own characteristics and complexity has grown considerably. Therein the development of the Common Maritime Transport Policy turns to a core part of European integration.

I need to express gratitude to all those without which completing this work would be an insurmountable task. Firstly, I would like to thank the several people whose advice, assistance, and time, to guide me to the depths of the phenomena under examination, have been sought and gratefully received. I am most indebted to Dr. Alan Butt Philip, for his intellectual inspiration and valuable guidance on fascinating theoretical paths. This book would be different if Ass. Pr. Constantinos Chlomoudis had not introduced me to the absorbing maritime transport world. His friendship and pressures to explore new research directions have been an invaluable inspiration. An award by the Hellenic European Community Studies Association has provided a critical motivation towards the publication of this work.

Finally, my dues and respect to my family, my mum, dad, Venetsiana, Alexia, for their love and support. Foremost, I owe much of this book to Valia for her love, patience, and faith. To each of them this book is dedicated.

List of Abbreviations

A	Austria
AMRIE	Alliance of Maritime Regional Interests in Europe
B	Belgium
BCS	British Chamber of Shipping
BIFA	British International Freight Association
BPA	British Ports' Association
BSC	British Shippers' Council
CENSA	Committee of European National Shipowners' Associations
CLECAT	European Liaison Committee of Freight Forwarders
CMTP	Common Maritime Transport Policy
CoR	Committee of the Regions
COREPER	Committee of Permanent Representatives
CTP	Common Transport Policy
CTWUEC	Committee of Transport Workers Unions in the EC
DG-III	Directorate General for Industry, European Commission
DG-VII	Directorate General for Transport, European Commission
DIS	Denmark International Shipping register
Dk	Denmark
DoT	Department of Transport, UK
DSA	Danish Shipping Association
dwt	dead weight tonnes
ECASBA	European Community Association of Ship-Broker Agents
ECJ	European Court of Justice
Ecosoc	Economic and Social Committee
ECSA	European Community Shipowners' Association
ECSC	European Coal and Steel Community
EP	European Parliament
ESC	European Shippers' Council
ESPO	European Sea Ports' Organisation
ETUC	European Trade Unions Committee
EU	European Union
Euros	European Register of Shipping
Fin	Finland
FoC	Flags of Convenience

Fr	France
GATT	General Agreement on Tariffs and Trade
Ger	Germany
GIS	German International Shipping register
Gr	Greece
grt	gross tonnes
HCS	Hellenic Chamber of Shipping
HSBA	Hellenic Ship-Brokers' Association
ICS	International Chamber of Shipping
ILO	International Labour Organisation
IMCO	Intergovernmental Maritime Consultative Organisation
IMO	International Maritime Organisation
Ir	Ireland
ISF	International Shipping Federation
ISM Code	International Safety Management Code
It	Italy
ITF	International Transport workers' Federation
Lux	Luxembourg
MAR	Madeira Registry of shipping
MARPOL	IMO Convention for the prevention of Maritime Pollution from ships
member state	A nation state which is member of the European Union
MEP	Member of the European Parliament
MIF	Maritime Industries Forum
MMM	Ministry of Mercantile Marine, Greece
MOU	Paris Memorandum of Understanding on Port State Control
NIMO	New International Maritime Order
NIS	Norwegian International Shipping registry
Nl	Netherlands
NUMAST	National Union of Marine & Shipping Transport Workers
OPA 90	Oil Pollution Act of 1990
PerRepsGR	Permanent Representation of Greece to the EU
PerRepsUK	Permanent Representation of the UK to the EU
PES	European Socialist Party
PI	Personal Interview
PLA	Port of London Authority
PNO	Panhellenic Seamen's Federation
PPA	Piraeus Port Authority
PPE	European Popular Party
Pr	Portugal
PSC	Port State Control

xi

QMV	Qualified Majority Vote
R&D	Research and Development
Ro/ro	Roll-on/Roll-off passenger ferries
SBT tankers	Tankers equipped with Segregated Ballast Tanks
SEM	Single European Market
SOLAS	IMO Convention on Safety of Life at Seas Convention
Sp	Spain
STCW	IMO Convention on Standards of Training, Certification and Watchkeeping for seafarers
Sw	Sweden
TENs	Trans-European transport Networks
TEU	Treaty of the European Union
UGS	Union of Greek Shipowners
UK	United Kingdom
UKAPTO	UK Association of Private Terminal Ports
UKMPG	UK Major Ports Group
UN	United Nations
UNCLOS	United Nations Convention on the Law Of the Sea
UNCTAD	United Nations Conference on Trade and Development
UNCTAD Code	UNCTAD Code of Conduct for Liner Conference

1 Setting the Scene

Since the completion of the Single European Market (SEM) the ratification of the Maastricht Treaty of the European Union (TEU), and the Treaties of Amsterdam and Nice, European integration has embarked on a new economic and political period. As the 'uniting of Europe' continues the politico-economic structures of the European Union (EU)[1] and its member states are vastly transformed. While monetary integration is part of the agenda, perceived with a mixture of hope and trepidation, common EU policies are developed in an attempt to give regional answers to sectoral (meso) economic problems.

One of the latter cases is the Common Maritime Transport Policy (CMTP). Since 1974 the European Union constitutes an additional supranational policy-making jurisdiction in the field of maritime transport. The first attempt to introduce a cohesive EU maritime transport policy took place in 1986. In recent years, the scope and depth of the particular EU policy have widened. Even though collective policy solutions do not always arise, discussions have shifted from the minimalist approach, which did not endorse the need for common initiatives, towards the consideration of a comprehensive EU policy.

In fact, the maritime transport system has been a highly institutionalised and politicised economic sector. Precisely because of its strategic economic significance, national governments are performing as market (de)regulators, as well as maritime infrastructure investors and owners. International intergovernmental organisations are consistently involved in the life of the sector striving for global solutions to numerous issues. In addition, an extensive industrial self-regulation has been frequently in application.

Taking into account the very international character of maritime transportation, the contemporary economic environments, and the preceding policy-making traditions, how are we to explain the emerging movement towards the Europeanisation of the maritime transport system's institutional and regulatory framework? Which factors induce, determine, or decisively interfere with this trend? What decides the course and the changes of the EU Maritime Transport Policy in the 1990s?

These are the questions that this book addresses. To begin with, it takes the view that political variables have a definitive impact on the character and direction of a common EU policy. Of course, EU-level policies do respond to the economic context. However, to see them solely as a response to prevailing economic conditions or as the resolution of technical issues is an incomplete view. Policy-making is also a highly political process. Stakeholders, either associated in interest groups or acting independently, demand or reject certain policy initiatives. National governments attempt to drive the integrative process towards their political targets. EU institutions jockey for influence over policy developments. For reasons such as these, it is a major challenge to correctly conceptualise the policy development process, so as to identify the factors that most influence it.

The emphasis is on the political dimensions of developing the CMTP. This book concentrates on the ways that governmental or non-governmental policy actors and their ideas interact within the contemporary structure and dynamics of the EU policy-making game, how these factors account for *why*, *when*, and *how*, the specific common EU policy is developed. In Chapter 2 the theoretical aspects of the relationship between policy actors and the process of developing EU policies are explored. The synthesis of this body of literature provides the background on which an analytical framework for research is developed. In essence, by bringing the theoretical account of (historical) neoinstitutionalism into the analysis of the CMTP, this volume examines whether a concept that puts particular stress on the critical role of EU political institutions during the policy making process and, consequently, the advancement and content of EU level policies is valid, or not. Two issue-areas, the establishment and the progress of the common policies on safe seas and short-sea shipping respectively, are detailed to test this framework.

Before this, however, the introductory chapter has a twofold intention. Firstly, to highlight the strategic magnitudes of the maritime transport system for the enhancement of integrative benefits. Second, to frame the politico-economic setting within which the specific policy is examined, by providing background information regarding the sector's politicisation, and the different policy-making levels.

The Strategic Significance of Maritime Transport

Maritime transport is a genuine sector, economically and environmentally of strategic significance for the European economy. A basic infrastructure of trade and an important lever of economic development, effective seagoing transport is, in the words of an ex-Transport Commissioner, 'a vital support to the concept of the Single Market' (Clinton-Davis, 1994). The provision of competitive services by a EU-fleet, the efficient operation of the port industry, as well as the maintenance and modernisation of infrastructure and superstructure, guarantee quality transport services to exporters and importers, and increase the welfare benefits of transport users, producers, and society as a whole.

The sector is important in its own right primarily because it is the dominant mode of transport. In 1999, 1215 million tonnes or 70.8% of the trade between the EU member states and third countries (extra-EU trade) were transported by sea.[2] Seaborne trade between member states (intra-EU trade) reached 295 million tonnes, or 28.2% of the total. In the case of some Member States, the flow of maritime transport accounts for practically the total of their international trade. According to the latest data available (1996), international short-sea shipping accounts for 13% of the total combined transport traffic in Europe (in terms of tonne-kilometres), with an average short-sea distance of 800 kilometres per tonne. In addition, the national coastwise traffic within member states (cabotage trade) was 162.5 million tonnes and a significant volume of the deep-sea cargoes was transhipped between one European port and another (feeder trade). The EU of fifteen member states, which represents the biggest trade area of the world, is unmistakably a massive user of maritime transport services. With the progress from a Common Market towards a European Union being accompanied by substantial increases in both passenger and freight movements, the EU has a growing economy with the demand for transport growing at an even faster rate. An unchanged scenario foresees that the amount of goods loaded at EU maritime ports will increase to 3385 million tonnes by 2010, when in 1980 and 1993 these goods aggregated 1836 and 2300 million tonnes respectively (ESPO, 1995).

The controlling interest behind 33% of the world merchant fleet is located in terms of parent owner in an EU member state. Operating either under EU-flags or third non-EU flags (44% and 66% of the total EU-owned tonnage respectively in 1999) many of these vessels, are routinely involved in cross-trade, this is, the carriage of cargoes whose origin and destiny are non-EU countries. In aggregate, EU-owned ships transport a significant part of the steadily growing international seatrade. They do so by providing either liner or tramp services. The former suggests the operation on fixed routes by fixed time schedules, the latter the carriage of commodities on a voyage, a limited number of consecutive voyages, or a short-term basis.

The sector is an important employer, both at sea and ashore. In 1994, the EU shipping industry alone employed 161,859 officers and seafarers on EU-flagged vessels. Besides, almost 74,000 EU citizens were employed on EU-owned vessels operating under non-EU flags (CEU-DG VII, 1996a). In total, approximately 2.5 million people are employed in maritime related industries of the EU (Power, 1994). Furthermore, maritime services make a substantial contribution to the European economy through earnings of foreign currency. Directly these earnings are attained through freights, wages, and the provision of port facilities, while indirect contribution is added by the maritime related industries, including insurance, banking, shipbuilding, ship repairing, and legal activities. Two examples highlight the significance of this contribution. The shipping exchange inflow in Greece represents over 12% of the total invisible receipts of the country's Balance of Payments. In 1994, the net contribution of British shipping was $3.81 (US) billion with $1.6 (US) billion earned by the maritime related activities in the City of London (BCS, 1996). Overall, the shore-based turnover of the EU-flagging vessels is estimated to average US$ 43,720 per dwt (CEU-DG VII, 1996b). The ratio shore-based/ship-based value added to the EU economy is estimated to exceed 50/50, with about 44% of this added value flowing back to the public authorities in form of taxes and social contributions (Core Group, 1995). The size of the maritime transport sector's endowment cannot be disregarded.

Moreover, as an inseparable part of the EU transport system, the maritime mode is of apparent merit at micro, meso, and macro-economic levels. Within the SEM, an interaction between transport and the location of economic activities takes place as a two-way process: transport serves a given spatial distribution of activities, but differential developments of transport to suit market conditions in different locations affect the future development of these localisations (Vickerman, 1992). Undergoing changes in the industrial structure, most notably the move from basic industries to manufacturing, upgrade the relative importance of transport in localisation decisions. Transport costs, as well as the operation of fast, flexible, and high quality freight services, take on greater weight because industries are increasingly functioning in wider geographic areas, and increasingly adopting operating and production methods that are transport dependent. Transport becomes an input to production, either by carrying finished goods or increasingly, as the pace of integration spreads, moving inputs and intermediate goods. Through operation and cost changes, consumption, trade and production patterns may be earned.

The transport system is also critical to regional production potential. It improves the core-periphery relations and result in the development of the necessary links for the spatial and economic development within and between the regions, as well as in the diversion of the current traffic away from traditional routes and modes (Vickerman, 1994). Within the SEM European nations are transformed into open-access economies whereas the potential of some regions to become losers and others to become winners increases, therefore the momentousness of the factors that can endow the balanced regional development is upgraded. In the case of the maritime mode this is underlined by the economic geography of Europe. The fifteen member states alone include a substantial coastline, many islands, and large peninsulas. The unique EU port structure (the largest concentration of ports in the world) directly interlinks a considerable part of the territory and many industrial centres. Due to these characteristics, as well as the geopolitical developments in Europe, the expansion and effectiveness of intra-EU maritime trade enhance the continent's socio-economic cohesion. By providing essential links to islands and remote regions, maritime flows are a critical force of balanced regional development, especially as a considerable number of maritime regions are located in the less prosperous member states.

Positive linkages between transport provision and economic growth exist, though their precise quantification remains difficult. Scholars, who concentrate on the economic impacts and productivity effects of transport infrastructure, conclude that the efficient operation of the latter and the value of the services generated, in short transport itself, favour the growth of an economy as a whole (cf. Kessides, 1993). An adequate transport system is a *sine qua non* for modern economic development.[3] This relationship contains a non-cost dimension as well. A high quality transport system is a precondition for enabling the economy of a country or region to grow without encountering bottlenecks and thus to change its sectoral structure; increasing the spatial mobility of citizens and goods; offering the freedom of choice to use different modes according to the potential of each mode and the requirements of the respective goods shipped; increasing the efficiency of energy use; protecting the environment; and promote further social and economic co-operation on an international level (Blum, 1985).

The aforementioned economic merits are positively related to the progress of European integration. The cost effectiveness and reliability of transport undertakings are one of the most fundamental factors influencing the maximisation of the economic integration benefits. Briefly restated, the framework of the Custom Union theory (Viner, 1950; Meadey, 1955), which forms the basis of European economic integration, anticipates economic benefits in terms of trade creation and trade diversion in all stages of integration.[4] At the national level they derive from trade specialisation, at the regional level from geographical specialisation, at the micro level they are fundamental about maximising economies of scale. Increased trade has to be realised physically; therefore, efficient transport is required. Failing that, transportation remains a 'natural trade barrier' (Nielsen *et al*, 1992), which replaces tariffs as an obstacle to further specialisation.

Critical approaches to this branch of neo-classical economics do not lessen the significance of the sector (cf. Tsoukalis, 1993). What they consider differently is the pervasive role that public authorities are demanded to develop as regulators of the economic activities to achieve the integration targets, among them an efficient transport sector. Importantly, when capital resources are becoming increasingly mobile, economic activities are helped to face the competitive challenges when they take place in the most adequate 'framework conditions', the transport system being one of them (Gönenç, 1994). Its irrational development can interfere with and make inefficient any other measures of structural adjustment policies. To conclude, irrespective of whether the maritime mode is regarded as a self-contained economic sector, or a part of a wider transport system, there is no denying that it is an important component of economic life.

An Environmentally Friendly Transport Mode

The ever-growing economic imperative of maritime transport is strengthened by the fact that it is an environmentally friendly transport mode. Since the contemporary transportation process results in an accelerating deterioration in environmental quality, the objective of minimising and if possible avoiding altogether transport activity externalities, that is 'the unintended by-products of the transport activity itself that disbenefit third parties outside the customer-carrier relationship, including social and environmental costs' (Whitelegg, 1993, p. 127), is an addition to the objective of carrying goods and people at least cost. Hitherto, phenomena leading to the qualification of this activity as a force of environmental destruction (i.e. road congestion increased energy consumption, the greenhouse effect, and intensification of land consumption) cannot be solved without the achievement of a new equilibria between development, movement, land use planning, and the environment. A solution within the current split of the transport modal pie remains a long unsettled issue, and Europe's commitment to sustainable mobility involves the qualitative improvement of all types of transport, as well as a shift towards the environmentally friendly modes. By providing an environmentally benign alternative, seagoing transport results in qualitative benefits beyond those directly attributed to transport users. When the emphasis is on economic resources, maritime transport uses the sea as the right of way and apart from the port does not take much scarce space. Congestion can be circumscribed, energy efficiency could be achieved, and capacity is almost unlimited. Only one segment of the modal pie has the potential to be transported by the maritime mode, yet the promotion of the latter can bear decisive benefits to the society as a whole.

Still, maritime transport may harm the marine ecosystem. It does so through operation pollution in the form of intentional and routine discharges of dangerous or polluting goods in the case of accidents at sea and in ports. Moreover, shipping accidents often entail the loss of lives onboard. It is of strategic importance for the citizens of Europe to be served by maritime operations that are effective and competitive in terms of financial costs. But it is of equal importance that such services take place at a minimal risk for crews, passengers, cargoes, and vessels, and operate into the lowest costs for the marine environment and coastal activities.

A Politicised Economic Environment

Maritime transport is a sector characterised by a remarkably high degree of institutionalisation and politicisation. Motivated by particular market features, social pressures, and the presence of substantial externalities, policy makers act either nationally or internationally in order to control, or alter, the economically and politically undesirable effects that the 'difficult' market structure and behaviour may create (Baum, 1993). Along with national governments and international organisations, industrial self-regulation is also a common practice. Aspinwall (1995a) remarks that shipping represents a 'curious paradox' of being highly protected by national governments but being a highly internationalised industry. Frankel (1987) notes a paradox of a different kind: international shipping is one of the most and yet least regulated industries. Its design, manning, cargo handling, stowage and other technical and operational aspects are highly regulated. At the same time the industry is largely free of economic and management regulations.

Transport policy is a structure (brought about in some process) of ends, ways, means and points of time, chosen by an actor concerning the satisfaction of needs of movement of persons and goods with the help of a relevant system of means of production (Kuypers, 1980). Maritime policy is an element of such policy. It derives certain characteristics regarding basic principles, targets, and means, while it remains the instrument that deals with the peculiarities of the mode itself. Policy targets entail the creation of the conditions that each operator makes efficient use of the assets at his disposal; the protection of owners', employees', passengers', and shippers' interests; the efficiency of maritime undertakings, which verges upon the facts that the total amount of transport provided is adequate and the operations are concluded with the minimal of undesirable externalities or other 'shadow' social costs; and the co-ordination and balance of traffic between maritime and other transport modes. Furthermore, maritime policy deals with the state and regulatory framework of ports. Public authorities frequently act as investors, constructors, and operators, of maritime transport infrastructure, either because they consider the latter as public good or because they merely want to overcome the negative results of infrastructure undercapacity.[5]

Gwilliam (1980) propounds four dimensions within which such policies can be described and appraised. The administration under which the policy is developed, the style of the policy approach (i.e. comprehensive or incremental), the objectives of the policy, and the instruments used to achieve policy objectives. These dimensions are interdependent. The nature of the administration and its jurisdiction determine the objectives, which in turn affect the choice of the instrument and so on. Nonetheless, all the distinct public policies have the same qualitative, multidimensional, and partially incompatible ultimate objectives whereas policy makers evaluate differently the means to achieve them (Table 1.1).

Table 1.1 Objectives of Maritime Transport Policies

The system should be:	In reference to:
Adequate	Capacity, routes, and schedules.
Economic and efficient	Pricing, Investment, Operations
Equitable	Shippers, ports, and nations
	Ship operators and employees
Acceptable	Participants and users
Adaptable	Changing needs
Reliable	Safety, performance and predictability

Source: Based on Lawrence (1972, p. 202).

National Governments and Maritime Transport

Recognising the importance of maritime transport for the prosperity of their economies, national governments have prompted policies impinging upon the commercial or trading aspects of shipping. Hitherto, the nature of these actions varies in different periods and among states. Ledger (1993) classifies them in three main categories: freedom of the seas; anti-trust policies; and protectionism. Although Ledger's classification is somewhat schematic and does not permit a strict allocation of any policy to anyone of these groups, it facilitates the illustration of the various governmental attitudes regarding the sector under examination.

'Freedom of the seas' refers to policies following the shipping liberalism doctrine.[6] The main principle is that merchant fleets should provide services without any intervention of public bodies, governments or their agencies. Whilst the application of this framework has not been observed in the 20th century (see: Sturmey, 1962; Davies, 1992), controversies within the shipping industry have led to suggestions that the laissez-faire model of economic relations cannot be fully implemented in seagoing transport (Crzanowski, 1985).[7] Others conclude that the distinction between liberalism and interventionism in the maritime sector has a broader meaning than the dichotomy between free trade and protectionism that is commonly used. Tzoannos (1989, 1990), an advocate of shipping liberalism, uses the intervention in aspects of competition as the prominent supporting example of this argument. The scholar holds that the exercise of 'anti-trust' public intervention is inevitable and the lack of actions against certain formats of market practices (i.e. liner conferences that have been subject to governmental, international or self-regulatory controls since the 19th century) can be taken as a form of protectionism. To Goss (1977), the field of maritime safety represents another paradigm that works against the classical free trade/protectionism dichotomy. Historical evidence supports that with negligible or inadequate regulations the forces of free competition do not work to an optimal solution in respect of those who sail on ships, a fact that has advanced the regulatory presence of public authorities.

However, the establishment of widespread worldwide governmental involvement, and the consequent politicisation of the sector, are primarily the aftermath of the dominance of the 'shipping nationalism' philosophy (Farthing, 1993). In other words, both developing and traditional maritime nations look at shipping from their national perspective, as an international industry the maintenance of which can benefit them as trading nations or provide significant foreign exchange returns. Thus, they intrude in the market, either permanently or *ad hoc*, to maintain and improve the size and position of their national fleets. Sturmey (1975) provides one of the most detailed reviews of the motives that lead to governmental interventionism. His list encompasses the promotion and protection of a merchant fleet for defence purposes; the establishment of a fleet capable of transporting the country's essential trade; the satisfaction of national prestige; the promotion of an infant industry; the advancement of trade and communications between the country concerned and other countries; foreign exchange savings; the provision or maintenance of employment for national seafarers; the protection of the fleet in times of severe competition; the counter of actual or suspected discriminatory practices by liner conferences or national trade groups; the improvement of the quality and the increase of fleet competitiveness; and the compensation of national shipowners for overvalued exchange rates maintained for other purposes.

On these grounds several national policies prevent the exposure of shipowners or state companies to market forces. The means include the provision of subsidies to reduce the total costs of vessels' operation (investment finance assistance, tax allowance programmes, direct subsidies) as well as preferential treatment, that is, non-financial measures of shipping protectionism that promote national flag shipping activities by providing a secure cargo base. A widely used practice to guarantee the supply of, and demand for, maritime transport services by a national fleet is the unilateral total exclusion of foreign flags from internal trade in coastal waters, known as 'cabotage restriction'.

Maritime economists provide rather ambiguous conclusions regarding the economic necessity of these measures. Several scholars question their economic efficiency (cf. Shier *et al*, 1985; Branch, 1988; Goss and Marlow, 1992)[8] and argue for the benefits of the immediate or incremental establishment of shipping liberalism (Yannopoulos, 1989). Others are advocates of interventionism on pure economic grounds, emphasising the retaliatory effects of some of these practices, like cargo reservations (Lawrence, 1972; Crzanowski, 1985).[9] Research on their perception by the industry in Europe is equally inconclusive. Hart (1993) surveyed the perceptions of companies and organisations within the maritime industries in the UK, a country with rather strong commitment to shipping liberalism and found that 25% favoured more 'interventionism' and some forms of subsidies. As Ademuni (1988, p. 218) remarks, when these policies are welcomed, especially when they provide relief or constitute positive reactions from one's own government, they are referred to as 'intervention'. However, when similar policies are adopted by foreign governments or consist of supposedly negative reactions from domestic governments, they are interpreted simply as 'interference'.

Nevertheless, it remains indisputable that interventionist practices are extensively employed even by nations that proclaim the acceptance of shipping liberalism, including the EU member states. A historical overview provides evidence of the consistency and multiplicity of assistance that EU member states have supplied to their merchant fleets since 1914 (Table 1.2).[10] Irrespective of the rhetoric, all the European along with other developed maritime nations have been involved in attempts to maintain a critical size of national fleet. Aspinwall (1995a) accurately comments that in most developed states, a hybrid policy of protectionism and liberalism has been in place for several decades, the relative mix varying by country and incumbent government.

These 'pseudo-liberal' regimes have been explained as the outcome of the conflict between traditional maritime nations defending the *status quo* of international transport and nations wishing to change it, either in terms of labour division in shipping or dependence of trade transport (Cafruny,

1987). The vulnerability of international markets and the protective national policies of non-maritime nations have increased the active involvement of traditional maritime states in the affairs of shipping. In a different vein, Goss (1989) holds that maritime transport should be seen as part of the economy and not in isolation. The scholar goes on to question the sense that piecemeal sectoral liberalisation would have when other economic sectors are heavily protected and sheltered from world competition. In his view, exposing one sector to competition without at the same time removing the burdens imposed on it from the protection of other sectors may actually undermine its ability for competitive survival, even if that sector enjoys comparative advantage in a fully liberalised regime.

Table 1.2 A Historical Overview of Policy Practices in the EU Maritime States

	Operating subsidies			Indirect subsidies			State Fleet			Preferences excluding cabotage			Cabotage Restriction	Second / Offshore Registry
	1919-39	1945-62	1990	1919-39	1945-62	1990	1919-39	1945-62	1990	1919-39	1945-62	1990	1990	1990
B				✓	✓	✓	✓					❶		✓
Dk				✓	✓	✓			✓				✓	✓
Fin	✓			✓		✓								✓
Fr	✓	✓	✓	✓	✓		✓	✓	✓	✓	①②④	❶❷	✓	✓
Ger	✓			✓	✓	✓					✓	❶		✓
Gr	✓			✓	✓								✓	
It	✓	✓	✓	✓	✓	✓	✓	✓	✓	✓	①	❶	✓	
Nl	✓			✓		✓								✓
Pr	✓		✓	✓							✓ ①②④	❶❷		✓
Sp	✓	✓	✓	✓	✓	✓					✓ ①③	❶❷	✓	✓
Sw				✓	✓	✓							✓	
UK	✓			✓	✓	✓								✓

① Bilateral trade ② Cargo reservations and preferences ③ Exchange control preferences ④ Tax and harbour concessions.
❶ Cargo sharing ❷ Cargo reservations

Sources: Sturmey, 1962; Bredima Savopoulou, 1990; Tzoannos, 1990.

The Presence of International Intergovernmental Organisations

International organisations whose work ranges from advisory to policy-making, regulatory, implementary, or a combination of these functions compound a major part of the politicised framework within which maritime trade is realised. In line with the trend towards the development of international intergovernmental organisations throughout the twentieth century (cf. Armstrong, 1982), an international mechanism of authoritative organisations has been created since the end of the Second World War. The juxtaposition of the transboundary character of the maritime transport process, the dominance of shipping nationalism, and marker practices (i.e. registration patterns and liner conferences), has invented long-term interstate conflicts (see: Knudsen, 1973), in turn leading to a growing demand for the expansion of global policy responses that would respect the international character of maritime flows. Furthermore, safety, pollution prevention, and environmental protection have become legitimate international concerns as an impressive number of international conventions have been adopted.

The United Nations (UN; founded in 1945) has been an organisation responsible for important maritime conventions. This has happened either directly, i.e. the successive UN Conventions on the Law Of the Sea (UNCLOS), or through its specialised agencies. A leading example of the latter is the United Nations Conference on Trade and Development (UNCTAD; 1964), a forum for the expression of views and legislation on, among other things, shipping. UNCTAD has been involved, *inter alia*, in the global scale regulation of liner trade through the introduction of the Code of Conduct for Liner Conference (UNCTAD Code). It also deals with ports policy and planning, training of port and shipping staff, conditions of shipping registration, the shippers-shipowners relationship, and the conditions of service of seafarers. The International Labour Organisation (ILO; 1919) also has a long history towards the improvement of working standards and conditions. Its specialised Joint Maritime Transport Committee has developed many conventions and recommendations. As in any international organisation, whereas conventions intend to create binding obligations to put their provisions into effects, recommendations merely provide guidance on policy legislation and practice.

Probably the main international organisation is the International Maritime Organisation (IMO). Its prime objectives are the improvement of maritime safety and the prevention of marine pollution (therefore, its work is examined in Chapter 4). IMO is in fact the successor to the Intergovernmental Maritime Consultative Organisation (IMCO; 1948). The initial idea was of an organisation that would consider political and economic issues under the UN auspices. However, because powerful maritime nations from both sides of the Atlantic opposed the creation of meaningful organisations having jurisdictions over maritime affairs including business arrangements, labour markets, safety at sea, and pollution, IMCO was established to solely examine technical issues. It began operation in 1958 and changed name to IMO in 1982.

Each of these intergovernmental organisations plays a leading role in the regulation of the sector, a role that intensified remarkably during the 1970s and 1980s (Böhme, 1984; Frankel, 1987). Other international organisations, notably the World Trade Organisation, and the International Standards Organisation, also have an input into the policy framework,[11] while maritime transport is affected by the wider multilateral negotiations that influence the terms of merchandise international trade worldwide, predominantly the General Agreement on Tariffs and Trade (GATT) rounds (cf. Krommenacker, 1989). In this context, most countries have explicitly expressed their preference for laying down 'internationally agreed regulatory frameworks for an international industry' rather than see a variety of conflicting unilateral measures exist. Still, different ideological principles, economic priorities, or social values have hindered such agreements. Moreover, ratifying agreed international rules has been a lengthy process. For instance, the UNCTAD Code was adopted in 1974 but enforced in 1983, whilst the 1978 UNCTAD convention concerning shipowners liabilities in the case of lost or damaged cargoes (the 'Hamburg rules') only entered into force in 1992.

Industrial Self-Regulation Agreements

In the area of regulation the largely privately owned shipping operation has critically relied on self-regulation based on bilateral or multilateral agreements among parties in voluntary association with a minimum of government involvement. The international character of the industrial pattern has been the logical drive towards global associability and self-regulation (Ronit, 1995). The International Shipping Federation (ISF; 1909), and the International Chamber of Shipping (ICS; 1921) have been lobbying on behalf of shipowners for some decades, while more special shipowners interests have also been associated internationally in recent times (i.e. Intercargo and Intertanko representing dry cargo shipowners and independent tanker owners respectively). The interests of maritime labour are represented for more than a century by the International Transport Workers' Federation (ITF; 1896), whilst European shippers formed the regional European Shippers' Council (ESC) in 1963.

This context produced several agreements over time covering the needs and furthering the economic objectives of the participants. An illustrative example is the Note of Understanding, which was signed in 1965 by the ESC and the Committee of European National Shipowners' Associations (CENSA) to regulate liner trade. It happened only because an *ad hoc* committee of European national shipowners associations, the Japanese association, and a committee of European shipowners representing individual liner companies and international container consortia, had developed a reasonable working relationship with the ESC and agreed upon certain elements. This CENSA/ESC Code of practice for conference agreements was finally ratified and published in 1971. Similar self-regulatory examples are the numerous directly negotiated agreements between the ITF and its counterpart the ISF regarding training initiatives and working conditions at sea. In recent years, however (for reasons discussed in later stages of this volume) the record of self-regulatory agreement has been comparatively insignificant.

The Registration Issue

Registration rules, particularly the eminent economic results of the Flags of Convenience (FoC, also termed 'open registries') phenomenon, contribute substantially to the politicisation of the economic environment. Registration gives a nationality to a ship. Any coastal or landlocked nation state having a separate system of municipal law may issue national regulations concern the vessels operating under its flag, the flag-state principle. Several small, even non-maritime, countries have been taking advantage of this capability, as well as of the fact that ships are highly mobile assets, and offer several incentives to register ships under their flags. They allow easy registration access and transfer of ships owned and controlled by non-citizens, low taxation, manning rules that are free of nationality requirements, lower management costs, but also ineffective application of international regulations, either due to countries' wishes, or due to the absence of the power to apply them (Rochdale Report, 1970). These characteristics contrast with the traditional registries' requirements of ships to be owned, and/or managed, and manned by nationals of the flag-state. In other words, these flags offer shipowners the convenience to avoid fiscal, manning, and technical regulatory obligations that would have been applicable if their ships were registered under their home countries.

FoC shipping is a phenomenon dating back centuries; as Carlisle (1981) argues it is probably as old as the invention of the flag itself and the emergence of seafaring. Controversies have been escalated in modern years since ITF began an intensive campaign against the tax-free rules governing the Panama (in 1930s), Honduras, and Liberia (in 1950s) registries (the so-called PanHoLib campaign: cf. Argirofo, 1972). However, the years after the 1974 and 1978 oil crises marked the beginning of the 'golden era' of FoC shipping. Many shipowners responded to shipping depression (trade stagnation, unjustified expansion of world tonnage and, consequently, fall in freight rates) by exploiting the cost advantages of re-registering vessels under FoC and lowering the overall operating costs by approximately 30% (Yannopoulos, 1988). On the other hand, the massive flagging-out produced a rise of several new maritime nations. Small countries with no national fleets turn to flag-states having large merchant fleets that contribute significantly to their Balance of Payments.

The operation of a substantial number of vessels under FoC is today a structural characteristic of the world fleet. In the beginning of 1997, the ten major FoC share 48.3% of the world tonnage (Table 1.3) compare to 18.2% and 36.1% in 1970 and 1980 respectively. Depending on the modifications of the advantages offered by such registrations the flexible shipping capital is continuously redirected to new favourable jurisdictions. Panama and Liberia remain the major of them (and represent the two biggest flags of the world) but Honduras registry has virtually disappeared from the maritime map. New, previously less visible, FoC have increased their market shares through continuous offers. Among them are Cyprus and Malta, two prospective EU members representing the fifth and seventh biggest flags in the world respectively. Noteworthy, the listing and quantification of FoC shipping are in fact complex and subject to varying interpretations and definitions. To give an example, under the very old but modern in application 'bareboat charter' registration system a shipowner might for an agreed consideration turn over all the operations of a ship to a second company formed in a FoC country without transferring the ship to a foreign flag. The ship remains entered on the original register and the shipowner affords the best of both worlds.[12]

Table 1.3 Merchant Fleet Shares of the Ten Major FoC

	No of ships	1000 dwt	%-share of the world total (in dwt)
Panama	4579	120950	16.7
Liberia	1574	94803	13.1
Bahamas	1031	37062	5.1
Cyprus	1552	36761	5.1
Malta	1171	31614	4.4
Saint Vincent	793	9713	1.3
Marshall Islands	112	7928	1.1
Bermuda	77	5070	0.7
Antigua and Barbuda	508	2837	0.4
Vanuatu	99	1856	0.3

Source: ISL Databases.

As most FoC offer a substantial degree of freedom regarding ships' manning conditions, this structural change has lead to the discontentment of organised labour which strongly oppose the employment of seafarers who do not work under collective agreements with resulting wage undercutting. Furthermore, non-open registry developing countries contend that the system exploits their cheap labour and comparative advantage. Since the 1950s and over three decades the reactions of these adversely affected interests took the form of politico-legal international conflicts, with trade unions and developing maritime nations trying to restrict FoC shipping through internationally agreed registration requirements.[13] These attempts were unsuccessful with western European countries being among those opposing them in alliance with FoC countries. The picture changed in the 1980s, as most of the European nations reformed their position under the pressure of an unprecedented decline of their flags. The latter decreased shipping revenues and produced job losses due to shipowners preference to use global sources of cheap labour. European countries did not look for international regulatory restrictions of FoC shipping but responded with the development of new types of registrations.

Regulating Liner Conferences

The organisation of liner trade in conferences represents another phenomenon contributing to the politicisation of maritime transport. Shipowners form liner conferences aiming to maximise profits through a sufficient degree of market control rather than through competing with each other. The contracting operators adopt wholly or partially practices like common freight rates; agreed frequency and allocation of sailings; specified degree of openness to new members; loyalty arrangements with the shippers; and deferred discounts after exclusive use of conference services for a certain period. The aim is to divide the trading area in a way that each operator has a particular sphere of influence at both the loading and discharging areas, sometimes in respect of ports as well.

Liner conferences have dominated the carriage of trade in several routes without being universally accepted. Their critics see conferences as private restraints to competition that enables the creation and abuse of dominant market powers. First, they effectively prevent the entrance of new carriers into their trades and control the tonnage supply at levels decided by them without shippers' cooperation and irrespective of their requirements. Second, they apply restrictive practices to secure the exclusive loyalty of shippers. Third, they fix tariffs at levels significantly higher than those that might exist under competitive conditions. Their supporters argue that in practice very few conferences can employ monopoly powers of the degree and security of the big land based monopolies. On the contrary, they prevent over-tonnaging of a route when they assure shippers of reliable, regular, at predictable rates, types of service, coupled with the assurance that they have received the same treatment as their trading competitors. To them conferences are essential in the interest of world trade and commerce.

In short, the debate on whether such agreements are necessary for the sensible conduct of business, or whether any advantages they might posses are overweighed by their disadvantages is inconclusive.[14] Thus, the system has produced overt disputes involving market forces and national administrations leading to several governmental and intergovernmental inquiries and investigations.[15] However, for a long period liner conferences remained self-regulated. Western European states, that were ruling a great part of world liner trade, refrained from any intervention advocating that this was the only way for international shipping to accomplish its task efficiently. A change was observed in the late 1960s, as several countries whose trade was covered by conferences tried to impose either a varying degree of regulation or cargo sharing provisions. These countries wanted to secure that cargoes would be transported by services provided by their citizens or state companies, so they also pressed for the establishment of an international system of regulation. Varying interests and philosophies were leading to contradictory legislation encompassing the danger for a disruption of international trade. These events provided the background to the development of a debate within the UNCTAD framework, a process that concluded with the agreement (1974) and ratification (1983) of the UNCTAD Code, which in turn upgraded the role of international organisations in promoting regulation as the principle governing maritime transport.

The UNCTAD Code was a compromise between those countries (mostly western traditional maritime powers) which did not want an international regulatory framework at all, or one that would be largely voluntary and those countries (mostly developing and socialist countries) which wanted specific regulatory policies based on balanced rather than unilateral considerations (cf. Ademuni, 1988). The agreement establishes the right of national lines of each trading country to equally participate in the transport of the generated traffic by allowing 40% of the cargo to be carried by the flag of the exporting and 40% by the importing country while it safeguards the right of third flag carriers to acquire 20% of that traffic (the 40/40/20 formula). It also lays down criteria and procedures for freight rates determination, in order to abolish discrimination and secrecy, and rules for the settlement of disputes between owners and shippers. Notably, the rule depended on the major maritime countries' decision to co-operate for its implementation. The Code would enter force after not less than 24 countries and at least 25% of the world general cargo tonnage has become contracting parties, hence, it would be difficult to do so without the support of at least certain of the major west European maritime nations. In fact, it came into effect following its ratification by Germany and Denmark, in turn the outcome of a EU decision.

European Union: An Additional Policy Making Level

Since 1957 the EU constitutes an additional policy-making jurisdiction in the field of transport. Within the framework of the Treaty of Rome (1957), the Common Transport Policy (CTP) was declared as an indispensable complement to the emerging Common Market, and was one of the two policy-foundations that gained 'certain autonomy' (Despicht, 1969) through a separate title devoted to it (the other was the Common Agriculture Policy). Nevertheless, for the next seventeen years policy actions regarding the maritime mode were excluded from the scope of the CTP. Following a European Court of Justice decision, maritime transport was included in the base of the CTP in 1974, a year after the first EU enlargement. In the succeeding years the EU developed a 'problem-orientated' maritime policy strategy. In other words, it was involved in the formulation of *ad hoc* measures responding to emerging problems, notably to the heterogeneous international policy developments of the time. The main policy development of the period was the adoption of a common positive response to the aforementioned UNCTAD Code in 1979.

The turning point towards a more systematic EU involvement in maritime affairs took place in the second half of the 1980s. In 1986 the Council of Transport Ministers adopted four Regulations that marked the beginning of a collective EU attempt to improve the competitive position of EU flagged shipping and terminate the deep and prolonged flagging-out crisis faced by member states flags. In 1989, when the limited results of the 1986 endeavour were realised, the Commission presented a second set of measures to improve the operating conditions of EU shipping. These developments represent a more consistent EU involvement in maritime transport issues than before. Notwithstanding that, the EU policy continued to be developed on a piecemeal basis and directed towards specific issues. In other words, the EU policy actions were based on a 'mosaic approach' (Cafruny, 1991).

This modus operandi was followed until 1991 when a new 'horizontal' approach was introduced. The radical differentiation from the earlier CMTP stages is that this philosophy addresses the entire maritime dimension. In the words of the Commission it implies 'a policy agenda aiming to give special attention to the maritime economy as a whole' (CEU, 1991, p. 5), within a predefined strategy. The EU has embarked upon a project of replacing what was a reactive policy, which 'may be characterised as the ad hoc response to specific perceived problems as they acquire some critical gravity', by a coherent proactive common maritime transport policy which 'involves a continuous attempt to establish and maintain rational comprehensive and well-integrated policies and institutions conforming to a clear logical structure' (Gwilliam, 1980, p. 39).

Understanding Policy Europeanisation

The foregoing discussion revealed the overt politicisation of maritime transport. Three well established policy-making levels have been contributing towards this direction: national policies; international agreements of states via their participation to intergovernmental organisations; and industrial self-regulation agreed by market players primarily at international level. Against this background in the years following 1974 a common EU maritime transport policy has been under development.

Those maritime nations that participate in European integration have been strong advocates of international solutions to the problems of the maritime sector, justifying this approach on the transboundary character of the latter. Notwithstanding that, they have also shown the willingness to maintain distinctive national policy initiatives in order to secure their national interests. Then, stakeholders have been keen to be associated globally and search for international (self)regulatory agreements. In spite of that background, the CMTP cannot be described anymore as a regional initiative to an industrial crisis like the one that the shipping industry faced in the post oil crises years. Although introduced as an *ad hoc* practice the EU activities have gradually transformed into a comprehensive policy that continues to expand, partially in parallel and partially at the expense of the pre-existing policy making levels. The current EU agenda embodies almost the totality of the sector's socio-economic problems. Meanwhile, the 1992 programme for the completion of the SEM and the ratification of the TEU together with wider geopolitical developments have introduced new economic and political dimensions.

Which are the factors propelling or restraining this evolutionary process? This is the central question that this study addresses. A point shared by the limited number of studies regarding the developments of the CMTP in the 1980s, is that the common policy initiatives have been the outcome of the interacting political and economical spheres of reality. However, their theorisation of this interaction within the EU policy-making process varies considerably (Chapter 3). Those who attempt to explain the factors that decide the progress of European integration *per se* put a similar argument forward. This growing branch of the literature has also been unsuccessful in producing a generally accepted theory. Being critical of early conclusions, recent studies turn to the examination of the EU as a 'polity-like' entity whose policies can be understood by the interactions of the involved policy actors in a transforming environment of growing economic interdependence (Chapter 2). Assuming they are right, the CMTP is the development of shared policies to govern economic activities within a changing economic context, but the distinctive institutional framework that governs this entity conditions the pursuit of this common policy. This framework generates in the narrower sense particular policy-making formats and mechanisms, and in the larger sense political relationships and behaviours of policy actors.

The juxtaposition of these theoretical arguments has provided the direction for this study. By considering the contemporary economic ambient factors and both the market and the policy answers, this contribution aims to examine and to conceptualise whether and, if so, which of and how the actionable factors are influencing the developments of the EU-level maritime transport policy during the chronologically, economically, and politically, distinct fourth period of the CMTP which started in the beginning of the 1990s.

The term '*actionable factors*' refers to all three clusters of actors that may influence the extent and the nature of the CMTP within the EU policy-making process. According to Van Patot's (1973/4, as rendered by Van Gent and Kuyvenhoven, 1980) conceptualisation of the making of transport policies, the existing economic situation of the sector forms the basis for the actions of authorities, the framework within which policy makers must take their decisions. Policy makers judge the present situation of the sector and indicate the situation to be expected in the future. Following their principles, they then target a desired situation and apply those means lying within their powers and competencies for changing the situation. Examining the politics on international shipping Knudsen (1973) observes that in most cases policy makers have a picture of a situation that would be at least satisfactory from their point of view. At any time they have a range of options including not addressing the policies they have in mind at all. In sum, policy developments are affected by their preferences as well.

As the focal point is the making of an EU policy, the decision making pattern involves two clusters of policy makers. One of them is the decision making institutions of the EU: the Council of Ministers; the European Commission; the European Parliament (EP), the European Court of Justice (ECJ); as well as the consultative Economic and Social Committee (Ecosoc) and the newly established Committee of the Regions (CoR). The second cluster includes the national governments of the EU member states. Furthermore, non-governmental interest groups, which try to promote the interests of stakeholders and influence policy-making at any or all of the possible levels (national, local, and supranational) represent the third type of actionable factors. Their policy demands and the manner of their articulation by their representatives may also have a vital input in shaping the EU-level policy outcomes. When solutions to any set of problems are anything but obvious, the logic of policy makers and choices of the market, or some parts of it, do not always coincide and this may affect the policy outcome. All these actionable factors have powers and use them, some being more powerful than others, and may promote, oppose, or be more favourably disposed to the development of the CMTP.

How these actors, their policy choices, and their respective interaction within the rules and norms of the EU decision making process, influence the policy developments of the CMTP in the 1990s, and *vice versa*, can be informed by this research. Following a qualitative case-study research method, this volume examines the remarkable policy developments towards the establishment of a common policy on safe seas and a common policy on shortsea shipping that took place in the 1990s.

Organisation of the Book

The book is divided into two main parts. The first part presents the theoretical framework and the factual background that have informed this volume. *Chapter 2* explores theoretical accounts attempting to explain European integration concentrating on the precise role envisaged for the actionable factors. This discussion leads to the introduction of a potential framework for understanding the CMTP in the 1990s. *Chapter 3* explores the progression of the CMTP in a historical perspective. Among others, this chapter reviews the contribution of previous studies on the understanding of the evolution of this common EU policy. It also justifies the selection of shortsea shipping and safety issues as two policy areas serve to explore and draw conclusions on the development of the CMTP in the 1990s.

The second part turns its attention to the CMTP in the 1990s, Chapter 5 discusses the new economic environment of international shipping and its implications for maritime safety, Chapter 5 examines the progress towards the establishment of a common policy on safe seas, and Chapter 6 discusses the findings of these developments. The next three Chapters turn to the second issue-area under investigation. Chapter 7 discusses the new economic context of shortsea shipping, Chapter 8 deals with the EU initiatives regarding the establishment of a common EU policy on shortsea shipping and Chapter 9 searches for within case conclusions. Finally, Chapter 10 proceeds to an explanatory assessment of the CMTP developments and formulates the conclusions regarding the determinants of the policy Europeanisation in the 1990s.

Notes

1   In this volume the focus is on the Common Maritime Transport Policy, which, in legal terms, is based on the 1957 European Economic Community Treaty. Following the ratification of the TEU on 1 November 1993, the European Economic Community was transformed into the European Community, which in turn encompassed by and became the 'first pillar' of a new European Union (EU). Therefore the latter term is used throughout this volume- even when reference is made to developments before 1993.

2   Unless otherwise stated, sources of statistical information are the databases of (a) Eurostat and (b) the Institute of Shipping and Logistics (ISL) as traced and compiled through various issues of ISL Shipping Statistics and Market Review (monthly publication) and Shipping Statistics Yearbook.

3   Controversies may be alive but as Button (1993, p. 225) summarises, 'sceptical studies accept that an adequate basic transport system is a sine qua non for modern economic development, but questioning whether opportunity costs involved in further improving transport are necessarily justified'.

4   For an analytical review of this economic doctrine: Swann, 1998; Healey et al, 1995; Mole, 2001. For a description of the history of economic thinking on integration: Machpul, 1977.

5   Transport infrastructure projects demands substantial amounts of capital and a long constructive period. Apart from the time lag between the start of capital formation and the beginning of financial returns, few of these projects are profitable enough to generate a cash flow that will service loan payment, secure the return on equity capital, and maintain the coverage ratios. Hence, they are unattractive to private investors (cf. ECMT, 1990).

6   The term 'freedom of the seas' is associated with the Dutch legal theoretician Hugh Grotius

who has defended it in his work Mare Liberum (1608; see: Bull et al, 1990).

7   Böhme (1989, p. 15), describes the operational framework that the ocean shipping enjoyed in the early post World War II years as 'the most liberal framework that could be conceived'.

8   Goss and Marlow (1992, p.56) assert that it is difficult to find any theoretical arguments to support protectionism because 'shipping is not necessary for promoting overseas trade; it is not an infant industry; investment in it has no special effect on balance of payments; as a capital-intensive industry it provides little employment; there is no general case for protecting shipping for defence purposes; and as a way of buying national prestige, it can become very expensive'.

9   According to Lawrence (1972) shipping subsidisation can be used to effectively advance economic welfare by i) correcting for inequalities of market values; ii) correcting imperfections in pricing of transport; iii) stimulating economic development; iv) stimulating trade; v) assure continuous service and enhance domestic economic stability; and vi) diversify sources of foreign exchange earnings.

10 This overview could go backwards to the great free-trade era between 1850 and 1914, when the prevailing doctrine of laissez-faire did not inhibit these nations from giving substantial support to the shipping industry (cf. Sturmey, 1962; Davies, 1992).

11 For presentations of the international organisations affecting maritime affairs: Frankel, 1984; Power, 1992.

12 German owners have made the greatest use of bareboat charters so far, while some other countries, like the UK, do not allow shipowners operating their flags to follow this practice (see: Spruyt, 1994; for the contribution of the phenomenon to the complexity of detecting FoC shipping: Northrup and Scrace, 1996).

13 The debate was transferred within the UNCTAD framework during the discussion of UNCLOS I, II, and III (concluded in 1958, 1982, and 1986 respectively) with affected countries demanding that a 'genuine economic link' should exist between the ship and the country of registration (for a comprehensive review: Ademuni, 1988).

14 For a detailed debate on liner conference agreements, but also the UNCTAD Code: Goss, 1968; Sletmo and Williams, 1981; Herman, 1983; Frankel, 1987; Farthing, 1993.

15 Examples of such inquiries are the Royal Commission on Shipping Rings (UK, 1909); the Alexander Committee Report (USA, 1914); Imperial Shipping Committee (Commonwealth governments, 1921); Congressional Hearings (USA, 1958-61); the Rochdale Committee of Inquiry (UK, 1968-70); and Consultative Shipping Group (Several W. European Countries and Japan Ministers, 1971-73).

2 European Integration and Policy Actors

This chapter reviews the theoretical endeavours to explain the dynamics of European integration and the process of developing common EU policies. The first three decades of the integrative experiment were studied from the standpoint of international relations with neofunctionalism and intergovernmentalism posing as the dominant paradigms. The theoretical terrain became progressively more perplexing. These approaches were revised and new theoretical frameworks relying on different assumptions and advocating different images of the political phenomenon and policy arena under examination were introduced. Bearing in mind this huge array of explanations of how European policies are made, this is a search for the role that each concept envisages for the actionable factors. The critical review of 'traditional' and more recent accounts leads to the introduction of (historical) neoinstitutionalism as a theoretical framework for understanding the developments of the CMTP in the 1990s. This is followed by a presentation of the governmental and non-governmental actors participating in the contemporary CMTP policy-making game, and the general decision rules of the latter.

Theorising the EU Policy-Making Process

Neofunctionalism

Neofunctionalism, the first approach developed with specific reference to the EU, conceives European integration as a *sui generis* incremental self-sustaining process of political change. Each step towards integration leads automatically to further supranational cooperation, a threefold expansive phenomenon known as 'spillover' (Haas, 1958). Spillover is 'functional', whereby the benefits reaped from successful integration in one sector lead to further action into related areas and further sections; 'political', whereby the formatted supranational institutions carry out increased and improved tasks enabling the growth in scope of the integration; and 'geographical' (Cram, 1996), whereby cooperation of some states affects excluded states (i.e. by altering existing patterns of trade) with the latter looking for inclusion in the integrative community.

The emphasis is on the major role of the societal groups, in particular that of the political and economic elites. The EU is the result of the complex interaction between autonomous non-state actors. Rational 'ideology-free' (Ioakimidis, 1993) expectations gradually persuade these actors to a self-interested shift of their loyalties and political activities to international organisations. Groups of non-political character become aware that their interests cannot be adequately served at the national level, therefore, they demand appropriate state action to further integration. When these groups emphasise collective action, the pre-existing pluralist pattern of political activity is directly transferable from national to international level. As societal groups can forge contacts, channels, and relationships, in a variety of directions and be loyal to several agencies simultaneously, thus the 'cobweb model' metaphor (Webb, 1983), they are considered as the carriers of integration.

Non-unitary member states are able to unify as much as a person (i.e. a state leader), or a group of persons (i.e. an interest group). Their acceptance of the integration process is best explained by the governance of demands within and among the nations concerned, not by a pattern of identical expectations (Harrison, 1974). National governments gradually forgo the desire and ability to conduct policies independently, seeking instead to make joint decisions, or to delegate the decision making process to a new supranational centre whose institutions possess, or demand jurisdiction (Lindberg, 1963). Regarding the necessary background conditions for the establishment of a transnational community, or the desirable end product of the co-operation between previously sovereign states, this account is not deterministic. Nevertheless, despite the belief that an overall equilibrium in the integrative process is not feasible, proponents of neofunctionalism foresee a gradual, possibly inexorable, move towards a federal system, an expectation that remains albeit gradually qualified.

Neofunctionalism allots a critical role to the institutional arrangements that accompany integration. When interest groups are the 'catalysts' of the process, European institutions are seen by the neofunctionalists as the 'organisers' (Corbey, 1995). Their precise role is that of the 'agents of integration' who act as the 'honest brokers' (Haas, 1958). The latter anticipates that, because decision-making is a positive sum game where a plurality of participants are ready to compromise on various issues if the total gains are more than the total losses, supranational institutions facilitate policy making, advance the identification of a new locus and ease the transfer of elite loyalties to the European level. Still, such institutions may involve the exercise of parts of the states sovereign tasks but without these tasks fully being relinquished to an autonomous institution. The territorial state remains the basic unit of analysis. It is the nation state that decides to participate in integration as a response to external constraints and opportunities, like the changes in international economy, or internal developments that create their own follow-up problems (Mutimer, 1994).

For the first decade of European integration, this was received as an account providing sufficient explanations. Governments participating in the formation of the EU had decided to promote European unification through a strategy consistent with the neofunctionalist interpretation.[1] But its heydays ended when events like the Luxembourg compromise (1966) challenged the automatic nature of the integration process. Attempting to explain why this model became redundant, its advocates wrote about 'spill-backs' and 'spill-arounds' (Lindberg and Scheingold, 1970; Schmitter, 1970). The notion that spillovers are unidirectional pushing steadily towards further integration and ultimately political union was dropped but the notion that spillover can occur if issues are linked has sustained. Haas (1976) focused on three vital, albeit ignored by earlier neofunctionalist studies, explanatory variables. First, the critical role of the changing objectives of the actors involved in the process. Second, that because there are many competing international forums, the EU has to demonstrate a unique capacity for winning its members' wholehearted support. Third, that the EU institutions were failing to develop as predicted, in part because national institutions had the administrative and political capacity to respond to demands made on them. Moreover, Haas stressed that research on regional integration should also take account of the wider economic context and specifically issues of economic interdependence.

Intergovernmentalism

Intergovernmentalism is largely a counterproposal to the pluralistic and mechanistic neofunctionalist apprehension of European integration. The core of this state-centric model is that sovereign participating states remain the 'obstinate' rather than the 'obsolete' players of international cooperation (Hoffmann, 1966). Inspired by Morgethau's (1948) realist theory, it intellectualises the EU as an international framework of policy coordination, constructed by egocentric Weberian nation-states[2] for the completion of their national objectives, namely their rescue from the new global pressures which are beyond their immediate control (Milward, 1992). Having interests and policy preferences of their own, the capacity to calculate these interests, as well as the ability to determine effectively the structure and the outcomes of any integrative step, the representatives of the states are the powerful and rational unitary-actors. The evolution of integration is a 'two-level' strictly zero-sum policy making game, where losses on vital issues are not compensated by gains on other issues (Putnam, 1988). Whenever national governments realise that individual 'non-vital' ('low') policies are insufficient, or want to remove them from controversy into the domestic arena of executive control, they have the power to Europeanise them. In areas of 'vital' ('high') importance to the national interest that may challenge their sovereign autonomy, governments can set limits, even prefer the self-controlled uncertainty, and prevent progress in European co-operation. By assuming that self-regarding rationally behaving nations interact in a structured system (Keohane, 1986), realists are not convinced that European integration is moving, or is likely to move, inexorably towards greater economic and political federation.

A subsequent point of the state dominance is the inequality of the participating actors. Neither the formatted institutions, nor the operating non-governmental groups do, or have the potential to, influence the integrative process. Because of the member states preoccupation with preserving national autonomy and sovereignty, it is impossible to establish supranational institutions that exercise authorities over the state (Keohane, 1984). Though the EU may move towards a supranational organisation and the supranational institutions may expand their powers, they do so only to the extent that its member states believe it to be in their national interest (Hoffmann, 1964). Similarly, societal and business interest groups turn to influential players only to the extent that they predispose policies and actions of the member states.

The (neo)realist emphasis on national autonomy gained credibility during the standstill of European integration in the 1970s. When the difficulties in progressing integration were explained as being the result of different nation-states preferences. In the beginning of the 1980s intergovernmentalists acknowledged that additional elements are critical facilitators of European integration. These elements include common knowledge, norms, rules, and procedures (Hoffmann, 1982), as well as the generated predictability of the policy making game which provides incentives to be attached to a Community having heterogeneous and differentiated membership (Taylor, 1983). Still, member states remain as the decisive integration makers.

The Theoretical Gap of the 1990s

The successful re-launch of integration in the second half of the 1980s created a gap between the reality of integration and the aforementioned conceptual frameworks. National interests and governments played, unambiguously, an important role in the history-making decisions of that period. However, the role of business interests in pressing forward the launching of the internal market and the political leadership of the Commission, are also identified here as core features of these events. Policy developments questioned the ability of the (neo)realist assumptions to describe efficiently the driving forces of European integration without re-establishing the dominance of the pluralist paradigm. Scholars recognised that the degree and pace of integration is decided in a different way to any of the two traditional accounts argued for.

The main shortcoming of intergovernmentalism is that it centres on the member states' rational and self-interest inputs but ignores the role of other actors. Even when realists acknowledge the role of European institutions and/or that of business interests in pressing forward for the single market project, the phenomenon is attributed to the failure of national policies (Hoffmann, 1989). Then, intergovernmentalism talks about an 'unrealistic hermetic national process' (Sandholtz, 1993). Apart from failing to sort out 'vital' and 'non-vital' national interests (Hix, 1994), it disregards that states find themselves increasingly drawn into immensely complex transnational relations that shape their preferences (O'Neil, 1996).

On the other hand, whilst the presence of functional spillover is widely recognised, its record has been uneven and much slower than the neofunctionalist idea of linear progression had assumed. Therefore, neofunctionalism is criticised for being an empirical 'apology' to the progress of integration, which fails to develop predictions about variations in the evolution of EU (Wincott, 1995) and neglects the impact of the international economic environment on the preferences of the participating actors (Sandholtz and Zysman, 1989). By assuming too much homogeneity of interests, and placing too much interest on the role of interest groups, it fails to appreciate the need for, and difficulties of, coalition building within the EU, and neglects the essential agreement of governments having different political ideologies and facing different political pressures. Shortly, it is criticised for overestimating the significance of the societal participation and ignoring other elements of the political arena.

Inextricably linked with the profound progress of European integration, this theoretical gap produced two distinctive, though not incompatible, conceptual developments. Firstly, it prompted the re-examination of the 'traditional' approaches. As it is frequently remarked (cf. Hix, 1994) much of the new debate parallels the traditional one. Of the most notable adjustments has been the greater emphasis on the influence of economic pressures, particularly the globalisation (internationalisation) of the economies. In a different vein, analysis is steadily moving towards a 'post-ontological stage' (Caporaso, 1996), where the nature of the EU is not the focal point anymore. Researchers are increasingly less concerned with how to categorise it than with how to explain the policy-making process and outcome.

Refinements of the Traditional Approaches

Departing from a state-centric position, Keohane and Hoffmann (1991a) synthesise the two traditional concepts, and the need of European nation-states to adjust to the changing economic environment. Their explanation of integration developments begins with governmental actions but embodies three hypotheses. First, the successful neofunctionalist spillover, which nevertheless requires prior programmatic agreements among governments expressed in an intergovernmental bargain. Second, the 'preference-convergence' hypothesis, which centres on the importance of the internal state politico-economic environment and concludes that integration proceeds as a result of converging policy preferences among member states, especially the most powerful of them. By introducing domestic politics as a device explaining EU policy-making, this hypothesis upgrades the importance of the different preferences and attitudes of the national, political, and economic, elites as well as that of party politics. Third, the 'political economy' hypothesis, which holds that change should be seen principally as a form of adaptation to pressures from the contemporary state of the world political economy. In this context, the EU is portrayed as a construction with common supranational functions where decisions are made as a result of negotiation and coalition building between a variety of actors but always within a context set by agreements between governments. Within this network of pooling sovereignty the Commission plays an indispensable role.

The essence of the last two hypotheses is also part of liberal intergovernmentalism a (neo)realist refinement, which claims that intergovernmentalism, the protection of national sovereignty, and the lowest common denominator bargain, can explain European integration (see: Moravcsik, 1995, 1998). Integration rests on governments' preferences but the increasing interdependence of nation states motivates them to protect sovereignty through inter-state bargaining. Common policies are the outcome of negotiations between independent but interdependent rational governments with different powers. These powers are figured out by the level of intensity of national preferences in a specific-issue area, the relative costs and benefits of potential inter-state agreements, the available alternative courses of action, the fear of exclusion, and the government's propensity to seek compromise linkage or side payment. In other words, domestic societal pressures and the international environment are the two factors that constrain the rational actions of the national governments.

In this theoretical path, European institutions have been developed as a result of conscious national calculations. Moravcsik (1991) advocates that their most important function is to supply sufficiently the exogenous intergovernmental demand for co-operative policies (and initially labelled his outline as 'intergovernmental institutionalism'). Pierson (1996) comments that this 'instrumentality' is implicitly acknowledged by all the realist intergovernmental variations. Drawing on the functional transaction cost approach intergovernmentalists (Keohane, 1984; Williamson, 1985) maintain that institutions have the main purpose and effect in monitoring the behaviour of the participants and providing information: in other words, to economising transaction costs. European institutions provide, without any substantive political authority or integrative power, a functional framework of negotiating major decisions that, on average, permit efficient bargaining and collective decision making. By acting as 'apolitical informational clearing houses' (Garret, 1992), they enable autonomous states to achieve efficient agreements and further their own interests. Moravcsik (1993, p. 507) concludes that 'the unique institutional structure of the EC is acceptable to national governments only insofar as it strengthens, rather than weakens, their control over domestic affairs', but appreciates that one of the EU institutions, the ECJ, has expanded its judicial power in such a way that it presents an anomaly to his theory.

'Consociationalism' (Taylor, 1996) offers another realist-based account focusing on the complexity of the integrative phenomenon. To the scholar, different outcomes posit different relationships between member states and the EU. Apart from the traditional 'hard intergovernmentalism', which sees common agreements as incidental by-products of the relation between the states, and the 'federalist position', which sees the EU as the primary actor, three more kinds of relationships are conceivable. Firstly, a 'soft' intergovernmentalism, where governments feel able to make concessions. Second, outcomes targeting 'the rescue of the nation state' (also: Milward, 1992). Finally, there is a 'symbiotic' relationship, which holds that each of the two levels has a degree of autonomy, its own policy, and is essential for the survival of each other. The focus is, apart from the relationship and balance between member states, on the interplay between states and the EU. His own conclusion, which essentially moves beyond the instrumentality assumption, is that 'symbiosis' and 'consociation' can describe efficiently the EU in the 1990s. Ascribable to the EU institutions is the active role of securing consensus on EU policies that maintain national elites' powers and increase the nations' own benefits from cooperation. Still, if the latter purpose conflicts with the former it is abandoned, the other way round is not possible.

Economic Interdependence

The preceding 'political economy' hypothesis is developed within the context of the 'theory of interdependence'. This theory maintains that the changing economic structures can convincingly and parsimoniously explain the notified trend towards international co-operation (Keohane and Nye, 1972, 1977). The focal point is the position of the states *vis-à-vis* the revolutionary transformation of the international economy. Precisely because the latter is dominated by the evolution of one global market, which needs to be managed within transnational perspectives, international cooperation and regional integration are seen as deliberate attempts to answer the diminishing importance of national economic boundaries.

Within this new reality the multiplicity and complexity of the contemporaneous transnational relations become of great significance. Despite the importance of national initiatives, the realist image of monolithic governments involved in intergovernmental linkages is only partially accurate. A variety of actors face new kinds of policy issues but also participate in new political interactions and may play a decisive role in policy developments. Intergovernmental negotiations and coordination coexist with influential transgovernmental networks between the bureaucracies of the nation states, and transnational linkages between governmental and non-governmental actors. The outcome is the evolution of international 'regimes' defined as 'networks, rules, norms, and procedures that regularise behaviour and control its effect' (Keohane and Nye, 1977, p. 19). These transnational relations affect the inter-state world and non-state actors and *vice versa*. Risse-Kappen (1995) argue that the structural differences of the political systems are likely to condition both the availability of channels for transnational actors into the system and the requirements for winning coalitions to change policies. Degrees of international institutionalisation interact in deterring the ability of transnational actors to bring about policy change.

This framework has been used to explain, at least partially, the driving towards further European integration, or some aspects of it. H. Wallace (2000) argues that globalisation makes the traditional state-level governance particularly inadequate for a number of important issues (even what intergovernmentalists may term 'high' politics) and induces needs for transnational cooperation. Given the specific geopolitical features of the west European region, European integration can also be seen as a distinctive west European effort to contain the consequences of globalisation. Rather than be forced to choose between the national polity for developing policies and the relative anarchy of the globe, west European invented a form of regional governance with polity-like features to extend the state and to harden the boundary between themselves and the rest of the world.

Theorising the EU as a Polity

From the beginning of 1990s onwards, a flourishing number of studies sketches a different theoretical path. These studies (among others: Marks, 1993; Scharpf, 1994; Richardson, 1996; Hooghe, 1996) suggest that the EU can be accurately understood if examined as a system that has been, or is, developed to a regional multilevel governance entity with 'polity-like' features rather than as an international regime. Within the new system, authority and policy making competencies are shared across multiple levels of actors participating in 'a political system but not a state' (Hix, 1999). Supranational, transnational, national, sub-national, actors are linked and fight in a 'n-person game' (Schneider *et al*, 1994) with the domestic and the international spheres not be clear cut. State executives and state arenas remain a central element of the system exercising substantial powers (cf. Sbragia, 1996). They articulate fundamental cleavages in EU politics, exercise long term executive powers, choose who holds short-term authority, are main actors in the EU legislative process, and are responsible for its implementation (Hix, 1996). However, EU policy-making is neither firmly under member state control, nor explicable in terms of conventional diplomatic bargaining among chiefs of governments or their representatives whose agreements require unanimity.

The EU institutions are also the locus of power and, to a certain degree, autonomous decision making control. Member states frequently support this trend, either because the costs of losing control may be outweighed by benefits of decisional reallocation, or because there are intrinsic benefits having to do with shifting responsibility for unpopular decisions of insulating decision making pressures (Marks *et al*, 1996). Yet, the created institutions do not only act in common with national governments. Their independent influence in policy making goes beyond their role as agents of state executives. They affect political behaviour and outcomes in at least three ways: by becoming autonomous political actors; by creating options for domestic actors in choice of allies and arenas (creating multi-level politics); and by inducing changes in domestic policies and institutions, thus, 'the distinction between conventional "national" and "interstate" politics blurs' (Sandholtz, 1996, p. 403).

These interlocked institutions, open multiple points of access for sectoral, socio-economic, national and sub-national interests representation. Such interests create transnational associations that seek to influence the new players or collaborate with them on behalf of shared policy objectives. In this perspective, national arenas remain important, in particular for the formation of national governments' preferences that are an integral part of the EU decision-making. But no longer do they provide the sole interface between national and supranational arenas nor do they monopolise control over many activities that take place in their territories.

Bringing (Historical) Neoinstitutionalism In

Recent studies of EU policy-making focus on the interplay between domestic and European (international) economic factors, in particular the complex interdependence of the national economies. That the continuous and rapid growth of economic internationalisation (i.e. location of production and services have become increasingly internationalised, time lags in the transfer of information reduced, transnational capital mobility exploded) has influenced European integration is a widely acknowledged concept. But the extent and the nature of the influence is a matter of dispute. There are those who insist that, although intra-European developments have been strongly influenced by changes in the world economy, European integration should not be regarded as simply another manifestation of the 'economic interdependence' phenomenon, not least because of the size and history of those that have been active participants in the process. Tsoukalis (1993, p. 5) observes that 'the difference between the European and the world level is both quantitative and qualitative and lies in the different degree and nature of economic interaction between national units and advanced form of joint rule-setting and management. Autonomous economic processes and policy co-operation have been mutually reinforcing'.

Whatever the degree of influence assigned to economic interdependence, the application of the paradigm to the EU is accompanied by a fundamental analytical implication. This is to 'stop arguing in an "either-or" fashion of interstate bargaining as if interstate bargaining were increasingly replaced by transnational and transgovernmental coalition-building' and 'focus on the interaction between interstate relations, supranational bodies and transnational transgovernmental bodies' (Risse Kappen, 1996, p. 58).

By emphasising the 'polity-like' features of the EU scholars have already begun to examine this interaction. These studies incorporate some earlier theoretical suggestions; the significance of national governments and domestic arenas, the active role of private interests, the influence of the economic environments. Simultaneously, they introduce an approach leading away from accounts that focus on the nature, the goals, preferences, desires, and plans of the member states (and/or the EU) towards an actor-centred approach which specifies particular individuals, groups, and organisations acting within the everyday policy-making. In this vein, the EU policy setting and decision shaping can be understood by sectoral analysis of the interlocked private and public actors who are involved in complex non-hierarchical formal and informal networking of varying density and (horizontal and vertical) depth. Policy integration progresses due to the fact that all these actors systematically attempt to influence the complex EU policy making game through the building of EU-level 'advocacy coalitions' (Sabatier, 1988), as well as due to the domestic and exogenous economic developments that create a fluid environment.

Certain analytical implications flow from the state of this discussion. Firstly, focusing on the nature and the role of the actors involved may enhance the understanding of EU-level policy developments. Secondly, as the governance of the EU is in a state of flux, and the interplay of the EU institutions, national policy traditions, and issue characteristics, vary across sectors (Andersen and Eliassen, 1995), the analysis of this governance can be promoted by paying attention to sectoral analysis. Caporaso and Keller (1995) suggest that without overestimating the division between 'history making' and 'day to day' decisions, which are in many respects reciprocal, studies of common sectoral policies might not simply occur alongside the development of macro-theories but also facilitate a rounder understanding of the integration process. Thirdly, the EU represents an emerging entity. Hence, the framework to analyse policy Europeanisation should combine the examination of the EU as a subset of international relations and its examination as an external projection of domestic politics (cf. Hurrell and Menon, 1996).

Foremost, if this alternative is plausible one critical issue that needs to be clarified is the precise role of political institutions in the development of common EU policies. In other words, is there a need to place all (or some) of the EU institutions central stage? The underlying assumption of conceptualising the EU as an emerging polity-like entity is that the contemporary institutional arrangements represent neither passive agents of national interests (as the instrumentality assumption of state-centric approaches suggests) nor of vested pluralist interests (as the neofunctionalist approach argues) but actors that matter.

The Neoinstitutionalist Account

To establish the aforementioned assumption it is useful to bring in the analysis insights from the comparative politics and political economy account of historical institutionalism (Skocpol, 1984; Hall, 1986; March and Olsen, 1989; Steinmo *et al*, 1992), also termed as 'neoinstitutionalism' (Hall, 1992). Even though it is much more 'a set of perspectives than a full-blown theory' (Peterson, 1995), this framework has been utilised to study the evolution of particular policy sectors or issues,[3] the dynamism of the Commission in the EU administration (Cini, 1996), and interest intermediation in the EU (Grande, 1996; Gorges, 1997).

Neoinstitutionalism posits that among the variables that have a definitive impact on the highly political processes of policy-making are political institutions. Without denying that the socio-economic contexts of politics and policies as well as the motives of individual actors are among the factors that most influence policy making process, neoinstitutionalists advocate that institutions can determine outcomes, affect behaviours and political powers in shaping policies. This emphasis is not an entirely original notion (see: Rhodes, 1995). Moreover, the range of scholarships postulating that institutions are critical to an understanding of policy making is diverse. Hall and Taylor (1996) review three contemporaneous analytical approaches using the 'new institutionalism' label. The first one is inspired by rational choice theories; the second by sociology, and the third is neoinstitutionalism. The last of these theoretical variants, however, brings two seminal features in the analysis of policy developments.

First, its conceptions of which institutions matter and, second, of how do these institutions matter.[4] In general, the definition of what should count as an institution may be either exclusive, and embody only the political institutions, or inclusive, and encompass both formal and informal rules and procedures that structure conduct. Neoinstitutionalism works within an inclusive but limited definition. Institutions are 'the formal rules, compliance procedures, and standard operating practices that structure the relationships between actors in various units of the polity and economy' (Hall, 1986, p. 19).[5] Second, and most critically, the focus is on the 'relational character' of institutions. In other words, the way a given institutional framework affects the degree of pressure an actor can bring to bear on policy and the likely shapes of 'political interaction' but also the ability of this interaction to induce changes in both policies and institutions.

On the one hand, either by design or evolution, institutions influence an actor's definition and articulation of its interests, the dissemination of ideas, the construction of market behaviour as well as its relationship to other actors. Other political actors pursue their goals, formulate policy, even create or alter institutions, but while they do so their decisions and strategies are shaped by the institutional context in which they operate (March and Olsen, 1984). Institutions that have interests of their own (e.g. growth, or survival) provide the lead towards particular calculations and potentially better social outcomes, as well as strategically used information that affects the very identities, self images, preferences, and perceptions of non-institutional actors. Neoinstitutionalism suggests both a 'calculus' and a 'cultural' approach to the problem of explaining how institutions matter (Hall and Taylor, 1996). Even if they are not liked or preferred by other actors, institutions and their initiatives create 'lock-in effects' (Pierson, 1993); thus, have to be appreciated as part of the rules of the game. On the other hand, the impact of a given set of institutions on an economic policy cannot be 'read' directly from the institutional structure itself, especially as the significance of political institutions ultimately depends on the particular circumstances in which they operate. Policies are a result of what institutions are pressed to do and what they can do in the economic sphere, specifically the pressures for a line of policy; the possibility of implementing it; the position of the nation within the international economy; and the organisation of labour, capital, and the state (Evans *et al*, 1985).

This dialectic conception of institutions, ideas and other actors, within the policy making process, avoids the deterministic character of older institutional interpretations which consisted of detailed configurative studies of different administrative legal and political, structures, in turn legal epiphenomena of self interest behaviour of individuals and groups (Thelen and Steinmo, 1992). Moreover, it differentiates this account to the contemporaneous 'rational choice' institutionalism. Both of them depart from an agreement at a definitional level of what is an institution. They also share the 'calculus' approach on the question of how institutions affect political behaviour. The vital point of divergence is that for neoinstitutionalists institutions and private actors are 'intimately intertwined' (Dunlavy, 1992) but for rational choice scholars the relevant actors have a fixed set of preferences and behave instrumentally so as to maximise their attainment. In the latter case, institutions provide incentives for certain actions but the preferences of both institutional and non-institutional actors are defined exogenously.[6]

Finally, the thrust of neoinstitutionalist argument unifies two dimensions, the historical and the institutionalist. It is 'institutionalist' because it stresses that many contemporary implications of the temporal processes are embedded in institutions, whether these are formal rules, policy structures, or norms. It is 'historical' because analysis does not look only at current social interests or at existing political alliances but recognises that policy development must be understood as a process that unfolds over time (Pierson, 1996). Keeping with the historical perspective, scholars have focused on the existence of 'critical junctures', when substantial institutional changes take place and create a 'branching point' that divides events into periods of continuity (Gourevitch, 1986).

Implications for the Analysis of the CMTP Developments

What then are the implications of this debate for the analysis of the CMTP developments in the 1990s? When scholars of European integration increasingly suggest that the conceptualisation of the EU as a 'system of multi-governance' provides sufficient explanation of the progress of such sectoral integration, the critical advocacy of the neoinstitutionalist thesis is that we cannot have a valuable explanation of policy making processes unless we locate the role of institutions and study the matrix of the interactions between them, other actors, and their ideas. This is because institutions can be more influential than their creators intended, though they cannot be in fundamental respects autonomous of socio-economic contexts, other actors' interests, ideas, and political activities.

Applying this concept to the EU implies that the latter is an overall interacting system where the institutional framework constrains and refracts politics and policies albeit is never the sole cause of outcomes. Those who have applied it conclude that European institutions represent indeed a distinctive and influential actionable factor of the multilevel governed European polity. Their functions and interactions between them, or between them and other actors, were found to be critical factors in determining policy integration. Furthermore, they advocate that the neoinstitutionalist account is a valid way of explaining the Europeanisation of sectoral policies, not least because its application offsets the 'intellectual apartheid' between comparative politics and the analysis of international relations (Bulmer, 1998; Peters, 1998). The analytical interest moves away from the debate on whether the progress of European integration involves a shift of jurisdiction to whether policy developments reflect an interaction of competencies and shared responsibilities, whereby the institutional framework is a causal variable.

If the governance of the EU policies responds to the neoinstitutionalism concept indeed, then the line of the CMTP is neither the sole outcome of rational governments that negotiate at a regional level in order to protect in a more efficient way their interests, nor the product of an arena simply dominated by exogenous defined policy demands of private actors. The progress of the CMTP is the outcome of a complex interaction between national governments, private actors, the EU political institutions and their ideas. Within this interaction the EU institutions have a decisive input. They posses a certain degree of autonomy as well as the ability to shape the ideas and interests, in short the policy preferences, of the other actors. In turn, their decisions and the ideas of each policy actor are influenced by both the socio-economic environment and the interactions that take place, thus, the Europeanisation of the policy may produce both optimal and sub-optimal answers.

In this perspective, the thorough understanding of the interaction between the aforementioned policy-actors generates knowledge on the factors that induce, determine, and interfere with the CMTP process. Finding what institutions matter and how they influence the policy-making process helps to achieve a better understanding of the CMTP progress.

Policy Actors and the Decision-Making Pattern

The Decision-Making Pattern

The Rome Treaty established a *sui generis* pattern of institutions, and decision-making procedures: 'the Commission would propose, the Parliament would advise, the Council would decide, and the Court would interpret' (Nugent, 1999). Functioning 'in complete independence', the Commission should initiate common policies and in certain cases administrate them. The Council of Ministers would represent the national interests and be the decision-making institution. Acting on the basis of Commission proposals it would decide unanimously (in limited cases under qualified majority) to adopt or amend them. This process should follow a consultation procedure. For most of its acts the Council was obliged to consult an advisory EP and the consultative Ecosoc, a body consisting of representatives of the various categories of economic and social life. All these acts were subject to the jurisdiction of the ECJ, which would act as a court of appeal against breaches of the Treaty and of Community legislation.

The projected decision-making pattern has been rearranged, with the SEA (1987), the TEU (1993) and the Treaty of Amsterdam (1997) representing the key turning points. SEA replaced the need for unanimity in the Council with the qualified majority vote (QMV), so that consensus by most but not all the member states is demanded for decisions to be reached.[7] The latter governs various articles of the Rome Treaty including Article 84(2) that forms the basis of the CMTP. However, Greece and Portugal in their statements that accompanied the SEA published their objections in respect of the abolition of the unanimity that Article 84(2) required, arguing that qualified majority should not work against the crucial sectors of their economy. Therefore, a paragraph was added stating that in the cases of vital consequences CMTP decisions would still require unanimity.

The SEA introduced a second major change, the co-operation procedure. This procedure set up a system of two readings of the Commission proposals by the EP; therefore it increased the participation of the latter within the policy-making process. During the first reading the EP has the right to amend draft legislative proposals drawn up by the Commission. The Council considers them and issues its common position on the basis of QMV. The EP has a second chance of amending the proposal at this stage if there is an absolute majority behind such amendment, or approves the proposal by a simple majority. After the second reading, provided that the Commission supports EP's position, the Council may only reverse EP's view by acting unanimously. A majority is needed in Council for the EP's view to stand. Both the possibilities to outvote minority views by the introduction of QMV, and the closer institutional cooperation were expected to facilitate policy developments and speed up the EU decision-making process.

The TEU led to the establishment of the 'co-decision' procedure, which consists of up to three EP readings. The Council and the EP jointly adopt the EU policies endorsed under this procedure, in other words the two institutions are co-legislators. However, co-decision does not apply in many policy areas including all aspects of the CTP but the development of the trans-European transport networks. A second important administrative provision contained in the TEU is the principle of subsidiarity. According to this principle the EU level policies must be developed only if, and insofar as, the objectives of the proposed actions cannot be realised adequately by lower levels of administration, i.e. local authorities or member states individually, and therefore, by reason of their dimension or scale of effects, are better realised by the EU. Among the further modifications introduced by the Amsterdam Treaty was the extension of the co-decision procedure and the inclusion of further policy areas under the QMV system. Regardless this further extension, the EU remains dependent on the Community method (Devuyst, 1999).

The Policy-Making Institutions of the EU

Council of Ministers This is the institution with the decision-making powers and the mandate to represent national interests. It is structured in sectoral Councils, where departmental ministers discuss matters falling within their competence. The Council of Transport is the earliest of them, first meeting in 1960 to elaborate a single transport market. Whilst decisions regarding the maritime mode are taken during its meetings, issues that cut across the competencies of more ministerial departments may be solved by joint (Jumbo) Council meetings. Although unanimity is not the principle decision-making rule anymore, the basic ethos is 'consensuality' and efforts are made to ensure that all the member states can agree to the proposed conclusions (Westlake, 1995). The pressure to ministerial representatives from each member state to compromise has grown and bargaining, trade off, and 'staying in the game' are seen as intrinsic goods (Garret and Tsebelis, 1996). However the discussions of the Council meetings are private and the conclusions are not always made public. Because of the notorious and contested secrecy of these 'tough and businesslike' meetings the state of knowledge about what really happens in the Councils is limited.

The specialisation and expansion of the Council have been accompanied by the establishment of a six-months rotating presidency that facilitates its working. The member state holding the presidency is responsible for advance preparation of the Council's agenda and the selection of the items to be discussed. The Commission has the *de jure* right of policy initiative but the Council can also request the Commission to draw up proposals. Although the Commission announces its own legislative programme for the year, other items are added through the presidency of the Council, a fact that allows the latter to push issues at the top of the agenda (Kirchner, 1992), and bring forward national priorities. That said, Hayes-Renshaw and Wallace (1997) advocate that the real ability (of the presidency) to deliver domestic expectations is heavily constrained as the Council remains an institution of diffuse concession and is deeply resistant to the explicit peddling of sharp national initiatives: any initiative has to work with the brain of a strong-minded national. The presidency may also play a strong role during the proceedings as it exercises pressure through mediation, compromise proposals, time-limits, and voting to persuade the members of the Council to agree. Its main aim is to have policy results through 'diplomacy rather than confrontation' (Westlake, 1995).

The Council secretariat provide practical and administrative backup. Its main function is that of collective memory more than policy formulation. When their opposite numbers in the Commission have a perspective on policy issues as well as a normative role, the only one aim of the Council secretariat is to assess discussions between the member states and advise on the procedure to be followed for proposing alternatives (Council, 1990). The secretariat members are close to the national governments and advisers of their permanent representatives in Brussels, and divided into ten Directorates. One of the latter deals with Research, Energy, and Transport (DG D), a subsection of which works exclusively on issues of maritime transport (DG D-II).

Apart from spreading along a horizontally articulated axis through sectoral Councils, the Council has extended downwards to the Committee of Permanent Representatives (COREPER), consisting of career diplomats whose task is to prepare the work of their political masters. COREPER operates at two horizontally divided levels consisting of the permanent representatives of the Member states themselves and of their deputies respectively. It feeds back to the national capitals formal and unofficial information ranging from the minutes of the Commission's weekly work to constant reporting back on meetings from forthcoming agendas. Hence, 'these diplomats yield considerable de facto executive and legislature power' because they are at the intersperse of a two-way information flow between the state apparatus and of the individual member states and the formal institutions of the Council (Lewis, 1998).

In theory, COREPER allows national control to be retained over the details of policy developments. However, Litner and Mazey (1991) propound a more complex reality where the interaction with Commission officials has resulted in the growth of bureaucratic interpretation or 'engrenage', within which the division between Community and national interests becomes blurred in the search for a proposal acceptable to all participants. Nevertheless, as ministers predominantly engaged with national responsibilities do not deal with all the EU policy matters, this mechanism becomes crucial. The Commission proposals are first submitted to COREPER, which searches for maximal consensus. So, the work of the latter determines the work-rate of the Council – almost 90% of decisions are taken at the level of COREPER and below (Edwards, 1996). The Council's mechanism extends downwards to a range of working groups. Significantly, it is COREPER and not the Council that supervises the lower level groups. In fact, COREPER discusses only the points on which lower committees have not reached agreement. Given this 'bottom up' work, van Schendelen (1996) argues that the Council meeting is to a high degree a clearing system that takes final decisions only on relatively few dossiers.

European Commission The Commission is the supranational institution that serves and promotes the interests of the EU. Its roles include the rights to propose and originate policy proposals (the initiative role); administer policies (the administrative role); guard the Treaties and the *acquis communautaire* (the normative role); coordinate the institutions in order to pilot its legislation through, and work with member states to operate policies effectively (the mediative role); and represent the EU in various international organisations and in the EU external relations with non member countries (the representative role). The Commission draft proposals fall broadly into two categories, those proposing the creation of completely new legislation and thus potentially with politically debatable content, and those proposing technical legislation merely amplifying existing rules. In all cases the Commission discusses its proposals with actors inside and outside the institutional framework. Where the first category may result in a highly political policy making process, the routes to adopt more technical legislation are less political (Edwards and Spence, 1994), and include the setting of consultative advisory, management, and regulatory committees where Commission officials debate the issues with technical experts and national civil servants. Bradley (1992), however, points out that this 'comitology' constitutes a compromise between the need for more effective EU decision-making and the member states' desire to preserve national influence over the Commission decision-making.

The Commission is involved in 'three simultaneous and linked games' (Peters, 1992): the national game in which nations attempt to extract as much as possible from the EU; the institutional game where institutions seek to gain more power relative to the others and thirdly the bureaucratic game which involves the formation of separate and competing policy communities. Studies have highlighted the importance of the Commission as the agenda setter (Pollack, 1997) and its role in promoting a regulatory regime (Majone, 1993). Yet, because its structure produces a considerable degree of inter-bureaucratic politics, scholars argue that the Commission should be conceived not as an actor in itself but as an arena in which action occurs (Greenwood and Ronit, 1994) and caution against over generalisations concerning the role of an institution having a highly differentiated structure (Bulmer, 1994b).

Since its formation, the Commission is divided into separate policy units of organisation, the Directorate Generals (DGs). These are predominantly sectoral in nature, and provide for the specialised technical and administrative know-how in the various policy sectors in which the Community is active, but there are also horizontal DGs dealing with cross cutting issues such as budget, personnel, or financial control. The internal structure of the DGs varies. The general model is to have a member of the Commission shadowed by a European civil servant at the top and served by a small cabinet and then a typical hierarchical proliferation of Directorates and sections underneath the top leadership structure. DG-VII is responsible for Transport (and Energy) issues and has an incentive to capture potential significant policy initiatives and shape them in a manner compatible with the assigned tasks of their organisation. After the inclusion of maritime transport in the scope of transport policy a division of DG-VII was devoted to this mode of transportation. While in the 1970s outsiders were hired to tackle the burning issues of the period, nowadays the maritime division has a staff of over 50. Given the sectoral specialisation of the DGs, maritime transport issues that cut across the Community's administrative division are a common occurrence. A draft directive can have a crosscutting theme and certain implications for other DGs, notably DG-I (External Relations), DG-

II (Economic and financial affairs), DG-IV (Competition), DG-V (Employment, industrial relations and social affairs), and DG-XI (Environment).

Coordination within a DG may be compared to a national government structure since there is a distinct hierarchy and the possibility for directors of the DG to impose a line. Still, given the sensitivity of the Commission's work and the possibility of trampling on national sensibilities, component sections of the directorates may work on a somewhat shorter leash from their political leaders than might be true in many national bureaucracies (Peters, 1992). Furthermore, the substantial mobility of senior officials between DGs questions the extent to which a cohesive civil service exists (Page, 1995). Finally, there are no close horizontal links between the DGs; this extremely compartmentalised and hierarchical structure is accompanied mainly by vertical organisational links. The 24 DGs appear to be developing their own organisational cultures and approaches to policy so that incoherent and inconsistent policy stances can easily emerge from the commission because the DGs make policy decisions separately rather than jointly.

European Parliament The European Parliament has been more assertive in the decision making process since its first direct elections in 1979. The SEA upgraded further its legislature powers and observers reported an increasing influence in the post-Maastricht period. Smith (1995) summarises that from an institute in search of a value, the non-deliberate increase of its powers in the 1970s, the direct elections, and the concern of the democratic deficit, have changed the EP almost beyond recognition. After the 1997 Amsterdam Treaty it has been argued that the European Parliament is measurably closer to being 'on equal footing with the Council' (Moravscik and Nikolaidis, 1998). This impact varies between policy sectors with the EP believed to have less impact in technical policy developments. The EP has also been discussed as a 'conditional agenda setter' (Tsebelis, 1994) because it can draft its own initiative reports on matters of concern and pass resolutions asking the Commission to introduce appropriate legislative proposals.

The elected MEPs are grouped into transnational parties with internal organisation but they also participate in a range of committees, one of which deals with transport issues (Committee on Regional Policy, Transport and Tourism). It is frequently the opinions of these committees that influence the way that the EP votes in plenary (Judge *et al*, 1994). The EP committees shadow the DGs within the Commission and this enables them to draw attention effectively to and report on the initiatives of the relevant parts of the Commission. The second source for committees reports are motions for resolutions by individual MEPs on a matter falling within the sphere of activities of the EU. A third common basis is when a committee decides that it wishes to draw up a so-called 'own initiative' reporting a particular subject on which it has not been consulted.

Through its committee structure the EP has developed a constructive staff contact and a 'symbiotic' relationship with the Commission (Jacobs *et al*, 1995). Each DG has a co-ordinator responsible for maintaining contacts with the relevant EP committee, while a member of the Commissioner's cabinet has a 'parliamentary attaché' who is in a permanent link with the EP and its organs. Council members may also participate in committee meetings to exchange views. Moreover, they are involved in extensive consultation with the EP, especially when the conciliation procedure is invoked to resolve disagreements. However, even though the EP has the power to dismiss the Commission by a two thirds majority it has no powers over the Council, neither can it exercise any control over COREPER decision making practices.

European Court of Justice The ECJ is the institution charged with ensuring that the interpretation and application of the EU laws are observed. Although it does not take a direct part in the decision-making process, its judgements settle the particular matter at issue and clarify disputed passages of legislation. Even though lawyers are regarded as by nature conservatives, they have taken decisions that have progressed integration, notably the application of the single market programme (George, 1991). Perhaps most importantly, the ECJ increases the likelihood that laws passed by the EU will be implemented at the national level (Wincott, 1996). Since the ECJ rulings in the field of the EU law override those of the national courts, the EU law decreased the legislative autonomy previously enjoyed by member states (Weiler, 1982). Unlike other institutions, the ECJ is not answerable to any other body in order to be independent from any form of political pressure either by national governments or within the EU. Yet, it cannot intervene unless requested and cannot sanction non-implementation of its decisions by member states. So, whilst the neofunctionalist vein suggests that this is an apolitical institution that has engineered legal integration in Europe (Burley and Mattli, 1993), others (Garrett, 1992) argue that the ECJ simply reflects the interests of dominant member states having little independent influence

Consultative EU Institutions The Ecosoc is an advisory body drawn from three groups: employers, workers, and consumers. It is outside the inner-circles of the decision-making process, but both the Council and the Commission are required to consult it where the Treaty so provides, or whenever they consider it appropriate. In fact, all Commission proposals are considered by this institution, which publishes its detailed reports and recommendations. The Transport Section of the Ecosoc prepares draft opinions in the field of maritime transport that are put to the plenary session for approval. This means that its final opinions reflect all the views of the representatives of the various categories of social and economic activity. These decisions are forwarded to the Council and the Commission, without however binding the final views of these institutions. That its most important contribution is made out of the legislative process is believed to result in a continued marginalisation (Greenwood *et al*, 1992). Since the ratification of the TEU, the Ecosoc has been joined by the Committee of the Regions (CoR), which has a similar status but brings together representatives of local and regional authorities. The members of the CoR aim to defend the subsidiarity principle and provide the local and regional point of view on EU proposals.

Interest Groups and the CMTP

A variety of private actors have identified with this decision making process an important new level of power and have re-targeted their lobbying strategies aiming to influence the making of the CMTP. Through the formation of EU-level interest groups they seek to 'shoot where the ducks are' (Mazey and Richardson, 1996) and influence what, how, and when will be changed.

European shipowners have recognised the possibilities of an association based on EU membership with the formation of a Committee way back in 1962 (Comité des Associations d'Armateurs du Marché Communnitaire). Following the first EU enlargement its secretariat moved from Paris to Brussels, aiming to facilitate closer and more permanent contact with the Community institutions (Hayman, 1978), and was renamed the European Community Shipowners' Association (ECSA). Today, members of ECSA are all the national shipowners' associations of the 15 EU member states, plus the Norwegian one. Working through its permanent secretariat and several specialised Committees, ECSA continues a long shipowners' tradition of collective interests representation but individualistic secrecy regarding commercial practices (Ronit, 1995). Yet, the Danish and the Italian associations keep small secretariats in Brussels, though they are seeking the representation of their interests through ECSA. Moreover, a year before Sweden's accession to the EU, the Swedish association established a temporary (two years) bureau in Brussels, its prime aim being to become familiar with the policy making process and the work of ECSA.

The European Shippers' Council (ESC) coordinates the political interests of European shippers. ESC also represents commercial interests in consultations with liner conferences and other groups of shipping lines or providers of services related to maritime transport. Furthermore, it provides the means for legal interests representation in the form of formal complaint to the Commission or the ECJ 'when normal commercial consultation appears insufficient to assure the maintenance of sound commercial market structures' (Baasch, 1996). These additional activities are the products of the initial configuration of the organisation, which was formed in 1963 more as a means to coordinate the commercial activities of shippers *vis-à-vis* liner lines which were for the most part without political intervention. However, ECS currently devotes around 80% of its time to EU making legislation and complaints and only about 20% to commercial matters, therefore, the organisation decided to relocate to Brussels in 1993, and became part of the intermodal European Council of Transport Users. The latter provides a secretariat for the ESC, while the Federation of Belgian Enterprises in Brussels provides further infrastructure facilities. This move was accompanied by the explicit recognition of the need to be closer to the Commission as the importance of its policy-making coincides with a diminishing task in relation to commercial issues, and direct consultations with liner conferences.

Trade unions are represented in the EU policy-making through the Committee of Transport Workers Unions in the EC (CTWUEC), in particular its seafarer section. At the early stages of the CTP, ITF, as well as the European Trade Unions Committee (ETUC) represented trade unions of all transport modes. Considering, however the rapid developments of the common policy, they agreed that a body following the pattern of ITF but representing transport workers at a European level would have political advantages and effectively safeguard their interests regarding EU policy developments. Still, in the case of the maritime mode ITF remains actively engaged in the EU-level debate. This organisation represents seafarer interests and co-ordinates their worldwide activities against FoC shipping. According to the chairman of the CTWUEC seafarer's section 'FoC is the intellectual property of ITF, all the policy decisions on this issue are monitored by ITF which has the experience' (Orrell, 1996). Therefore, whenever subjects related to this aspect are discussed at a EU-level, ITF co-ordinates and represents national level trade unions.

In response to a growing perception that a body should represent their interests within the EU, port authorities set up the European Sea Ports Association (ESPO) in 1993. ESPO, is organised in three Committees (environmental, maritime and transport committee respectively), and comprises of national representatives of (private and state owned) ports from all the 13 member states having access to sea, together with observers from Norway, Malta, Cyprus, and Iceland, which may ultimately seek membership. Interestingly, in some member states port authorities are organised in different national-level associations. However, all of these national associations have become members of ESPO. Also in 1993, private port operators from 9 member states,[8] representing the 80% of all European private operators, formed the Federation of European Private Port Operators (FEPORT), as through contacts with the European policy makers, they 'realised the necessity to create an organisation that would represent their interests on a European level, serve as a contact with EU officials and other interest groups, and monitor all EU activities which concern ports and transport' (Verhoeven, 1996). At the beginning of 1994 FEPORT established its own secretariat in Brussels, located at the same building as ESPO. The two organisations have developed a cooperation discussing and formulating, whenever possible, common points of view with regard to European policies. Like ESPO, FEPORT has united port operators that at national level are organised in different associations.

The stakeholders that have been less actively involved in the policy-making process are the mediators in the maritime transport process. Although national associations of both freight forwarders and shipbrokers are associated in respective Euro-federations, these groups are primarily engaged in commercial activities rather than interest representation. A revealing example is the European Liaison Committee of Freight Forwarders (CLECAT) that associates forwarders and custom agents in all transport modes. This is not irrespective of the fact that national forwarding associations are involved in training, education and the provision of professional certificates in freight forwarding, lobbying is only a small part of their activities. Similarly, the European Community Association of Ship-Brokers Associations (ECASBA) considers itself as a professional organisation concentrating on the coordination of commercial and training activities of its national associations and is the only Euro-federation still located far from Brussels (in Rotterdam).

A different kind of interest group started work in 1994. This is the Alliance of Maritime Regional Interest in Europe (AMRIE), which has been formatted to bring together authorities and stakeholders interested in the future of the maritime regions in the EU. AMRIE works to ensure that these regions have a political voice and are able to influence developments that affect their employment prospect and quality of life increase the political profile of maritime activities and the awareness of their massive contribution to the prosperity of the Community (AMRIE, 1995).

Lobbying Practices The Euro-centred format of interest representation is not a new phenomenon in the EU policy-making process. A boom has been observed since the SEA reformed the decision-making process and the QMV became normal practice for policy decisions. By extending the EU policy-making competence and upgrading the role of the EP to co-legislator, the TEU increased the appeal of and necessity for rapid, transnational interest definition, aggregation, and coordination, and raised the pressure to improve the effectiveness of EC-level interest association.

Federations of nationally based groups representing a given interest are the most common organisational form of business collective action. These highly political specialised, representative groups of restricted membership are the most likely to be consulted by the EU institutions (Mazey and Richardson, 1993b). The value of the federation structure has been challenged (Jordan and McLaughlin, 1993) yet, given the opportunities these associations offer to influence collective sectoral positions, gather consistent reliable sources of information, and maintain network contacts, the generalisability of the 'weak Euro-federations' thesis has been questioned (cf. Greenwood and Ronit, 1994). There are also national branches of European industry and employer associations, national and multinational companies which prefer individualistic lobbying, direct firm membership associations, and 'half-way house' structures that include both associations and firm membership (Greenwood and Cram, 1996). When more than one type of these intra-sectoral interest groups arise one can come across instances of 'competition' and 'collaboration' between them. Other interest groups operating at EU-level include European 'peak' (all business) associations of employers and labour, sub-national, regional, and local authorities, trade associations of non-EU member countries, law firms and professional lobbyists.

The EU policy developments affect directly the ways that interest groups exercise influence and indirectly their organisational structure. While in the 1980s Euro-groups used to monitor development at an EU level, communicate information to their national member associations, and facilitate some policy coordination, recent observations stress that they have developed functions enabling them to act more autonomously, speedily, and effectively (Greenwood, 1997). Small secretariats, insufficient membership and/or geographical spread, location in various European capitals, and inability to reach a common position other than the lowest common denominator, have been replaced by wider membership rather than just the EU, a trend to be based in Brussels, and at least some majority voting, so as to speed up decision making and reach a common position at the early stages of the policy making process.

The unregulated Brussels game differs from the national one, as the EU system is less 'corporatist' and more 'lobbying oriented', with interest groups having a number of access points. In addition to the formal linkages, there are the infinitive informal ones every actor is free to develop. There is not an independent autonomous public decision-making body that is clearly defined but a policy arena where power is fragmented and more than one institution integrated into networks of joint decision-making (Grande, 1996). This structure obliges interest groups to adopt complex multi-level strategies for the successful pursuit of interests. Organised interests are involved in a (variable) interaction with all the EU institutions aiming to overcome the fluidity and unpredictability of policy making (Richardson, 1993). Then, although the 'tried and tested' (Grant, 1993) national route has lost momentum to spontaneous, or formal, 'Brussels' lobbying (cf. Greenwood, 1995), the operation of both routes is a frequently observed lobbying strategy. Therefore, 'the master lobbyist like the chess master must be able to play several games at once at different tables' (Butt Philip, 1983).

Interest groups tend to shift their lobbying to Brussels in the early stages of the policy-making process aiming to influence the content of the initial Commission draft proposal. They concentrate their attention on the Commission, which represents a small but relatively open bureaucracy that may depend on outside governmental and non-governmental experts to develop comprehensive policy proposals. Top-level officials are the prime lobbying targets but because they are not easily influenced medium or low-level contracts, as well as the comitology, tend to be important. Business interests have responded in different ways, nevertheless, issue identification and policy drafting of the Commission proposals are influenced by this representation (Lodge, 1989). That said, Greenwood *et al* (1992) conclude that the relationship between organised business and the Commission is by no means characterised by simple unilateral pressures, Business is represented by various actors and relationships are always of a reciprocal nature.

The EP was initially considered as a less attractive source of power, however, as the relative power of the institution increases this pattern changes (Andersen and Eliassen, 1995). In the aftermath of the TEU the formerly weak EP has enough power to be taken seriously by the interest groups, notably as a useful means of achieving amendments to the EU legislation. As a professional lobbyist firm states, the EP 'has the powers to shape the regulatory environment with the EU at all levels ... In addition to passive observance however it can be used to curtail the action of other governmental institutions both European and non-European' (Hammond-Suddards, 1994, p. 31). The lobbying targets are primarily individual MEPs, especially the Rapporteur appointed for drawing up the draft text of a report that will eventually form the basis of the EP opinion, as well as the other members of the Committee, which is primarily responsible for the preparation of the draft. Notably, interest groups consider the EP less important on technical matters and more important on wider issues like the environmental and social policy fields. As regards the consultative Ecosoc, this is not considered an important focus of lobbying.

The Council, COREPER, and the Council working groups, represent the last opportunity to influence a policy proposal. Although perceived as the less accessible and more secretive EU institution, interest groups try to influence the Council mostly by using the 'national route to Brussels'

(Calingeart, 1993). Considering its role and legal status, national associations lobby their own governments to achieve collective or individual targets, though that lobbying is regarded as less effective than that during the early stages. Cross border cooperation at that stage is increasingly evident, as the introduction of the QMV has increased the probabilities of member states to seek allies in other member states in order to achieve the formation of a blocking minority.

These activities do not end with the adoption of a policy proposal and interest groups continue to exert pressures at the stage of implementation. The importance of national lobbying is re-emphasised once a proposal has been agreed by the Council and is to be implemented. Lobbying at that stage is also directed at the EU level. The Commission monitors the implementation process through working groups, consultative committees, and 'committees for adjustment to technical progress'. The activities of these bodies are highly valued by many interest groups (Butt Philip, 1991). As these committees may also be involved in the preparation of new proposals, in a sense lobbying activities at that stage represent the lobbying of future policies. Finally, EU level actions during the implementation phase may also take the form of complaints at the ECJ.

On the other hand, the EU institutions are a set of actors seeking the industry's participation. At the stage of translating ideas to workable policies, policy-makers regard interest groups as essential sources of unique knowledge and help them to overcome the information deficit. Intensive consultation, information exchange, interests accommodation, alliance formation, have all been seen as essential to achieve maximum efficiency of legislation and its implementation (Andersen and Eliassen, 1993). Thus, interest groups have acquired a close relationship with the Commission, which seeks to reward (i.e. with access) the 'most efficient' of them (Gorges, 1993). Hix (1994, p. 13) describes the EU as 'a system close to post-pluralism ... where decision makers are no-longer neutral arbiters but proactively take account of countervailing interests'. The generic term 'policy networks' (Rhodes and March, 1992) has been used to describe the involvement of public and private interests in symbiotic, close, and mutually dependent relationships from which the meso sectoral policies are formulated.

A large number of private actors are apparently interested in establishing channels of influencing EU policies, still the exact nature of their activity remains the subject of various interpretations. This is closely related to the significant sectoral variation regarding interests' organisation and the different decision-making procedures employed over the administration of different policies. McLaughlin *et al* (1993) anticipate that European policy studies should distinguish between the process of representing an interest which leads to a diversity of methods of representations and interest group activity that is merely one aspect (albeit an important one) of this phenomenon As the goal of this volume is to understand the development of a sectoral EU policy, the major target of scrutiny is the influential policy participant rather than the narrow pressure group structures. In other words, the primary concern is on what Greenwood (1995, p. 4) terms as the 'logic of influence', that is 'the extent to which such actors influence policy outputs (means) and outcomes (ends)', without however ignoring the, inextricably linked and possibly reciprocal, 'logic of collective actions', that is 'the factors which impact the ways in which business interests work together'.

Summary

This chapter reviewed the theoretical accounts developed to explain the wider issue of European political and economic integration. The critical discussion of the various conceptual paths suggests that a great emphasis should be given to the role of the actionable factors in the context, content, and process, of policy integration. Scholars increasingly concentrate on the examination of the EU activities as the outcome of a new multi-level governance system, which displays its own dynamics. In this context, they have recently brought into the analysis the neoinstitutionalist paradigm as 'a useful "conceptual lens" through which to view policy change in the EC' (Bulmer 1994b, p. 442). The critical thesis of neoinstitutionalism is that an interpretation of EU-level policy integration needs to focus on the interaction of three dimensions: the EU institutions, its member states and interest groups, and place the impact of the EU institutional framework centre stage. Furthermore, scholars studying policy integration from different perspectives, seem to agree that the actions of public and private policy actors towards further integration are largely influenced by the 'new' economic context within which they operate.

Informed by these theoretical developments, and the preceding examination of the involved policy actors, the next chapters examine the

CMTP-making process in the 1990s to conclude on whether it is valid to advocate that *policy Europeanisation progresses as in the contemporary political and economic interdependence context EU institutions, member states' administrations, and interest groups, develop a dialectic relationship, wherein the EU institutions play a decisive role in the dissemination of policy-ideas, the definition and articulation of other actors' preferences, and the determination of policy-outcome.*

Notes

1   The 'Community method' involved a democratic process towards political unity by integrating specific fields and sectors, and by extensively relying to the existence of central institutions, which according to the treatises would take more formal power of decisions of the national governments in some aspects (cf. Coombes, 1970).

2   For the Weberian concept of the state: Dahl, 1961; O'Neil, 1996.

3   In particular: social policy (Pierson, 1996); European merger control (Bulmer, 1994a; 1994b); fraud (Menindrou, 1994).

4   Critics question whether the paradigm consists of a 'new approach' or represents just a renewed, hitherto familiar and part of the political science mainstream, interest in the complexity and multifaceted nature of politics (Almond, 1988; Jordan, 1990; Rhodes, 1995). This debate is beyond the scope of this volume, not least because it does not challenge the content of the arguments that the neoinstitutionalist paradigm adduces.

5   Therefore, this account differs from the new sociological institutionalism which by including in the term institution 'not just formal rules procedures or norms, but the symbol systems, cognitive scripts and more templates that provide the frames of meaning guiding human action (sociological institutionalism) breaks down the conceptual divide between institutions and culture' (Hall and Taylor, 1996, p. 947).

6   Interestingly, Norgaard (1996) argues that rational-choice theorists have reconceptualised rationality in a way that partially embraces this approach, hence, the different traditions share a converging course.

7   Following the 1995 EU enlargement 87 votes are allocated to member states roughly in proportion with its population size. Ger, Fr, It, and UK, have 10 votes each; Sp has 8; B, Gr, Nl and Pr, have 5 each; A and Sw have 4 votes each; Dk, Ir, and F have 3 each; and Lux has 2. Agreement under QMV demands 62 votes and decisions can be blocked only by a 'blocking minority' of 26.

8   The nine member states are: B, Dk, Ger, Fl, Fin, Nl, Pr, Sp, and the UK. There are no private port operators in Greece, and, of course, in the landlocked member states Austria and Luxembourg.

3 CMTP and Policy Actors: A Historical Perspective

As the CMTP is a sequence of events that unfold over time, it would be difficult to understand the contemporary developments without considering how the specific EU policy has evolved. This chapter examines the progress of the CMTP, the changes of its nature, scope, and objectives within a historical perspective. Although the beginning of this policy is traced to 1974, the analysis looks back to the developments in the field of transport since the beginning of the European integration. This is because developments concerning the maritime mode are part of an integral Common Transport Policy (CTP). The latter is a matter of bringing out the comparative advantages of each transport technique and each mode of transport, and putting them to the best possible use. It is valuable, therefore, to analyse special aspects or specific parts and modes without loosing sight of the overall view of the transport sector. The next sections provide more than a mere descriptive survey of the main policy developments. The focus is on the interaction and influence of policy actors on the progress of the CMTP, therefore, integrated in the analysis is a discussion of how scholars have assessed the impact of these actors during this evolutionary process.

Towards a Common Maritime Transport Policy: The Four Periods

Succeeding a period characterised by the absence of any policy interest regarding the particular transport mode, the elaboration of a CMTP became part of the European agenda in 1974. To understand the kind of progress that has been made in developing a common policy, as well as the form that these activities have taken, the overall EU period can be divided into four phases. They are from 1957 to 1974 ('excluding maritime transport from the scope of CTP'); from 1974 to 1986 ('the problem-orientated approach'); from 1986 to 1990 ('the mosaic approach'); and the 1990s ('the horizontal approach'). Table 3.1 illustrates the keystones of this process, all of them to be discussed within the forthcoming sections.

The determination of the actual moment that marks the introduction of a new approach, and consequently the ending of its predecessor, is not always clear. The EU policy-making process is a structured and complex sequence of events. Similarly to any agenda building (cf. Kingdon, 1984), it implicates various interrelated phases, including identification of problems, formation of draft proposals, formal decisions and their implementation. The distinctive moment of a new policy strategy may be defined either by the 'discourse' of an approach, that is, the intellectual developments that the Commission initiatives and policy proposals put forward, or by the 'policy output', that is, the legislative and political decisions that the Council of Ministers adopts (Porter, 1995).

Table 3.1 Towards a CMTP: Main Policy Developments

	Year	Development
1st Period	1957	Signing of the Rome Treaty (Introduction of the CTP)
2nd Period	1974	Expansion of the CTP to include maritime (and air) transport
	1979	Adoption of the 'Brussels Package'
	1983	EP takes Council inaction to the ECJ
	1985	Commission Memorandum: The first proposals
3rd Period	1986	Adoption of the four Regulations
	1987	The Single European Act comes into force
	1989	Publication of the second set of Commission proposals
	1991	Introduction of the horizontal approach
		Signing of the Maastricht Treaty of the European Union
4th Period	1992	White Paper on the future of the CTP
		Green Paper on the impact of transport to the environment
	1993	Publication of the Common policy on safe seas document
	1995	Publication of a policy document on shortsea shipping
	1996	The two maritime strategy documents
	1997	Green paper on sea ports and maritime infrastructure
	2000	Commission proposals on the safety of seaborne oil trade
	2001	White Paper on a European Transport Policy for 2010

In fact, the Commission frequently issues communications and consultative documents (such as Green and White Papers) all of which require a Council response. Legislative output is not always the aftermath of the conceptual development of a policy approach, and whenever such legislative output occurs it is largely pre-empted by the policy discourse. Nevertheless, ambiguities would surround the selection of the 'policy discourse' as the definite point of the introduction of a new EU approach. A specific policy output might influence the future approach of the Commission. Then, in many cases the conceptual innovations, informal discussions, and proposals necessary for actions are evident before the formal expression of the Commission's new policy thinking. For instance, the Treaties and the successive enlargements of the EU, both 'policy outputs', have been identified as influential agenda-setters (Westlake, 1995). It would be misleading, however, to conclude *a priori* the moment they began to affect, at least intellectually, the nature of a common EU policy. Since there is a time lag between when agreements are reached and when these changes actually come into effect, it is only the start of their legal influence that can be precisely defined.

On that account, although a ECJ decision on the application of the rules of the Rome Treaty to the maritime mode (1974) is commonly considered as the point that marked the beginning of the CMTP, this point could also be determined a year earlier when the first enlargement of the EU took place. Respectively, in spite of the widespread embracing of the adoption of four Regulations in December 1986 as the turning point towards systematic EU involvement, the latter could also be traced in 1985 when the Commission issued its communication and proposals well in advance of the adoption of these regulations. Preferences ultimately depend on the conceptualisation of the policy-making process, thus we will return to this discussion later. For analytical purposes, however, this volume utilises the commonly preferred points and defines four distinctive periods of the CMTP.

1957-1974: Excluding the Maritime Mode from the CTP

By including distinct provisions for a CTP in the preamble of the inaugurating Rome Treaty (1957), the original six member states of the EU gave a special status to the transport sector. As attempts to formulate such policy had first been made during the inception of the older European Coal and Steel Community (ECSC)[1] this was not a surprising decision. The free movement of goods and persons was, along with the free circulation of services and capital, the *raison d' être* of the newly established common market. As all commodities have to move in space and time, a reduction in expenditure of transport should stimulate cross-frontier movements and trade increase. The decline of transport costs related to production would widen the range of international commodity exchanges and push into international trade products which had been previously excluded, or traded over short distances.

Article 3 of the Treaty mentioned that the adoption of a common policy in the sphere of transport was an indispensable complement to the new customs union. Transport was the only economic sector apart from agriculture that had a separate title devoted to it in the Treaty context (Articles 74-85). This chapter officially recognised transport as an area in which action should be taken and provided the broad lines of what this policy should be. However, the transport injunctions of the Treaty were remarkably general and limited in scope (Bayliss, 1979). Article 3 did not have any reference to transport modes but Article 84(1) stated that 'the provisions of this Title shall apply to transport by rail, road, and inland waterways'. Maritime transport was mentioned only in Article 84(2) which provided that '[T]he Council may, acting unanimously, decide whether, to what extent, and by what procedure, appropriate provisions may be laid down for sea and air transport'. The interpretation of the latter paragraph led to the conclusion that maritime (like air) transport fell outside the scope of the CTP, as well as of other provisions of the Treaty like competition.[2] These provisions were followed by a visionary memorandum targeting a CTP that in the very process would replace national transport policies (CEU, 1961), and an action programme defining three objectives to be achieved by the EU policy: removing obstacles; integrating transport systems through liberalisation and detailed regulation with respect to market control; and technical, social, and economic, harmonisation.

Subsequent events were to show that these goals were over-ambitious as none of them progressed significantly. The first period of the CTP was characterised by a 'disappointing performance' (Despicht, 1969; Button, 1984), and an 'output failure' under which the system was unable to translate a general commitment to participate in a collective decision-making effort into an acceptable set of policies of rules (Lindberg and Scheingold, 1970). The presence of different regulatory regimes in the national markets disfavoured any policy progress (Gwilliam, 1990; Button, 1993). By trying far-reaching proposals the Commission found little support for the different national preferences, as some national governments (i.e. Germany) advocated the 'social service philosophy' and others were endorsing the 'commercial philosophy' (i.e. the Netherlands). This situation led to the critical absence of any leadership towards policy developments. Other studies question, however, whether any category of policy actors, including the EU institutions, really perceived a CTP to be in their vital interests. Abbati (1986) and Vickerman (1992) suggest that the CTP was a component of the Treaty due to a commitment to a gradualist 'sectoral' approach of integration and not because the founding members were conscious that such a policy was an essential precondition of the common market.[3] To Swann (1988) the introduction of a CTP was the result of a delicate political compromise among the Netherlands, which had significant interests in the Rhine transport, and the five other states.

The latter may explain why, having come from the experience in the area of international road haulage policy in the context of the ECSC, the founders of the EU decided to include inland waterways in the provisions of the Treaty but neither maritime nor air transport. Given the major difficulties that had already arisen during attempts to find a compromise formula for inland transport, it seemed preferable at that point to exclude these two modes from the *lex specialis* of the Treaty. A high-ranking Commission official adds that the functioning of the EU and the shortcomings of the policy-making procedures were revealed in the shaping of the common transport policy. Specifically, Erdmenger (1983) propounds that the strongly legalistic even dogmatic in nature work in the field of transport during these early days should be expected, because of 'a certain institutional dogmatism'. Decisions had to be taken according to what the Treaty said and in no other way (for a similar argument in a wider context: Dahredorf, 1971). Whilst the decision to exclude maritime transport has been attributed to the absence of any maritime interest by the original six member states, the willingness of the European institutions to follow dogmatically the letter of the Rome Treaty was not insignificant.

In a different vein, Cafruny (1991) emphasises that in the case of maritime transport, even if the six member states wanted to develop collective policy measures they would face the shipping industry's strong resistance on the logic of transfer policy powers in maritime affairs from national governments to the EU institutions. That said, in 1962 all the coastal founding members of the EU, UK and Denmark (which were to access the EU in 1973), Greece (to access in 1981) Sweden (to access in

1995), and Norway responded in unity against the manner of implementation of US anti-trust laws, arguing for a collective European policy as the best way to oppose them.

1974-1986: The Problem-Orientated Approach

The first EU enlargement in 1973 had an enormous impact on the content of the CTP. The accession of three maritime nations (Denmark, Ireland, and the UK) remarkably changed the economic structure of the European experiment. Among others, it substantially increased the relative importance of the maritime mode. The bulk of the trade between the three new members and the rest of the EU was carried by sea, so that maritime flows represented 25% of the trade within the EU of nine members compared with 8% in the EU of six. The size of the EU-flagged fleet almost doubled, and the number of ports within the EU increased as well. The second enlargement and the accession of Greece, a traditional maritime power, in 1981 furthered the importance of the maritime transport for the EU economy.

A major policy reform was the extension of the EU interest to include the maritime mode within the common transport strategy. As the Commission later reviewed, the enlargement to include island states made it urgent to bring sea transport within the common strategy (CEU, 1984). In 1974 the Commission took a test case to the ECJ attempting to resolve whether the provisions of the Treaty were applicable to the maritime mode.[4] The ECJ confirmed the EU policy making authority, a judgement with legal and political implications: it incorporated this mode in the process of European integration, hence considered as the most important ECJ case in the field of maritime transport (cf. Power, 1992). Subsequently, the focus turned on whether the EU could help to bring about solutions to specific sectoral problems. In 1975, and reacting to the ECJ decision, the French government presented a memorandum on the development of EU action on shipping[5] and the Commission chaired a Working Group composed by representatives of the EU ports, which investigated the management of various ports from institutional, structural, and administrative angles. In 1976, the Dutch Presidency of the Council opened discussions on competition rules and shipping, the Commission submitted a communication on shipping matters and relationships with third countries, and an interim EP report emphasised the need for further EU coordination in the field.[6]

Apparently, all the EU institutions launched discussions related to the possibilities of formulating common policy measures. In line with the working pattern of international organisations involved in maritime affairs, in these first years the EU endorsed a 'problem orientated approach' (Erdmenger, 1983), which was summarised by R. Burke (1978, p. 13), the then member of the Commission whose portfolio included transport as well as consumer affairs: the Community was working on the emerging problems in respect of which it seemed profitable to examine whether the Community might be able to act more effectively than member states individually; or indeed supplement member states activity.

The Brussels Package

The most important policy decision of this second period was achieved after five years of discussion. A Regulation, which was adopted in 1979, known as the 'Brussels package', enabled the member states to accede and ratify the UNCTAD Code (Chapter 1).[7] An international agreement on the latter was initialled only two days after the ECJ ruling and opinions on how to respond on it ranged from support by three member states (France, Germany, Belgium) to total opposition (UK, Denmark) or neutrality on the part of others (cf. Couper, 1977). Against this background, and based on the significance of the UNCTAD Code for the organisation of maritime trade worldwide, as well as the fact that the EU fleet was particularly strong on a proportional basis in the liner section, the Commission tried to develop a common stance. As Hayman (1978) observed, the Commission had provoked the ECJ ruling and was interested to give some reality to it, when the unilateral accessions of the Code would widen the divergence between national policies. Its actions achieved an agreement with the three pro-code member states not to proceed with ratification until the ratification period elapsed, or until a common policy could be reached (Bredimas and Tzoannos, 1981). Two years later the British government and shipowners put forward a compromise solution that remained in principle in firm opposition to the Code (cf. Davies, 1992). Yet, the Commission published a draft of an accession Regulation and an official consultation procedure begun in September 1977. This procedure led to the Brussels package, which obliged member states to ratify the Code subject to some reservations: the cargo sharing formula envisaged by the Code would not apply to the liner trades between EU and other OECD countries; and the share allocated to the EU lines would be redistributed among them on the basis of commercial criteria.

Several observations highlight the dynamics generated during the process of making this policy decision. First, the unanimous EU stance was achieved despite some of its members having earlier officially expressed a negative position in the UNCTAD framework. Second, the Code could never come into force without the support of at least certain of the major maritime nations, or the EU as a group, would become contracting parties. Third, liner conferences in the UK had never been subject to any form of regulation in national law. To sum up, the EU involvement was an admission that the questions covered by the international agreement were of importance not only to individual member states but also to the EU as a whole. Notably, Finland, Norway, and Sweden, which were supportive of the Code, associated their final position to the outcome of the intra-EU negotiations indicating that they would not ratify the agreement unless there was a positive EU response. Nonetheless, the implementation of the Brussels package was slow, as member states continued to sign bilateral agreements with non-EU countries that included cargo-sharing clauses conflicting with it.

Other EU Policy Developments

Cafruny (1987) suggests that the Brussels package was more of a common response to the growing political turbulence in international shipping than a movement towards integration of national policies. The second part of the 1970s was indeed a period when two successive oil crises resulted in major changes to maritime transport. Of the most critical economic phenomena were the stagnation of seaborne trade and the subsequent worsening of the surplus of world shipping tonnage. The employment of flag discrimination and other protectionist practices by many countries who wished to control their trade through state trading shipping, particularly in the liner trade, were expanded. West European and other traditional maritime nations, which had dominated world shipping saw this dominance challenged more intensively than ever by FoC and other third-world countries.

In this context, an alteration of the shipowners', shippers', and trade unions' stands towards the EU administration and the potential of common

EU measures became evident. ECSA put its first detailed proposals to the Commission in December 1973, calling in particular for the inclusion of shipping clauses in the EU trade agreements. Shippers were seeking, according to the ESC chairman of its standing committee, a collective European policy with regard to shipping in general and liner shipping in particular (Muheim, 1978). Trade unions were demanding the development of EU initiatives regarding social issues (CEU, 1984). Still, none of them was looking for a coherent EU policy. The growing politicisation of the economic environment of shipping and the UNCTAD activities encouraged shipowners to consider EU policy, as a mean of asserting their interests, but the preference was the development of *ad hoc* policy measures. Similarly, the only priority for shippers was liner conferences regulation. Finally, trade unions were seeking self-regulatory agreements through EU-level meetings arranged and chaired by the Commission.

A similar change was observed in the stance of national administrations. In the face of serious problems with the rate dumping and cargo reservation practices followed by state trading countries, in particular by the COMECON fleets,[8] the UK decided to request the assistance of the Commission. In spite of the limited potential for a unanimous decision, this was an effort to mobilise EU discussions as an additional pressure on the state-trading countries. The British view was that these countries would not adopt a more flexible negotiating position *vis-à-vis* the west European nations unless the EU agreed on common policy action. Early in 1977 the EP also called the Commission to assess these practices. The Commission took the recommendations on board but member states could not agree on the proposed concerted retaliatory action, due to the strong French opposition (Abbati, 1986). Still, the 1978 Council common position was a decision to monitor the activities in question for two years and prepare for further actions. As this was a much weakened version of the original Commission proposal, that provided for executory rather than monitoring actions, the British administration continued to ask for more concrete EU action (Davies, 1992). The issue was finally superseded by the provisions of the UNCTAD Code, yet these events highlight a growing interest in exploiting the newly established policy making level. However, when Denmark, the Netherlands and the UK were interested in cross trading and open to international competition, France and Italy were more protectionist. Within this environment, the implementation of a problem-oriented approach was mainly supported by the more liberal maritime nations as an attempt to forestall integration, which at the time it believed to be a danger to the traditional system of shipping (Cafruny, 1987).

Following a number of maritime accidents and disasters involving oil tankers on the EU seaways (including the infamous *Amoco Cadiz* accident) issues of marine pollution also came into discussion at a EU-level, albeit followed by an insignificant policy output. The most notable development was a Commission proposal for a directive to improve the enforcement of international standards of safety and pollution prevention for all shipping using EU ports.[9] The directive was not adopted at a EU level but provided the basis of a wider European agreement (the 1982 Paris Memorandum of Understanding on Port State Control). Policy measures in the field of maritime safety were restricted to recommendations for the implementation of the international rules.

Beyond policy developments produced with direct references to shipping, some of the trade and economic cooperation agreements that were concluded between the EU and third countries had a bearing on shipping. For instance, the Lomé II and III Conventions (signed in 1979 and 1984 respectively) contained declarations on the objective of cooperation between the EU and the African Caribbean and Pacific countries in the field of shipping. Other agreements also referred to the need to examine problems arising in the maritime relations between the EU and other countries in a cooperative spirit, yet such references were of little practical use. The bulk of shipping agreements with non-EU countries were still an issue primarily considered by each member state at national level, with the EP stressing that a common external economic policy cannot work if it overlooks sea transport.[10]

The CMTP initiatives were directed to a different path than that followed in other transport modes. The rest of the CTP concentrated on the potential alignment of the internal inland transport systems into a single competition-oriented market organisation. The maritime internal market was also subject to divergent national traditions (Chapter 7) and provided considerable scope for policy integration. However, traffic flows within the internal market did not become part of the agenda. With national governments dealing with shipping as a special case, because of its international character and its substantial economic returns, there was no sign by the Commission of an intention to confine it as part of the establishment of the common market. In the heydays of the Luxembourg compromise, which emphasised the national veto potential, it was questionable whether there was a common maritime philosophy on the part of the member states. Moreover, stakeholders explicitly opposed the development of an EU policy concerning the internal market, as an unnecessary interference to an efficient market.

The absence of any policy initiative concerning the problems of ports and the state of their connection with the hinterland emphasises the difficulties in introducing new policy measures requiring unanimity as well as the continuation of a certain institutional dogmatism. The Commission and the EP had discussed such issues since 1970 but no initiative followed the 1974 ECJ decision. The absence of any reference to the word 'port' in the Treaty of Rome, continued to make unclear whether ports fell into the scope of the transport or the industrial common policy; and if the former was the case, whether ports should be considered as part of sea or land transport (Pallis and Chlomoudis, 2001). The Commission did not try any proposal that could be objected to but directed its activities to the continuation of its cooperation with the industry to identify potential common philosophies, build alliances, and prepare the ground for future initiatives. The sole notable outcome was the submission of an official report to the EP, which in turn adopted a report on the role of ports in the CTP and a ten-point resolution.[11]

The integral CTP developments of that period were marginal. At the end of the 1970s, the EU was no nearer to a real CTP than twenty years before (Bromhead, 1979; Button, 1984) and in mid-1980s Whitelegg (1988:16-17) argued that the record of the CTP 'is characterised by little development of its basic thinking about transport and much repetition and bureaucratic non-activity which passes for a common policy. Its resilience to popular academic and critical transport policy is remarkable and exists in isolation from transport policies'. In the opinion of the then chairman of the EP Transport Committee it was a period of a 'theological strife' between supporters of liberalisation and supporters of harmonisation (Anastasopoulos, 1994). The former group insisted that liberalisation was the precondition of any policy harmonisation; the latter argued that harmonisation was a *sine qua non* for liberalisation. Thus, national governments were inclined to make only limited commitments with reasonably clear implications. Bayliss (1979) points out that, lacking any 'grand design', member states thought that a compromise could only make each of them worse. Because they did not see any great political advantage stemming from an agreement about a CTP, failure to agree was not perceived as damaging to the European idea.

To some scholars, the variation of the institutional priorities was critical. Ross (1994) suggests that whereas the Commission and especially the EP realised the importance of the CTP at every stage, the member states via the Council were reluctant to follow. The unanimity requirement strengthened the position of the *status quo* oriented parties, which in the aftermath of the Luxembourg compromise defended their interest effectively by using a veto. Both the Dutch and the British governments used this power on a long list of transport issues in the 1970s, including infrastructure pricing and investment, and apparently apolitical matters became great stumbling blocks (Bromhead, 1979). Abbati (1986) concludes that the short-term interests of the Transport Ministers, and the fact that the Commission was seeing itself as an arbiter for a consensus, were clearly revealed in the framing of transport policies. In a similar vein, Gwilliam (1979) holds that when the Commission found it difficult to reconcile the antithesis between liberalisation and harmonisation, it decided on a change of emphasis away from the field of operation to the field of infrastructure. Still, the difficulties surrounding the decision making process and the problems to implement and administrate EU level initiatives resulted in negative effects on the production of policy outputs.

However, it was the institutional background itself that provided the impetus for the progress of the common policy in all transport modes. The absence of such progress led the EP to institute proceedings against the Council alleging inaction in the field of transport. It did so in 1982, arguing that the Council had infringed the Rome Treaty 'by failing to introduce a common policy for transport and in particular to lay down the framework for such policy in a binding manner'.[12] In fact, the EP had already expressed its discontent with the slow progress towards a real EU transport policy without any practical effect. Perhaps at the specific point of time, the motivation of the first elected EP was not the slow CTP progress *per se*, but a test of the institution's mandate to press for further integration. Nonetheless, the ECJ confirmed the Council's inability to convert proposals to actions and ruled that the Commission was obliged to elaborate proposals for the establishment of a common transport market by 1992.[13] This was the first time in the life of the EU that the ECJ found the Council guilty of breaching the Treaty of Rome provisions. The EP action and ECJ judgement provoked the Commission's reactions, including the publication of policy papers on maritime transport in March 1985.

1986-1990: The Mosaic Approach

The Four Regulations

The adoption of four Council Regulations on December 1986 is frequently conceived as the starting point of the systematic EU involvement in maritime affairs (cf. Power, 1992). Like previous EU actions, these Regulations were devoted mainly to aspects that may be called the 'external relations' of shipping. Notably, they provided means for coordinating member states' policies in the face of practices by countries outside the EU. This was a period when the operating conditions of vessels under EU-flags worsened due to the continuation of trade stagnation, oversupply of services, and the subsequent fall in freight rates. As European shipowners were prone to re-flag their vessels, and exploit the FoC advantages, the size of the EU-fleets was declining steadily (Figure 3.1). The objectives of the responsive EU-level initiatives were to implement the application of the principle of the freedom to provide maritime transport services between members states and between member states and third countries;[14] to ensure that competition is not distorted by laying down detailed rules for the application of Article 85 and Article 86 of the Treaty to maritime transport;[15] to discourage unfair practices by non-EU countries;[16] and to provide conditions necessary to co-ordinate action and safeguard free access to cargoes and ocean trade.[17]

These initiatives continued 'on the same path of blending a general liberal orientation with specific acts of protectionism, which has been followed by the EU in its past actions in the maritime sector' (Tzoannos, 1989, p. 55), and aimed at ensuring the continuance of a commercial regime by taking action to deal with non-commercial attacks upon it (Erdmenger and Stasinopoulos, 1988). According to Whitelegg (1988), the nature of the specific EU intervention was designed to protect the EU shipowners share of the market and the economic value of this sector of the economy, and under that view it stands in a relatively good order and shows the benefit of a Community response. However, by introducing global regulations for extra-EU trade in maritime transport, the impact of this European framework extended over a considerable part of the international market for maritime transport (Yannopoulos, 1989). The EU was already the world's largest trading area and a significant part of shipping, irrespective of flag, was engaged in the transportation of the EU seaborne trade, thus it was affected by the introduction of a CMTP.

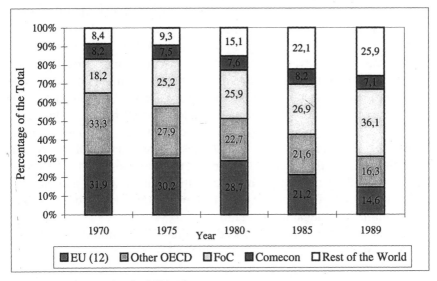

Source: Lloyds' Register of Shipping

Figure 3.1 Flag Distribution of World Shipping Tonnage 1970-1989

The Commission had annexed these measures in a memorandum aiming to set in motion a mechanism 'towards a common maritime policy' (CEU, 1985a). Thereby, the decline of the EU-flagged tonnage was attributed to a loss of comparative advantage due to internal as well as external pressures, the latter being the growth of protectionist practices by third countries. The memorandum also expressed the view that the interventionist practices of the member states had not significantly distorted competition between the various EU flags; stressed the need for excluding liner conferences from the application of the EU competition rules; and favoured the facilitation of policies that would lead to a continuing concentration of EU shipping into fewer but larger groupings, partly to generate the capital necessary for development and partly to create the strength necessary to resist the competitive pressures. To the Commission, shipping should be treated as a special case and be privileged by generous legal exemptions and financial aids that no other industry or transport mode had.[18]

The adopted Regulations were the outputs of a two-year debate between the EU institutions, interest groups, and national administrations. Apart from them, the Commission had also proposed the liberalisation of cabotage services but the proposal proved remarkably controversial and a decision was not achieved before 1992. The second controversial proposal was that for a definition of the 'beneficiaries' of a common policy, in other words, the conditions upon which nationality should be granted to ships and companies. The definition of who should 'benefit' by the provisions of a common EU policy is difficult in the case of the shipping industry. International law provides that a vessel has the nationality of the country whose flag it is entitled to fly.[19] By contrast there are no specific provisions of EU law dealing directly with the conditions upon which nationality is granted to ships and companies. The matter remains unsettled and subject to different national legal interpretations.

During the consultation procedure the EU institutions expressed diverse opinions. The Ecosoc (1985) criticised the Commission for a static review of the situation and a failure to consider the effects of the fundamental changes in the level and patterns of the world trade. Its opinion was that EU should favour a liberal approach but intervening when necessary in certain trades and sectors. Then, a stormy debate took place in the EP Transport Committee (see: Bredima-Savopoulou, 1990). The initial report supported that 'the diagnosis of the EU shipping sector was correct but the cure wrong', rejected the total of the Community approach, which to quote the Rapporteur was a 'shipowners charter',[20] and proposed an alternative approach.[21] This rejection was not supported by sufficient members of the EP Committee, leading to the resignation of the Rapporteur and the appointment of a new one. The second and final report welcomed the proposals as a first step and a 'pragmatic approach'. However, it remained critical of the Commission's views, particularly regarding the assessment of the FoC problem, and became more so after the position of more than one hundred amendments by the plenary session of the EP. To the EP, the Commission was wrongly adopting the view of shipowners that FoC are an economic necessity, while in reality they are not consistent with the obligations of the Rome Treaty to enhance the working conditions and living standard of seafarers.[22]

The EP Transport Committee developed its position after a public hearing where interest groups advocated divergent views on the character that a common policy should have. Shipowners offered a clear support to the initial proposals. In fact, the European shipowners association had expressed the opinion that measures in specific fields should be taken by the EU as early as October 1983. On the contrary, shippers believed that the Commission had failed to interpret the situation in the logic of the changing nature of international trade. To their view, the proposals had left wide scope for interference in the market mainly because there were significant omissions, like no clear references to liner conferences, and to the inherent risks of large consortia and shipping companies achieving a dominant position in specific trade markets. ITF criticised the proposals as inadequate, predicting that the regulations would not give any real improvement unless there was a major policy reappraisal.

Notably, these Euro-groups faced substantial problems in reaching these collective positions. Shipowners were divided on the liberalisation of cabotage trade and the Greek Union of Shipowners (representing more than a third of the EU fleet at the time) did not favour a common EU stance on unfair pricing practices in cargo liner shipping. Mainly engaged in tramp shipping, Greek shipowners were concerned more than liner operators about the possibilities of a reaction by the countries towards which the EU countermeasures would be addressed. As for the consumers of the services, Aspinwall (1995a) observes that those shippers' councils composed of numerous small firms, like the British and French Councils, were more dogmatic in their positions regarding shipping cartels than those shipper groups that are dominated by large industrial concerns (i.e. German Shippers' Council). Finally, trade unions were divided on the liberalisation of the cabotage trade, with those enjoying the advantages of protective markets not appreciating the specific proposal.

The Commission Proposals of 1989

By the end of the 1980s, it was recognised (CEU, 1990a) that the first package had not achieved its objectives. The EU fleets continued to experience significant losses of capacity (Figure 3.1), employment, and a slow rate of modernisation. When national governments were readjusting their domestic policies, the Commission presented a second set of proposals (CEU, 1989a), which were advocated to be in line with the non-protectionist shipping policy of the EU, based on the principle of free and fair competition, and capable of speedy introduction. The target was to provide sufficient incentives for European shipowners to register their vessels within the EU without driving up freight rates to the detriment of shippers.

The centrepiece of the Commission's strategy was the proposal for the establishment of an EU-flag, the European Register of Shipping (Euros). Euros would operate in parallel with the national registers offering a high-quality register and motivated by financial and practical benefits, as well as political symbolism. According to the Commission, the proposal was expected to be in the common interest because it could help both the retention of community ships under EU flags and the employment of EU nationals, as well as facilitate the solution of the other controversial issues (Smith, 1993). The recommended measures also included the liberalisation of cabotage; technical harmonisation and standardisation; social measures to improve working conditions, establish training programmes and promote the mutual recognition of diplomas, licences and certificates; and the implementation of international safety standards. The Commission declared that only a combination of concerned measures taken at a national level with the necessary participation and cooperation of the industrial patterns could have the required positive impact. This was not irrespective of the fact that DG-VII had needed four years to conclude a report on the possibility of a group exemption for consortia agreements as the shipping industry did not make sufficient information available to the Commission to constitute a satisfactory basis for analysis.[23]

Euros, in particular its provisional manning requirements, proved to be too ambitious an idea. Neither shipowners detected any economic incentive from such an establishment, nor were trade unions convinced that the recommended Euros structure would create jobs. In 1994 the Commission proposed a revised plan for a draft Regulation. The initial idea of having 100% officers and 50% ratings from the EU has been watered down to a minimum of the master and 'several' officers, in an attempt to reduce the manning costs of the register. While seafaring unions attacked this plan, shipowners argued that the proposal was realistic; otherwise they would have to continue flagging-out, which intrinsically results in job losses for the European seafarers.[24] Policy makers, either national administrations or

EU institutions also had diverse opinions regarding the rules that should govern a EU registration. When some member states were supportive of the idea (i.e. Greece, Germany) others were sceptical (i.e. Denmark, the UK), with all of them objecting to the link of Euros to issues of external EU relations (i.e. transportation of state aid). This was a different stance than that of the EP and the Commission that favoured such linkage, arguing that vessels under Euros should also benefit from fewer controls in European ports, state aid, and possible financial support for the training of seafarers. For a long while, and despite various amendments, the idea was close to failure. Finally, the Commission formally withdrew its proposal in 1996.

The publication of the 1989 proposals was accompanied by a second advisory paper (CEU, 1989b), wherein the Commission reaffirmed the approval of subsidies offered to shipowners under some circumstances (i.e. approval of subsidy plans by the Commission before they could be implemented). The industry was already heavily subsidised, and this was grossly distorting the market, but fiscal measures were justified under Article 93c of the Rome Treaty as a means to combat subsidies and similar measures adopted by fleets outside the EU, including US, Japan, Australia, and Norway (Brooks and Button, 1992). As the Commission asserted, 'in a situation where the Community is completing its internal market for goods and services in general it cannot allow a fading away of its presence on the world shipping market and a drifting apart of member states' own national policies of assistance to their fleets, with the consequent danger of increasing disparities inside the Community and distortion of the competition between Community shipowners' (CEU, 1989b, par. 12).

The third period was marked by the evolution of EU measures concentrating on the maintenance to the highest possible proportion of three elements, namely EU ownership, registration, and employment. By amending the regulatory framework that was governing the provision of services by vessels operating EU-flags, the policy proposals and legislative output were attempting to reverse the negative economic trends that shipowners were facing and to halt the unprecedented decline of member states' fleets and European seafarers' employment. Overall, the EU policy remained responsive to external developments and the problems that the latter were posed with, and continued to be characterised by what may be called 'disjointed incrementalism' (Lindblom, 1968): despite its greater consistency, many issue-areas remained peripheral topics. Maritime safety, or the state of maritime infrastructure and of the port industry, was sporadically included in the EU agenda and the policy process was confined to little more than an occasional exchange of ideas and information.

Studies of the Mosaic Approach

All the scholars who have studied the progress towards a CMTP over this period confirm that interplay between private interests, national governments, and the EU institutions, has taken place. Cafruny (1987, 1991), Bredima-Savopoulou (1990), and Aspinwall (1995a, 1995b), also verify that changes of the sectors' politico-economic environments influenced the CMTP content by acting as the determining factors of policy makers' and stakeholders' preferences and policy expectations. However, these studies balance the role of each actor on the development and terms of the common policy differently. Cafruny and Bredima-Savopoulou conceive the EU as an intergovernmental organisation of regional character. The format, progress, or rejection, of certain policy initiatives is the outcome of the member states' decisions to react, or not, collectively to the domestic or international adjustment pressures that traditional maritime nations face. The distinctive difference of Aspinwall's account is the conception of the EU as more than a typical international intergovernmental arena. Within this arena, organised interests, depending on their power, decisively influence the policy outcome. To the scholar, these powers are the result of the international economic conditions and especially the power of capital mobility.

From Intergovernmentalist Approaches...   Cafruny (1987, 1991) suggests that the framework to understand CMTP is to see it as an element of national policy by a coalition of states that attempt to respond to the development of a new regime. This is the New International Maritime Order (NIMO), which in the second half of the 1980s was posing several tangible problems like the general increase of protectionist laws and policies, the increasing competition from the third-world and East European fleets, the continuing USA predominance, and the need for rapid technological adaptation to maintain a competitive fleet (for NIMO see also: Laursen, 1982; Ademuni, 1988; Yannopoulos, 1989). Reflecting efforts of both governments and EU shipowners, the EU functioned as a maritime bloc acting in defence of the *status quo* in a period of these nations' declining hegemony. To the scholar, the dominance of liberalism motivated the nature of the collective actions, however, the agreed policy changes in the 1980s were influenced by international developments and by the differences among member states. On the one hand, international registries were giving rise to unemployment and weakening the ability of the EU to implement policies. On the other hand, divergent maritime traditions, commercial interests, and domestic structures, undermined the ability of a universal agreement on a unified policy. In short, Cafruny (1991, p. 294) argues for 'the continuing relevance of an approach that views progress toward integration in terms of bargains among sovereign states' because 'national interests provide an indispensable guide to the formulation or lack, of policy'.

Bredima-Savopoulou (1990) places an analogous significance on the views of the member states. In retrospect, the influential variables of the CMTP development before 1985 were the divisions between the 'fundamentalist' states, led by France, and the adherents of the 'petit-pas' approach, led by the UK. The preferences of the UK dominated policy developments, especially as they were further enhanced by the accession of Greece in 1981. Since the two biggest maritime states of the EU were in accord on the shape that a common policy should take, policy developments were adapted to their views. Examining in detail the 1986 Regulations, Bredima-Savopoulou argues that the possibilities and the nature of policy outcomes were determined by the views that member states expressed and the concessions that they were ready to accept. The failure to agree on the cabotage issue was the product of the substantial divergence of the views between the Mediterranean and the northern EU front. Similarly, the issue of 'beneficiaries' would have been solved by an agreement between Greece and other member states if the accession of Spain had not reopened the discussions. Successive enlargements of the EU were eventuating the need to reconsider policies as the balance of national views was shifting (also: Button, 1993).

This intergovernmentalist path is implicit in a collection of essays by Hart *et al* (1993) and the CMTP studies conducted by Tzoannos (1989; 1990). Smith (1993), for instance, argues that no relevant legislation to the 1989 set of proposals was passed by 1992 because of the remaining fundamental differences between member states, with both free market advocates (UK, Ireland, Denmark) and protectionists (Greece, Spain, Italy, France) rejecting the proposed policies. However, Tzoannos (1989) maintains that the significant political power of shipping groups exercised domestic pressures, influencing the national governments' political will to achieve an agreement on the liberalisation of cabotage trade.

...to Interest Groups Power   Studying both the 1986 Regulations and the 1989 proposals, Aspinwall (1995a, 1995b) challenges this 'member states' dominance' and criticises the preceding studies for an insufficient examination of the role of interest groups. Based on the assumption that member states consider shipping as a 'low politics' sector, the scholar concludes that the actions of elite non-governmental interest groups played the major role in outcomes. His observation is that 'a competitive pluralistic lobbying environment was emerged over the course of the 1980s in which the interests of shipowners, consumers, and labour were represented at the peak level albeit not equally effectively' (1995a, p. 129). This inequality was partially the result of the limits that the economic environment (and predominately the shipowners' ability of asset mobility) possessed to the relative power of the stakeholders, and partially the result of the organisation and the lobbying practices of these peak associations. Notwithstanding these, Aspinwall does not reject that national governments constitute a significant part of the process, in particular when policy decisions have wider implications. Antithetically, he stresses that states do have particular identifiable interests and preferences regarding the sector and their preferences occasionally deviate from their domestic elite constituencies. In the case of state aid issues, where shipowners, trade unions and the Commission were for once united in supporting a mandatory fiscal regime, their influence was limited by the fact that this was a highly sensitive matter where domestic policy remains guarded by state power.

Aspinwall (1995a, p. 126-127) suggests that the 1986 Regulations struck a balance between the interests of carriers and consumers while the participation of labour was limited, and advocates that these Regulations can be parsimoniously explained by five variables: domestic nation-state priorities, including efforts to protect and foster the domestic merchant fleets; collective competitiveness, which stems from the perceived need to promote the entire EU fleet as a collective unit; spillover pressures, produced by previously agreed policies; the changing global regimes that limit regional or national action; and the dominance of the prevailing ethic of liberalism. All these variables motivated pressure groups and determined their actions. The largely unsuccessful second phase was an attempt to build on the 1986 legislation and the policy outcome determined by similar variables. Once more the developments of the EU policy hinged upon the powers and influence of the pressure groups. This time shipowners and labour were active in the process, with the Commission attempting simultaneously to split the difference between liberal and protected shipowners, as well as, shipowners and labour. Agreement on Euros was impossible because labour and owners opposed the idea demanding diametrically different alternatives.

A critical parameter that affected these developments is the relevance of capital mobility, that is 'the movement of financial or physical assets to a new national jurisdiction', and the critical constraints that it possesses to regional authority-building. Aspinwall (1995a) argues that public policies are closely related to foreign direct investment of capital because "mobile business with access to a range of production jurisdictions throughout the globe is less willing to bear new regulatory and distributive burdens at either the European or state level than otherwise would be' and shipping is 'the apotheosis of capital mobility', as unlike other investors shipowners are not concerned with local markets and factors of production. The combined effect of the exposition of the shipping industry in international competition and the capability of high asset mobility produce a significant degree of sensitivity to different regulatory frameworks. In other words, the globalised natures of the industry, and the power of shipping capital to disinvest, limit the opportunities to legislate competitiveness both autonomously at national level and collectively at regional levels (also: Aspinwall, 1996). Examining the loss of the comparative advantage of European shipping, Goss (1989) also notes that in an international market where both national and FoC coexist the shipowners' opt out option is of the most important factors limiting a common policy in tackling problems of competitiveness.

What Role for the EU Institutions? All the aforementioned studies of the mosaic approach have made important contributions to the understanding of the progress of the CMTP. However, in part because they examine the progress of specific stages of the CMTP and in part because they conceptualise differently the relative importance of the actionable factors, various questions arise. It is worth examining whether the conclusions of any of these endeavours can explain contemporary developments or not, and whether economic changes and/or the dynamic of European integration shift the balance of influence in such a way that a different conceptualisation is essential. Should we maintain that member states are the powerful players that induce the progress of Europeanisation as early studies suggested? or is Aspinwall's conclusion that the interest groups and their relative power are the most influential factors more useful? Foremost, is the question about the largely unidentified impact of the third cluster of actionable factors, the EU institutions? Do they simply provide the bureaucratic infrastructure and secretariat that facilitate the interaction of (or the most powerful of) the two other clusters of actors? Or do they represent variables that advance, shape, or restrain the progress of the common policy?

Unsurprisingly (Chapter 2), the intergovernmentalist approaches to CMTP developments focus on the 'instrumentality' of the institutional framework. To give an example, Bredima-Savopoulou (1990) maintains that an agreement and the final idea of a package of four Regulations emerged within the Council after an assessment of the possible realignments of the positions of the national delegations and the detection of possible breakthroughs. The scholar acknowledges that the publications of the Commission triggered debates at several levels: between the EU institutions; within the member states between interest groups and governments; and within interest groups at EU level. But such debates are 'brainstorming exercises' when policy formulation remains an issue of member states agreement. Cafruny (1991) suggests however that the analysis of shipping suggests that EC institutions have become more important in determining policy; as the transfer of power from member states to EU institutions was an inevitable part of the 1986 policy outcome. This is in line with Erdmenger and Stasinopoulos (1988), two high-ranking Commission officials whose 'view from within' also emphasises this institutional impact and the reinforcement of the EU role in international organisations. On the other hand, Aspinwall (1995, p.63) puts forward the argument that the interaction between private interests, national, and supranational actors, is an influential factor in the development and terms of the CMTP, and asserts that: 'supranational institutions have acted in ways that limit state choices and that further their own particular interests. For instance, the Commission's proposals often feature an institution building element'.

The CMTP in the 1990s: The Horizontal Approach

The beginning of the contemporary CMTP phase is traced to a Commission report publicised in 1991 (CEU, 1991). As already indicated, in the beginning of the decade several initiatives had been undertaken or were still under discussion without, however, a comprehensive European policy being in place. Against this background, the Commission pronounced the promotion of a coherent 'horizontal' EU answering to the challenges and prospects of the several interrelated maritime industries. In its own words this strategy 'does not follow the more traditional approach on concentrating on sector specific aspect ... is a general and horizontal one, as it addresses the whole maritime dimension – which is of common concern to the different parties involved' (ibid., p. 2). The EU became engaged in the development of a CMTP that tackles the contemporary challenges of the European fleets' competitiveness in combination with other critical policy issues. The latter include wider transport developments, the achievement of the internal market, the improvement of the sector's safety and environmental performance, personnel training, promotion of research and development (R&D), and aspects of competition. Essentially, the objective is a cohesive EU policy with real impact for the whole of Europe's maritime industries.

The introduction of the new philosophy took place contemporaneously to a re-approach of the slowly progressed CTP, attempting to transform it into a more comprehensive policy design that ensured the proper functioning of the EU transport systems into the post-1992 period (CEU, 1992a) and constructed a framework for sustainable development (CEU, 1992b). Moreover, guidelines have been introduced for the establishment of a unified trans-European transport network, in part to fulfil the goal to integrate the environmental dimension to the EU transport policies (transport became one of the five main economic 'target' sectors of the Fifth Environmental Action Programme) and in part to promote the competitive position of the sector (CEU, 1992c). This network should gradually integrate in operational terms all the national transport modes in a multimodal approach. It might be argued that all these moves were the first efforts to meet the provisions of the TEU that demands the development of a CTP incorporating economic, social and environmental dimensions. When the completion of the SEM entered the final phase, and the TEU provided evidence of greater political priority to the function of the transport sector, the Commission presented a new approach trying to implement these priorities.

These moves were followed by several Commission initiatives, including those referring to a common policy on safe seas (CEU, 1993a), and the prospects and challenges of shortsea shipping (CEU, 1995a), the content of which are analysed as part of respective case studies. In 1996 the Commission published two parallel strategy documents aiming to readjust the maritime strategy (CEU, 1996a) and the ways that the EU strategy attempts to shape Europe's maritime future (CEU, 1996b).

Grounding on the absence of a collective EU answer to the problem of the EU shipping competitiveness, the former of these two documents concerns the possible new policy initiatives to be pursued through the EU legislative institutions. In this vein, the Commission has called for a debate on the formulation of a future maritime strategy on securing the competitiveness of the EU shipping sector, state aid, maintaining open markets, and maritime safety. This readjustment formally withdrew Euros from the EU agenda, as well as the proposal for a 'common definition of Community shipowner'. The second document suggests policy elements and initiatives in order to contribute to the industrial competitiveness of all maritime industries of Europe. Therein, the promotion of tangible investments, the development of industrial cooperation, the elimination of the distortions of competition and the barriers to market access in third countries and the reconsideration of the role of the public authorities *vis-à-vis* the industry are pronounced as main fields of the future EU action.

Summary

Apparently, the establishment of the CMTP and the expansion of the EU competencies over the various policy areas (Table 3.2) has been a continuous process divided into four phases. The early one was marked by the exclusion of the maritime mode from the basis of the CTP. The next phase was inscribed by the first involvement of the EU institutions in the development of a CMTP through a selective, problem-orientated approach. The improvement of the EU-flagged fleet's competitiveness was the central theme of the third stage. Since 1985, agreements have settled both non-controversial and controversial issues, though compromises in the latter cases have been essential, yet the EU policymaking process has not necessarily produced collective policy outcomes (i.e. Euros). Scholars interpreted the whole process in an intergovernmental vein suggesting that the process has been subject to national governments' desires in a changing economic context. This view, however, has been recently challenged by Aspinwall (1995a) who suggests that attention should be given to the role of the interest groups with various powers, notably defined by the ability of the shipping capital to relocate into more favourable regulatory jurisdictions.

Table 3.2 Policy Areas and Competencies

	1974	1985	1990	2000
Liner Code	Global	EU	EU	EU
Other competition issues[a]	National	National	EU	EU
Trade agreements	National	National/EU	National/EU	National/EU
Registry	National	National	National[b]	National[b]
Manning rules	National	National	National[b]	National[b]
State aids	National	National	National	National[c]
Intra-EU market opening	National	National	EU	EU
Cabotage trade opening	National	National	National[d]	EU
Shortsea shipping	National	National	National	EU
Safety/Environment	Global	Global	Global	Global/EU
Crew conditions	Global	Global	Global	Global/EU
Maritime Infrastructure	National	National	National	National/EU
Research and Development	National	National	National	National/EU

[a] Except in Rules of Liner Code
[b] Unsuccessful attempts to sift competence at EU-level. Proposals were withdrawn in March 1996.
[c] Commission guidelines were published in June 1996.
[d] Unsuccessful first attempt to sift competence at EU-level. Proposal adopted in 1992.

Source: Based on Aspinwall's (1994) comparative survey of policy areas and competencies in the years 1982 and 1992.

The contemporary spur towards policy integration is marked by a widening agenda attempting to address the totality of the sector's problems. Along with issues of competitiveness, new spheres of EU policy interest have emerged. The state of European shortsea shipping, intermodalism, R&D, and maritime infrastructure are currently conceived as parts of the policy repertoire in which action should be taken or coordinated at an EU-level but were absent from the agenda of the 1980s. Furthermore, the EU is increasingly involved in more traditional maritime issues, like maritime safety and competition laws (i.e. regulation of trans-Atlantic liner trade agreements, consortia, and new types of multimodal operators' agreements, or the abuse of dominant positions by port operators) increasing its competencies in these policy areas. The *ad hoc* crisis interventions of the 1970s and 1980s have expanded into an all-embracing CMTP. Meanwhile, the EU became even more maritime oriented with the entry of Finland and Sweden in 1995.

The rationale that the interactions between private interests, national governments, and supranational actors, are among the influential factors of these developments, provides a theoretical basis to analyse the fourth, chronologically and contextually distinctive, period of the CMTP in the 1990s. Associating this concept with the theoretical strands focusing on European integration, this analysis tries to locate and understand the precise role of this interaction, and conclude on whether the causal arrows are in fact more multidimensional than the previous CMTP analyses have assumed. In line with the greater emphasis that has been recently given to the developed, or under development, 'polity like' features of the EU, it is anticipated that a greater emphasis should be given to the EU institutional framework as a causal factor of what the Europeanisation of the maritime transport system's regulatory framework is about.

Two sets of policy issues are examined to generate knowledge about the validity of this anticipation. The first refers to the common policy on safe seas, in other words the attempts to promote a common policy concerning safety of ships, safety of persons onboard, and prevention of environmental pollution. Policy issues regarding European shortsea shipping form the second case-study. The choice of these cases was influenced by a number of factors. Firstly, both of them are more than single important issues. They represent clusters of related policy measures that have gained momentum since the beginning of the 1990s and, moreover, they span considerable time and are rather distinct from each other. So, they have the potential to give rise to differences in policy actors' behaviour in each area. Moreover, these issues are characterised by their significant diversity in respect of their degree of 'internationalisation' as well as their place in a 'traditional policy' index (Figure 3.2).

Within a historical perspective maritime safety and environmental protection can be classified as highly 'traditional' policy issues. The maritime transport process, irrespective of whether concerned with the transportation of goods or persons, is intrinsically associated with safety externalities and costs. Safeties at sea and at shore and the minimisation of environmental deterioration have long been issues of public concern and integral parts of any maritime transport policy. Then, partly because maritime operation is a transboundary operation, and partly because environmental problems are of a global dimension these issues have historically been regulated at an international level, either by intergovernmental organisations or industrial self-regulatory agreements. European policy initiatives in this field are gaining momentum either at the expense of, or in parallel with, such international level policy developments.

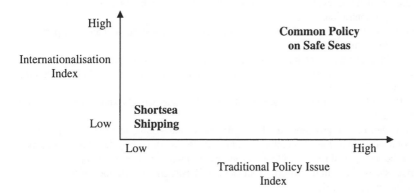

Figure 3.2 'Internationalisation' and 'Traditional Policy Issue' Index

On the other hand, attempts to promote the competitiveness of shortsea shipping refer to activities previously regulated, in some cases highly protected, by national-level policies. Adding that the EU authorities have, to a significant degree, regulatory access in both countries of origin and destination of the shortsea transportation process, policy measures regarding shortsea shipping can be placed on the lower part of the internationalisation index. These measures, then, deal with a comparatively new policy issue, as far as interstate level policies are concerned. A dialogue based on the recognition of European shortsea shipping as a sector with particular political and economic demands and potentials begun in the early 1980s (ECMT, 1983). The concept was absent from the EU policy concerns during the previous phases of the CMTP but attracted attention during recent years and especially in line with the completion of the European internal market. Policies concerning the particular market segment had been in place before that but the national or local maritime transport dimension was dominant in all these cases.

Notes

1   Specifically, the founding Treaty of the ECSC (Treaty of Paris, 1951) had explicitly laid out a number of basic requirements regarding transport charges for carrying coal and steel, publication of rates, and the use of discriminatory transport charges, during a transition to eventual harmonisation.

2   The Council Regulation 141/62, of 26.11.1962, excluded maritime (and air) transport from the common competition policy.

3   The 'sectoral approach' of integration is a process 'i) limited to particular industries or sectors of the economy, or the economies concerned and ii) gradual proceeding successively from sector to sector' (Machpul, 1977, p. 33).

4   Case 167/73 Commission v. France (1974) ECR 359, alternatively known as the 'French seamen case'.

5   In particular, France proposed 'the harmonisation of intra-Community sea transport from the point of view of intra-Community trade' because 'a common policy on sea transport cannot be achieved through scattered efforts which might weaken the competitiveness of member states' fleets in the world' (10th General Report on the Activities of the European Communities, point 451).

6   For details: 11th General Report on the Activities of the European Communities.

7   Council Regulation 974/79, of 15.5.1979.

8   The usual practice through which these countries allocated cargoes to their national flag was by selling their product on a CIF and buying on a FOB basis. This practice was reinforced with a network of freight bureau established in other countries which directed cargoes to the state trading country's own fleet offering low shipping rates often up to 40% less than the rates of Western countries. An additional impediment imposed on foreign shipping companies was that these were prohibited from setting up their own agencies in the state trading countries; and thus depended on the latter for cargo accessibility (cf. Frankel, 1987).

9   OJ C192, of 30.6.1980.

10   EP Doc. 5/77.

11   OJ No C96, of 11.4.1983.

12   OJ C49, of 19.2.1983, p. 10.

13 Case 13/83. European Parliament v. Council of Ministers (1985)ECR 1513.
14 Council Regulation 4055/86, of 22.12.1986.
15 Council Regulation 4056/86, of 22.12.1986.
16 Council Regulation 4057/86, of 22.12.1986.
17 Council Regulation 4058/86, of 22.12.1986.
18 Kreis H., Commission administrator, interviewed in: *Seatrade Review*, A different ball game, August 1993.
19 UN Convention on the Law of High Seas, 1958 (Article 6), UN Convention on the Law of Sea, 1984 (Article 92), and UN Convention on Conditions of Ship Registration, 1986 (Article 8).
20 Stewart, K. (1986). EC Maritime Policy: Shipowners Charter. In: *ITF Seafarers Bulletin*, No. 1, 1986.
21 EP Doc. A2-53/86; Rapporteur: K. Stewart, PSE, UK.
22 EP Doc. A2-95/86. Rapporteur: K. Anastasopoulos, PPE, Gr.
23 The Commission had undertaken the task to submit such a report within one year from the adoption of the regulation 4056/86. A copy of 23 consortia agreements was submitted in September 1989 when the Commission's information led to the conclusion that at the time were at least 40 consortia which operated in Community liner trade (CEU, 1990).
24 Cf. *Lloyd's List*, Euros register crew plan angers unions, 12.5.1994.

4 Maritime Safety: Critical Aspects of the New Economic Context

This part of the book analyses the establishment of an EU policy concerning safety of ships, persons onboard, and the marine environment, with reference to the interaction of the actionable factors during the policy-making process. Chapter 4 begins, however, with a discussion of the features of the new economic environment of international shipping that have been the result of changes in the recent past, setting them within the framework of safety issues. Given the transboundary character of shipping, most of the EU initiatives, like any policy measure relating to maritime safety worldwide, have a clear reference and several implications to the international policy making machinery. Thus, the impact of the new economic environment to the policy developments at that level is also taken into account.

Quantitative and Qualitative Market Changes

From 1974 onwards maritime transport has been experiencing profound changes, the most radical being the generation of new registration patterns that alter market structures and modify the powers and actions of policy makers. As reviewed in previous chapters, the stagnation of trade, the unjustified fleet expansion, and the subsequent fall in freight rates that followed the two oil crises produced a massive flagging-out from traditional maritime countries to third cheaper flags and the rise of new maritime nations. Nowadays, more than half of the world merchant fleet operates under FoC. The decline of the EU-flagged fleet continued throughout the 1980s. Declining by 28%, the combined tonnage of EU(12) reached its lowest point in 1990. Since then the flagging-out trend has been halted without, hitherto, the EU flags regaining their substantial losses (Table 4.1).

Table 4.1 Registration Development of EU-Owned Merchant Fleet

	Merchant fleet under Member States Flag[a]					Flag Composition of the Major EU owned Fleets[b]			
	1990		1999		Change (%)				
	000 grt	% of the EU fleet	000 grt	% of the EU fleet		EU-flags	Affiliated flags	2nd Register	Other Flags
Gr	20716,2	37,2	24833,3	33,3	19,9	44.6	0.5		55.0
UK	6620,7	11,9	9061,5	12,1	36,9	6.8	24.8		68.4
It	7335,7	13,2	8048,5	10,8	9,7	78.0	1.7		20.3
Ger	3655,4	6,6	6513,8	8,7	78,2	35.7	1.8		62.5
Dk	4754,7	8,5	5912,8	7,9	24,4	4.3	1.3	51.6	42.8
Nl	2987,6	5,4	5923,4	7,9	98,3	47.2	13.1		39.7
Fr	3986,2	7,1	4925,0	6,6	23,6	28.8	28.7		42.5
Sw	2317,8		2946,9	3,9	27,1				
Sp	3181,1	5,7	1903,1	2,5	-40,2	19.3	8.0		72.6
Fin	829,8		1658,4	2,2	99,9				
Lux	3,6	0,0	1343,0	1,8	37205				
Pr	587,1	1,1	1164,8	1,6	98,4				
Ir	127,0	0,2	218,9	0,3	72,4				
B	1806,3	3,2	132,1	0,2	-92,7				
A	204,1		71,1	0,1	-65,2				
EU 12	55761,6	100,0	69980,2		25,5				
EU 15	59113,3		74656,6	100,0	26,3				

[a] Including affiliated and second registries;
[b] GIS not split out from German Register due to lack of information; as in 1995.
EU flags include: Azores, Madeira, Canary Islands, French Guiana, Guadelope, Martinique
Second Registries: Danish International Shipping, German International Shipping
Affiliated (Offshore) Registers: Anguilla, Bermuda, British Indian Ocean Territory, British Virgin Islands, Cayman Islands, Channel Islands, Faeroes Greenland, Falkland Islands, French Antarctic Territory, French Polynesia, Gibraltar, Hog Kong, Isle of Man, Kerguelen Island, Macao, Mayotte, Monserrat, Netherlands Antilles, New Caledonia, St Pierre, Turks and Caicos, Wallis and Futuna

Sources: Lloyd's Register, 2000; CEU-DG VII, 1996a.

As in 1999, the EU-flagged tonnage is 74,6 thousands grt, or 13,7% of the world total. This aggregate remains higher than in the beginning of the 1990s, even when the most recent EU enlargement is considered. However, the trend is imbalanced, and the product of the positive development of half of the EU-flags. The member state distribution of the EU-flagged fleet is remarkably concentrated, with six nations (Gr, UK, It, Ger, Dk, Nl) controlling over 80%, and nationals from some member states having limited interest regarding the provision of maritime services. Hence, the tonnage of some major flags has increased reversing the declining trend.

The main reason for this reverse has been the introduction of offshore, or 'affiliated', registries based in dependencies or colonies. Prominent examples are the Isle of Man (UK), Kerguelen Islands (France), Madeira (MAR, Portugal), Netherlands Antilles (Netherlands) registries. All of them are offering to various degrees similar incentives to FoC, i.e. they permit the use of non-domiciled crews from the ruling country, but with a better reputation and a more stable politico-economic environment.[1] Other European nations established, in parallel with their national registry, second 'international' registries allowing vessels to carry the domestic flag but rules are detailed internationally. The successful example of the Norwegian International Shipping (NIS; established in 1984)[2] was followed by Denmark (DIS; 1988), Germany (GIS; 1989), as well as the development of the Luxembourg flag, which is used mainly by Belgian shipowners. These registries have prevented the expansion of flagging-out. The enlargements of the Danish and German flagged fleets have been the outcomes of the introduction of DIS and GIS respectively. The UK flag would be cited as the one that continues to experience the biggest decline of all if the tonnage operating under offshore registries was excluded. The analysis with view to the tonnage beneficially owned by EU shipowners gives an accurate picture. Whereas 56% of the EU-owned fleet are registered under FoC, a pattern similar to that of the total world fleet, a further 10% is registered under affiliated or second registries.

Remarkably, the most substantial tonnage increase has been noted in Greece, a case where both social partners and the national administration have rejected the idea of introducing a second registry. The third biggest flag in the world remains one of the cheapest in terms of registration costs, a policy that has been continuously readjusted by the Greek government in post war times.[3] Greek shipping is 'a tax-free business, and that has accounted for the rapid growth in the Greek fleet'.[4] Moreover, the Greek regulatory system enables ships of Greek interests to be registered and contribute to the Retired Seamen's Fund but the selection of their crews remains free of nationality requirements. This provides an additional explanation for the absence of shipowners' demands for the introduction of a parallel international registry (Goulielmos, 1996).

Against this background, member states continue to search for ways to develop their market share either through further development of the existing second registries, the introduction of an international register, or, to follow the successful Greek paradigm and establish similar forms of financial aid to ships operating under their flag (including tax cuts, employment of non-nationals, and fiscal packages for those who select to hire nationals – i.e. Italy).

The apparent benefits of retaining ships under non-traditional registries or attracting them back from FoC, include nominal home control, reduction of direct subsidies, and advance of employment. However, negative effects such as reduction of tax revenues and seafaring job losses accompany these registries, as well as the other preceding concessions. The relaxation of nationality requirements in respect of crews' composition decreases the employment opportunities for European seafarers. The phenomenon is accompanied by the reduction of crew sizes, induced by technological progress, and the progressive increase of skilful (or at least holding qualification certificates) low cost labour from developing countries (Table 4.2). Precisely because they enhance the employment of low cost labour from developing countries onboard EU-flagged ships, these 'captive open registries' (Yannopoulos, 1989) have been objected to by organised labour. All western European unions participate actively in the ITF move to designate several second registries as new forms of FoC, despite that some of them have accepted the introduction of second registries as a response to flagging-out (ITF, 1996a).

Table 4.2 Employment on EU-Flagged Vessels

Year	No of Ships	EU-nationals	Average per Ship	Non-EU nationals	Average per Ship	Total	Average per Ship
1990	5.671	158.457	27,9	27.579	4,8	186.517	31,8
1995	5.336	128.728	24,1	33.031	6,2	161.589	30,3

Sources: ISL Databases; CEU-DG VII, 1996b.

Overall, EU resident companies control 33% of the world fleet (in dwt). Greek, British, and German interests own 47%, 23%, and 17% of this tonnage respectively, however, the commercial interests of the major EU maritime nations differ significantly. Greek owners maintain their major interest in oil tankers and bulk carriers, traditional vessels mainly involved in tramp shipping. The other two nations have more interests in general cargo and containerships, which are more sophisticated vessels operating on a liner basis.

A decade ago EU shipowners controlled 37% of the world fleet, but in part because of tighter finance and in part because of changing behaviour, they do not expand their tonnage at the level that the rest of the world does. This is not an intrinsically negative phenomenon. The 'casino mentality', that is the tendency to develop great self-fed expectations of seaborne trade booms, thus, over-invest in building up tonnage, avoid scrapping, and continue to buy vessels on the second hand market (Peters, 1989), has been an inherent characteristic of shipowning that in the past produced a critical overcapacity in all segments of the market.[5] Throughout the 1990s the low levels of broken up tonnage and steady fleet additions have lead to a 2.1% average yearly growth of the world tonnage, so that the world is still approximately 10% oversupplied (Core Group, 1996). The situation is unlikely to change unless there is either a sudden and massive increase in world trade, supply is withdrawn from the market, or no new tonnage is ordered in the forthcoming years. As none of these scenarios seems probable, and though they have not followed the expansion trend of the 1990s, EU owners have inevitably to share the negative effects.

Another critical development is the increasing depersonalisation and reorganisation of shipowning. Responding to the geographical restructuring of international trade, multinational shipping companies have been established to overcome political and economic barriers. An increase of intermodal operations, in turn the result of widespread application of new forms of production and distribution organisation, have resulted in vertical and horizontal integration, with shipowners increasingly involved in more economic activities. Then, the slump in world seaborne trade after the oil crises increased the selling of ships facilitated the ease for newcomers to enter the trade and the growth of 'asset players' who speculate in the second hand markets (Stokes, 1992). Most importantly, purely ship management companies operate substantial number of vessels (cf. Spruyt, 1994). Their contribution to a profound reorganisation of shipping is such that they are considered one of the two defining 'waves' in modern shipping history (Sletmo, 1989). They fragment traditional shipowning into separately managed activities, making shipping more footloose as an industry, and facilitating relocation in least cost markets. Along with flagging-out, the second defining wave, they have generated new maritime countries. In conjunction with second registries, they produce the phenomenon of the so-called 'straw-companies', whereby the real shipowner remains unknown.

Favourable economic conditions in recent years have ensured a positive effect on the demand for maritime services. Especially since 1987, world trade grows significantly faster than the world output driving to seaborne trade expansion. In 1997, seaborne trade reached a new record volume of 5092 million tonnes (Figure 4.1), Medium term forecasts suggest an average annual growth rate in world seaborne trade of 5.9% until 2010, expecting these positive developments to affect all types of trade. The prospects are even more dynamic in the container market, as the globalisation of the manufacturing process influences both volume and composition of the word seaborne trade.

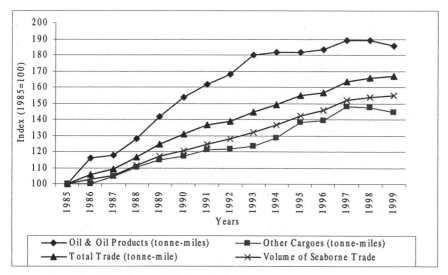

Source: Fearnleys' Review, 1999; Predictions for 1999.

Figure 4.1 Development of World Seaborne Trade

In spite of these developments, and due to the aforementioned fleet overcapacity, the expansive demand for maritime transport services is accompanied only by modest freight recovery. Freight rates in dry bulk markets are an evident example. In 1985 the Lloyd's Shipping Economist combined index had a value of 247. Following several fluctuations it reached a 285 average in 1995 to return to the lower 209 in 1996, largely the outcome of a tonnage overcapacity between 10.4% and 9.5% of the total demand. As seaborne trade induced lower increases in tonne-miles, rates for large size vessels experienced their worst year since the mid-1980s in 1994. In the oil market, which maintains the most important share in world seaborne trade (37% in 1999), freights have shown a moderate increase. Nevertheless, there are indications that in this market segment freight rates are increasingly developed in parallel with the demand. Despite the rewarding market for container vessels, respective rates did not suffer from rapid growth. In general, it is only the situation of the liner market that has improved substantially in recent years (OECD, 2001).

Implications for Maritime Safety

Challenges to the Existing Regulatory Mechanisms

It has long been a common belief that, because of the transboundary nature of maritime transport, actions to improve safety would be more effective if devised internationally and applied co-operatively and universally. This induced a tradition of twofold policy developments. There is a substantial record of international self-regulation, with agreements regarding working conditions at sea, or training initiatives, directly negotiated between the social partners. Then, the first ever international body devoted exclusively to maritime matters, the International Maritime Organisation (IMO), was established with the responsibility to promote maritime safety.

However, the preceding changes of the economic environment have had a critical impact on the progress and the effective implementation of agreements achieved in both fields. The development of both FoC and new European registries have generated increasing tension between shipowners and organised labour. The latter has seen its negotiating powers eclipsed and recover only in cases where pressures have been generated by the shortage of trained seafarers. ITF tries to certify that FoC shipping, as well as vessels operating second or affiliated flags, are covered by acceptable collective agreements (ITF, 1994a). This campaign to upgrade and standardise total crew costs has produced strong reactions by shipowners. ISF has organised an International Maritime Employers' Committee to oppose the ITF policy (cf. Northrup and Scrace, 1996). The synergy that was developed between the social partners during the 'years of plenty' has disappeared. Furthermore, the depersonalisation of shipowning and the presence of new players (countries, operators, or ship management companies) have generated fundamentally different commercial and policy principles. A change in business ethics encumbers self-regulatory agreements between the social partners, but also between shipowners themselves. For instance, a number of tanker owners have expressed the view that industry itself has not done enough to secure an adequate level safety, attributing this to the presence of 'mavericks'.[6]

These difficulties are reflected in the work of IMO, and its ability to provide long-term solutions. Since its establishment, IMO has evolved as the prevailing machinery in promoting policies relating to maritime safety, pollution prevention, crew quality and legal issues arising from environmental impacts. The convention on Safety Of Life At Sea (SOLAS), first adopted in 1960 and coming into force in 1965, is still the basic instrument in the field of safety onboard. In response to developments it was substantially amended in 1974, but at many other times it proved difficult to bring new requirements into force. The 1978 convention on Standards of Training, Certification and Watchkeeping for seafarers (STCW; came into force: 1984) establishes internationally acceptable minimum standards for crews. The most comprehensive IMO instrument to curb the impact of pollution is the 1973 convention for the Prevention of Maritime Pollution from ships (MARPOL). Whilst economic pressures made it difficult for many states to ratify it, a series of tanker accidents led to the adoption of the 1978 IMO Protocol that absorbed in effect the parent convention and introduced additional measures. This combined instrument, commonly referred to as MARPOL 73/78, came into force in 1983. In summary, IMO succeeded in setting standards where none existed. Meanwhile (1977) it became the first UN body to institutionalise a technical cooperation programme aimed at helping its expansive membership reach the standards contained in its instruments.

Today the IMO has 153 members, plus two associates, and a coherent organisational infrastructure. Its secretariat of some 300 civil servants and its functions are assisted by other UN specialised agencies, more than 30 governmental and nearly 50 non-governmental international organisations (including the EU) which have been granted consultative status. However, the juxtaposition of inclusive membership and changing registration patterns implies that the progress of the organisation's decisions depends on nations which, at least within the current environment, share non-identical social and economic priorities regarding maritime transport in general, and maritime safety in particular. IMO decisions are reached on the basis of consensus. The agreed conventions come into force and become mandatory only after fulfilling certain requirements, which always include ratification by a specified number of countries and world tonnage (IMO also adopts non-binding codes and recommendations). The more important the convention, the more stringent are the requirements for entry into force (i.e. SOLAS 74 coming into force in 1980 as ratification was required by 25 countries representing at least 50% of the world fleet). Over the last decade this process has been underlined by growing disputes of flag-states even for the agenda of IMO, undermining the organisation's ability to ensure safety. The main interest of several rising flag-states is to extract large revenues from the expanding registries, or create onshore employment in associated maritime industries. They have different priorities to flag-states whose prime purpose is to promote shipping and employment and to regulate the industry to proper standards.

The major problem arises from the failure of significant, in terms of registered tonnage, flag-states to implement instruments that they have agreed to. A clear hierarchy of responsibility for ensuring compliance with international rules and standards exists. Responsibility lies, in addition to the market, with the flag-state. The latter is responsible for converting the international conventions into national laws and applying them to individual ships. It is also supposed to help the shipowner meet the requirements of its own maritime laws. Maritime safety largely depends on the ability of flag-states to carry out their responsibilities effectively. The expansion of FoC shipping and the growing interest of developing countries to increase the tonnage registered under their flags have allowed the creation of maritime nations that, due to the lack of either the essential infrastructure or the necessary political willingness, do not become parties to IMO instruments. Alternatively, they sign these international agreements and then do not comply with the totality of the resulting obligations. Evidently (cf. Hindell, 1996), neither all, nor only, FoC countries are neglectful in respect of international standards. Still, the flags that are growing most rapidly have relatively poor records compared to the records of the declining traditional flags.

These inefficiencies have been recognised by the IMO secretariat which in the late 1980s proposed the establishment of an 'implementation sub-committee' to monitor and assist national administrations to fulfil their obligation. Whilst its members agreed to it, the decision disappointed those countries that were seeking the introduction of an enforcement mechanism.[7] The remarkably different attitude of the IMO membership to international rule making is leading many countries to complain about the unavailability of essential firm and rapid action. In addition, there is a noticeable lack of willingness by many nations, including some EU member states (reportedly Germany and the UK), to back financially the work of the organisation. The 1995 row over the IMO budget for the period 1996-97 is illustrative. The IMO finance comes from various sources (i.e. the UN Development and Environmental programmes) but individual countries remain the major and critical contributors. When the IMO council proposed a 10.7% budget increase, a 3/5 majority of its assembly, voted for 6.3%, and the setback was confirmed by the finally agreed 6.7% rise. Shipowners have not been helpful to the organisation either, as they have rejected the IMO calls for a more proactive approach on the grounds that quality initiatives are already in place.[8] To give an example, the suggestion of the establishment of an international ship information database which, *inter alia*, would either disassociate or prove the association of substandard ships with certain flags, has been rejected not only by some flag-states but also by shipowners, who have always jealously guarded their independence, as a threat to their traditional secrecy.[9]

Negative Implications of the Contemporary Market Practices

Safety problems inflate as the current situation generates considerable scope to deliberately avoid compliance to internationally applicable rules and obtain the subsequent financial advantages. For instance, the oil trade and the charter market operate in a highly competitive atmosphere. Finding the cheapest oil tanker carrying capacity on the market is an essential part of the operation. The volatile nature of the market is also resulting in a move-away from long-term contracts between charterers and carriers towards short-term charters (the so-called 'spot market'). Prices on this market are fiercely competitive. In reality, the age of the oil tanker plays little part in the decision-making process; often it is the cheapest available tonnage offered by the oldest ships that dictates prices. It is therefore difficult to create a situation where quality pays, so much so that small operators with low overheads are winning over parts of the market at the expense of companies with well-established reputations. This phenomenon poses a risk to safety.

Moreover, the chartering practices, though peculiar to the oil trade, also add to the complexity of the situation. Thus, the oil companies have largely lost control over their oil tanker fleet. In reality, they control only a quarter of the world fleet. What we are witnessing is a process of 'atomisation' among the oil tanker owners. By dispersing their fleet among single-ship companies, often taking the form of dummy companies registered in offshore financial centres, the owners are able to reduce their financial risks. Consequently, it is often difficult to identify the real decision-makers and hence to determine where responsibility really lies.

Shipowners have to put resources in order to satisfy the demands of each regulation. In difficult economic circumstances, some of them take advantage of their freedom under FoC to set operating standards failing to conform to existing rules and standards. Most non-compliance is minor and represents only small savings, but financial implications are larger when the substandard vessel continues trading before the deficiency is detected (OECD, 1996). As the less safe ships drives out the better one, the market operates to a significant scale under a kind of 'maritime Gresham's Law' (Goss, 1994) and the safety performance of maritime transport deteriorates. In policy terms, different flag-states approaches create a 'distinct dualism' (Yannopoulos, 1988) that increases the opportunities to the supplier of shipping services to avoid specific regulatory frameworks. Shipowners have available the option to opt out for a new environment which affords lower factor costs and offers conditions of comparative advantage. The tendency towards the introduction of second registries highlights its influence on policy makers' thinking: to counterbalance the competitive handicap of their traditional flags they offer regulatory concessions that were unthinkable a decade ago.

Nonetheless, flagging-out is not without limitations. Loyal owners that stay with home flags are rewarded with financial aid or other inducements that progressively offset several advantages enjoyed by FoC operators. They also enjoy the benefits of political stability, a strong and influential shipowners' association and active diplomatic administrations of the flag state around the world. In conditions of relative prosperity in the industry, traditional register shipping is able to effectively promote its, deserved or not, higher market and social image in the interests of its own success. Furthermore, when second registries counterbalance FoC tax incentives, differences of labour costs are the most important element in determining the international competitiveness of ships. Vessel specialisation depends on smaller but high quality crews; therefore, absolute manning cost advantages offered by FoC are of less importance. Training grants for crews may also be enjoyed by the operation of a traditional flag, when new flag-states have limited interest. Certain benefits are extracted by the avoidance of potential delays and cost from ITF activities.

Finally, given the relatively bad record of FoC, classification societies exercise an indirect pressure by insuring different registers that stick to safety principles and are concerned about operational quality. For instance, the Norwegian classification society Det Norske Veritas has established an optional class, which audits conformity with safety and environment protection rules. Ferry owners operating in Sweden have requested their classification societies to confirm that the companies' management systems conform to certain IMO guidelines.

Irrespective of flag choices, the most critical development is fleet over-ageing. This is produced by the combination of positive but low rates of build up with lower scrapping trends. The responding strategy of many owners to the low levels of freight rates is to keep the existing shipping assets beyond commonly accepted life spans. At the beginning of 1998 the world merchant fleet has an average age of 17,8 years when in 1993 this average was 16,7 years. Only the age of containerships decreased from 11,5 to 11,1 as more than 30% of such ships were built during this period. On the other hand, 40% of all tanker ships are older than 20 years and many oil companies look like extending the life of their tonnage to more than 25 years. Seven years ago the age profile showed quite different patterns, as only 29% of the total number of tankers were attributable to the over 20-age category. The age pattern of the EU-flagged vessels is not comparatively uncompetitive, its average age and that of the total world fleet are almost identical. The development of the EU-flagged fleet by ship type confirms the absence of structural uncompetitiveness. The share of the containerships has raised 7.5% of the EU fleet in 1990 to over 10% in 1997, which is significantly higher than the respective world fleet share (6.7%). Still, the slow modernisation of the EU-flagged vessels is a significant long-term structural problem with negative implications for its safety record.

Combined with the tendency to cut costs through curtailing maintenance expenditures, over-ageing frequently leads to risky operations. An increasing number of substandard ships raise casualties, with structural failures being the most commonly identified cause. Of the 943 ships total losses in the six first years of the 1990s, 522 (55.3%) were vessels of 20 years and over, and 240 (25.5%) of the 15-20 category ships (ILU, 1996). Sixty of the 77 oil tankers lost between 1992 and 1999 were more than 20 years old (CEU, 2000a). Age alone may not be responsible but it is incontrovertible that old ships are distinctively more dangerous than the younger vessels. Accidents are often attributed to human error (navigation or pilotage error). Crew training and crew skills have been recognised as key elements in improving safety at sea. In addition, working conditions constitute an equally important factor, in particular since fatigue has come to be increasingly recognised as a growing cause of accidents at sea. Still there is a general correlation between the age of the vessels and the accidents that have occurred.

Effective financing arrangements for the mobilisation of considerable sums in order to replace critically overaged tonnage seem remote.[10] In turn, the poor safety record augments operating expenditures. Insurance costs have been increased by substantial margins, in many cases representing more than 20% of the operation, and further increases are likely as long as the safety performance is not improved. Whilst the poor maritime safety record is negative for those employed in the sea, and from a societal point of view, it also generates a counterproductive vicious circle undermining the prosperity of shipowners themselves.

Notes

1   For example, the Isle of Man registry offers the tax haven of the island, while seafarers are employed without payment of employers national insurance and pension contributions that would be payable under the UK rules and crewing agreements.

2   The main rules of NIS include: no nationality requirements in respect of crew or equity capital; freedom to negotiate employment conditions with any representative union regardless of nationality; shipowning company may be incorporated outside Norway provided there is an owners representative in Norway and part of operating functions are located there; no taxation of foreign owners; minimum registration fees; liberalisation of currency requirements; regulations to accord fully with OECD standards (Kappel, 1988).

3   In 1953 extensive privileges were given to owners flying the Greek flag, including

allowances to hire foreign executives; buy ships free; administer freely their earning from shipping activity, ship sales, or insurance claims; pay reduced sums to the Retired Seamen's Fund, and tax between 2% to 4%. In the 1960s shipowners were allowed to use the dual registry system without being taxed on overseas earnings. Since 1975, similarly to FoC countries such as Liberia and Panama, Greece does not tax shipowners earnings but charge an annual fee based on tonnage. In 1979 a further effort was made to attract vessels to the Greek flag by creating the so called 'maritime company', enjoying all the previous benefits plus lax establishment criteria. In the 1980s the Greek administration reviewed the rules governing crew synthesis (1983, 1986, 1990) and minimum payments of foreign crew (1983), and cut the total tax paid by ships up to 75% (1990). Further reviews are currently under consideration.

4   Tudball P., Chairman of Baltic Exchange, quoted in: *Industrial Review*, Doldrums and Maelstrom: Currents in Greek Shipping, p. 5, May 1994.

5   When seaborne trade increased by 30% between 1970-1986 the size of the world fleet almost doubled.

6   See: Seatrade, *Conference Papers of the 1995 Tanker Industry Convention*, London, UK.

7   *Seatrade Week Newsfront*, New Year Resolution, Vol. XII, 1-7 January 1993.

8   *Lloyd's List*, International Chamber of Shipping attacks IMO over safety, 25.5.1995.

9   *Lloyd's List*, IMO move to establish International Ship Information Database, 31.12.1994.

10   Peters (1993) points out that the costly scenario to correct world fleet deficiencies, including inflation calculation, implied the mobilisation of a sum exceeding US $400 billion before 2000, hence, there are more doubts than assurances hanging over the international maritime industry and the markets it serves.

5 The Establishment of the Common Policy on Safe Seas

In the mid 1980s the EU record in the area of maritime safety was minimal. The rights and responsibilities of the EU members as flag, coastal, and port states continued to be negotiated at an international level. Discussions on a Commission proposal for unilateral action of its port states to ensure the enforcement of international standards were suspended. Discontent by the lack of implementation of the flag-state principle, member states agreed with the objectives pursued but accepted the French invitation to discuss the content of the directive within a geographically broader alternative form of cooperation. In 1982, Norway and all the current EU port states bar Ireland (which did so later) signed the Paris Memorandum of Understanding (MOU). These countries voluntarily made the commitment to harmonise their Port State Control (PSC), that is, their system of inspection of the foreign flagged ships that visit ports under their jurisdiction, and in case of deficiencies to detain them until their correction of such deficiencies.

The development illustrated appreciation for the Commission's concerns that the expansion of new registries had 'brought into the shipping market vessels which present both operating hazards (substandard ships) and a threat to the marine environment', which had been expressed as early as 1977 (CEU, 1977), and admitted that port-states should also have a responsibility for ensuring an adequate level of safety. The geographical scope of the EU(9) was judged to be restrictive to the inclusion of non-member countries into the measure but member states feared that the adoption of the directive would lead to the establishment of a new EU competence.

The CMTP progress in the second half of the 1980s dealt with the area of safety only as a secondary theme. Yet, grounding on both economic and environmental interests, the 1985 Commission memorandum expressed an increasing consideration of the extent to which some international rules needed to be modified, or rendered stringent (CEU, 1985a). This was accompanied by suggestions for the exploitation of the EU external relationships to help in the training of labour and maritime administrations around the world, and on the development of the PSC within the EU. The latter was in its early days and the Commission was of the thought that if competitive pressures among the various EU ports were undermining its application, the way to deal with the problem would be the writing of rules into EU law. Therefore, it was deliberately leaving its option open with this end in view.

The proposed by the Commission 1989 positive measures associated issues of safety and pollution prevention, like most of the CMTP themes, to the establishment of Euros (CEU, 1989a). The requirements of the latter would be such that highly skilled personnel and obligatory compliance of international standards would ensure that vessels operating this EU flag would meet high standards of quality and reliability. As for the problems arising from non EU-flagged shipping, there was an increasing emphasis on EU actions in the context of PSC. Initially, this was in the field of seminars and recommendations on the better enforcement of the PSC, lately transformed to a recommendation for the inspection of the 25% of the ships visiting European waters. The Commission, which had begun to participate in the appropriate meetings, announced its decision to take the lead in conjunction with the PSC secretariat and the ILO maritime branch in achieving agreement among the countries subscribing to the MOU on the integration of this convention into the manual of their surveyors.

The 'Safe Seas' Document

Between 1986 and 1991, the rate of total losses of ships fluctuated at around an average 230 vessels per annum, some of them seriously damaging the EU ecosystem. According to published figures, 7.952 persons lost their lives at sea within the same period.[1] Events generated public attention but policy makers and stakeholders continued to insist that the key to maritime safety lay solely with the presence and enforcement of international rules. Member states started to enact laws and develop policies regarding the environment at a pace never seen before but few of them had any direct relevance to shipping (Power, 1992). However, following several pollution accidents in the last fortnight of 1989,[2] the Council passed a resolution which, although sustaining the commitment to the implementation of international rules, called on the Commission to start promoting and improving EU action in the form of a 'task force'.[3] Responding to major ferry disasters,[4] the Council called on the member states and the Commission, as members of the IMO and the MOU and as an observer of these organisations respectively, to press for urgent identification, elaboration, adoption, and implementation of measures to improve the safety of passenger ferry vessels.[5]

In this setting, the introduction of the 'horizontal' CMTP approach pointed out the potential of European standards, which would help with the implementation of international rules but also lead to the creation of new ones (CEU, 1991a). The 1992 White and Green Papers on the Common Transport Policy development (CEU, 1992a, 1992b) emphasised the same policy direction, emphasising the benefits that could be expected by the establishment of Euros. In the meantime, the TEU had underlined the importance of goals like sustainable growth, and improvements in the safety of the transport sector. But the absence of concrete measures dissatisfied MEPs who questioned the Commission's inaction and called for practical steps towards a EU policy.[6] Similarly, the critical Ecosoc opinion on the White Paper demanded EU measures for the uniform implementation of international provisions to be put into effect as soon as possible (Ecosoc, 1993a). The Ecosoc was also concerned 'about the contradiction of the emphasis on EU maritime fleets when non EU-flagged vessels that frequently do not meet safety standards carry more of the EU trade'. Before the MEPs' questions responded, or the Ecosoc opinion was formally published, actions towards that direction had been published.

Following the preceding publications, the Commission had started to draft a report[7] on an area which at the time was one 'where the EU has not yet formulated a policy' (Slot, 1992). When public awareness was fuelled by new incidents in the European waters at the end of 1992,[8] the Transport Commissioner, A. Matutes, decided to rush the publication.[9] This decision was impelled by the conclusions of an 'Extraordinary Council of the Environmental and Transport Ministers', which expressed the intention of concrete EU-action to improve maritime safety and contribute to the prevention of maritime pollution.[10] Some member states made apparent that they would like to see the urgent introduction of higher European safety standards, similar to those that the US had unilaterally inaugurated. The German administration called for translating to EU law aspects of the US Oil Pollution Act of 1990 (OPA 90) that would make it compulsory for tankers to fit double hulls, a 10-years age limit of tankers entering the EU waters, and the establishment of unlimited shipowners' liability. These measures were explicitly supported by France, Italy, and Spain, but forcefully opposed by two major maritime member states with strong interests in the tanker market. These were the British and Greek administration that during the Council meeting were also supported by the (Greek) Commissioner for the Environment.[11]

A month later, the Commission documented its proposals for a *Common Policy on Safe Seas* (CEU, 1993a). Therein, it prioritised common initiatives targeting the uniform implementation of existing international rules (measures concerning the flag-state); the convergent enforcement of international rules through a tighter and more effective control of ships visiting EU ports (measures concerning the port-state); the development of maritime infrastructure (R&D, modernisation of traffic control and navigation, reception facilities in ports, training and education); and further international rule making. The scope was to provide a framework for policy actions that would make the most of both flag- and port-state capacities of the EU member to eliminate substandard vessels from its waters. With the Euros proposal remaining controversial, the Commission suggested, antithetically to previous proposals, an EU policy approach irrespective of the ships' flag. Still, priority should be given to adequate international actions, the promotion of which could be enhanced by a more proactive EU role. To establish this role, the Commission proposed the creation of a special Committee to coordinate the international efforts of the member states, and 'put forward for examination' the possibility of an EU membership of IMO.

The Commission continued to adhere to the view that negative competitive advantages could result from the introduction of a regional regulatory framework. However, a worrying safety record was accompanied by a correlation between vessel accidents and registration under certain non-EU flags, as well as wide variations in the safety performance of flag states within EU membership. Having monitored policy initiatives taken by member and non-member governments and those of other international organisations, the Commission 'was forced to act', firstly because of the absence of a fully effective and coherent European approach to the implementation of international rules and, secondly, because of its obligation in the interest of the EU to complete the loopholes that exist in the international level when required.

This was not considered as a framework to bypass IMO, but a search for an interactive relationship to assist IMO to become efficient: According to a Commission official, 'the principle of the document is implementing IMO rules, it is not to substitute or work in parallel with IMO. The

Commission started from the IMO work and tried to build on that. In IMO you have a lot of loopholes, so from time to time derogations make IMO conventions empty boxes. EU action is meant to ensure a better and harmonised implementation of the Conventional obligations of the member states. Second, we should at least ensure that those commitments that are binding by the IMO, plus the no favourable treatment law, are applicable to those that are not contracting parties to the conventions' (De Dieu, 1996).

Interest Groups Mobilisation

This initiative received a mixed reception from European shipowners. European shipowners have always maintained that despite the legitimate cause of concern and the adverse publicity generated in the wake of maritime accidents, it should not be forgotten that problems of a worldwide character like safety and pollution of the seas involve an international industry and are best dealt with through international agreements that set uniform standards. Hence, they had strongly opposed the development of an EU policy. So, the Commission's framework was welcomed only insofar it was based on the principle that 'the IMO should decide'. To the extent that this policy initiative represented an intensive trend towards EU intervention on IMO issues, they rejected the approach as an unjustified challenge to the international rule making machinery, where it may be extremely difficult to decide but the final decisions are extremely significant. To them, this challenge could have negative rather than the positive results anticipated by the Commission (Mavrommati, 1996).

Attributing particular importance to what could follow the Commission initiative, ECSA issued a special publication of its position stressing that the central problem was a lack of compliance with existing regulations, and that IMO was the obvious forum in which to take matters forward. The main concern was that, despite this need being acknowledged by the Commission, there was a danger of the initiative leading to a regional approach that would cause confusion. The publication also made clear ECSA's opposition to a potential EU membership of IMO, because it could lead to a bloc voting system and increasing politicisation through the establishment of other blocs. The shipowners' view was that more effective enforcement by flag states, with compliance ensured through the development of the existing PSC mechanism would make the single most effective practical contribution in the short term to enhanced safety and pollution prevention standards (ECSA, 1993). Therefore, ECSA was satisfied by the fact that the Commission seriously and usefully addressed the role of preventative measures regarding the human factor through emphasis on training, together with action in areas of maritime infrastructure. In this vein, ECSA demanded financial incentives for efficient owners who have to cover the high costs of quality manning. Finally, the publication mentioned as 'encouraging' that the Commission had avoided 'the suggestion made on occasions' of banning ships over a certain age from European waters.

In the aftermath of the Jumbo Council, shipowners had been increasingly anxious that the publicity on maritime incidents could tempt European institutions to follow the US path and impose higher, more costly, standards than those agreed internationally. The most affected market segment would be the tanker industry. So, apart from lobbying through ECSA, Intertanko submitted a 'memorandum on tankers operated by independent owners' appealing for the avoidance of a panic reaction which would have opposite results from those intended and its representatives continued to lobby the Commission in Brussels (Greek Shipping Cooperation Committee, 1995). When the 'safe seas' document was published, shipowners were happy that several of their objections were taken into account.

They realised, however, that the traditional notion for exclusively international regulatory developments, with an absence of any EU initiatives, was undermined by the noticeable 'flexibility' on the enforcement of IMO rules by the national administrations. Moreover, shipowners 'could not continue to argue that if IMO adopts a Convention then there is not a role for the EU, as to adopt and apply IMO decisions at a Community level means in practice to transform the IMO Conventions to mandatory regulations' (Economou, 1996). Still, they remained troubled with the concept of translating IMO resolutions into EU law arguing that a resolution is by its nature a recommendatory advice for the formulation of national rules and should remain so. The presence of substandard non-EU flagged vessels enjoying competitive advantage may explain the positive attitude towards the strengthening of a regional initiative like the PSC. Although the system adds to operational costs (i.e. port delays, increased vessels' scrutiny), it is conceived as an instrument that might develop a more balanced implementation of existing regulation and, eventually, improve the competitive position of EU flagged operations. In this context,

ECSA expressed the need for the system to be improved by a more selective approach to ship inspections but also asked for financial incentives in case future EU measures created increases in costs.

With shipowners sharing the principle that IMO and MOU should be the main fora to promote maritime safety, ECSA achieved a line that satisfied all of them. Yet, national associations recorded a variation of positions that reflected domestic policy developments and divergent commercial interests. British shipowners welcomed the new EC common policy as a major contribution and expressed support for the measures provided the right balance is achieved between regulation at national, EC, and wider international level (BCS, 1993). Following the Braer grounding, the British government initiated a public inquiry regarding national level actions to protect the UK coastline from pollution. Although British shipowners submitted several recommendations for national level measures they would like to see them adopted by other countries as well. On the other hand, Greek shipowners rejected the development of any EU measure. Pollution from the tanker industry dominated the debate; hence, Greek shipowners could face more financial burdens than shipowners mainly interested in other market segments. Moreover, as their major involvement is in tramp cross-trade shipping, they worried, more than those operating in ports, which are subject to PSC, that EU action could adversely affect their business by imposing higher standards. Therefore, the Commission could bring about positive results as long as unilateral or regional action would be avoided (UGS, 1994). Even essential preventive measures, i.e. the development of infrastructure relating to safety and pollution prevention, should be pursued through IMO (similar was the reaction of the Danish association: DSA, 1994).

The EP became the focal point of shipowners lobbying, with ECSA intensifying its contacts with MEPs to put across the views of the industry in a positive and proactive manner (ECSA, 1994). National associations emphasised their own priorities at national and EU level simultaneously. Realising that pressures in environmental issues were coming from the EP, the British Chamber of Shipping decided to build contacts with national MEPs aiming to clear up the ambiguities. The UGS submitted a memorandum to all Greek MEPs, 'so that they would be able to support and promote the Union's views', while it also expressed its position via the Ecosoc, as the opinion of the latter was drafted by one of its consultants.[12]

Trade unions were particularly satisfied by the 'clear mark of political intention for the development of an EU policy' (Orrell, 1996). In fact, organised labour had already supported that safety and the environment should come back to the political agenda because the shipping industry was not prepared to fulfil its long-term responsibilities and invest in such aspects. Two interrelated parameters were critical to the approval of the EU approach. First, the issues raised by the Commission were not isolated from international developments. Second, those countries subscribing would effectively implement any future regulations. Increasingly dissatisfied by the international policy making machinery, wherein 'there is a tendency of everybody to agree because no flag-state takes care of these agreements and no government will transform anything in law', they put less emphasis on the regional character of the Commission's framework (De Villele, 1996). The main issue for the unions was not whether solutions would be given by regulations adopted at a regional, national or international level but to find the 'necessary' solutions. Still, labour recognised that given the global nature of the industry the establishment of international rules standards should remain the first priority of the EU institutions.

Since the target was to improve the quality of maritime services, the recommended policy framework would upgrade their profession. Therefore, the first attempt to enforce preventive measures was welcomed although labour did not necessarily agree with all the details. In this context, ITF set a panel of safety experts to advise trade unions on the Commission proposals on maritime safety and substandard vessels. Labour representatives focused on the inadequate support of the national administrations for the IMO work and especially its conventions regarding the human element, pointing out the inconsistent application of PSC by the member states, and lobbied for more concrete action regarding the establishment of minimum levels of training for maritime professions.[13] Notably, the increase of the PSC powers was a central theme of their support campaign as 'one solution to create more employment opportunities for the European seafarers; To them, the outcome of a strict enforcement of a European PSC would be the strict application of rules on safety, insurance, employment, anything that is linked with the quality of the crew and the ships; and all these mean, by induction, more employment for European seafarers' (De Villele, 1996). Moreover, they suggested that the potential of the Commission speaking on behalf of the member states at the IMO would be a negative development, though they argued that the

Commission has a valuable coordination role to play in promoting a common EU stance.

The Commission's initiative was also utilised by labour on the domestic front. The British trade union found it an immense assistance to influence an unhelpful British government to initiate a public enquiry (and the subsequent 'Donaldson report') regarding the Braer incident even if it was a ship that did not carry the UK flag and was not even coming to the UK. Moreover, as the document underlined an increasing concern for the level of training of European seafarers it had, along with the ongoing discussions on Euros, an effect on this union's decision in following the 'Brussels route' to the representation of its members interests: The recognition that was made, and accepted, was that they may better influence the maritime strategy in Europe through the various avenues that the Commission provides than with their government. NUMAST continued to have problems and limited influence to the British government. Any valuable initiatives adopted were tickling with the edge of what it needs to be done. The Safe Seas document and a concentration on maritime safety were the reactions from Europe to the Braer incident; so to represent effectively their members, trade union representatives had to change their attitude (Orrell, 1996). Since the safety record in the UK had worsened, and the conclusions of the Donaldson report provided another voice of warning, the union looked for collective European actions that would counterbalance the safety cuts of its national government.

Policy Makers Reactions

The Council committed itself to actions on the Commission's proposals before the ending of the consultative process. A few days after the communication (March 1993), the Council expressed its satisfaction at the quality of the objectives outlined by the Commission and instructed COREPER to expedite this matter.[14] Such agreement was facilitated by the fact that the controversial proposals discussed in the Jumbo Council were not brought forward by any minister. In June 1993, the Council adopted a resolution which was important in that member states did not only stress the role of international policy making machinery but also 'the need for intensified action as appropriate at Community or national level to ensure an adequate response to the requirements of maritime safety and the prevention of marine pollution'. In this vein, it invited the Commission to submit further reports for collective EU action, to develop common criteria for more thorough PSC, and to identify IMO resolutions considered necessary for improving maritime safety of vessels entering EU waters. Notably, although the resolution provided for 'a more effective common monitoring of the work of IMO and MOU and the preparation of, or contribution to, a closer coordination of member states towards a common position in these organisations achieved through the usual Council procedures', it also agreed to the Commission's proposal for the establishment of a Committee on Safe Seas to coordinate actions of national administrations and the Commission itself. A Council working group monitored on a daily basis by COREPER had previously undertaken this role.[15]

Although welcoming the 'timing' of the Commission's initiative, the Ecosoc remained critical. Its opinion, rejected the idea of promoting EU standards, since they 'could lead to regionalisation', and emphasised the already present 'extensive corpus of rules at the international level' (Ecosoc 1993b). It acknowledged, however, that if member states acting in a coordinated manner are not able to succeed in incorporating an appropriate IMO resolution into a convention, there could be merit in rendering it mandatory at an EU level. Such action should be examined on a case-by-case basis. The Ecosoc also rejected the idea of an *en bloc* membership of the EU in the IMO, as it would politicise the forum and greatly hamper its effectiveness. This opinion also focused on two issues concerning the nature of the policy-making process. By adopting the resolution despite the pending consultation procedure the Council had bypassed both the Ecosoc and the EP, so the opinion expressed 'misgivings about the timing' of the Council's action. Furthermore, it opposed the establishment of the Committee on Safe Seas, arguing that it would be more appropriate given the prime role of member states if the existing Council working group machinery were used, adjusted as necessary.

The EP endorsed the Commission's framework but called for the establishment of a far-reaching European policy. Contending that the safe seas document was 'a breath of fresh air', the EP report stressed that enforcement legislation was necessary 'if the Commission and the Council are serious in tackling the maritime problems'. While the Commission was focusing on PSC implementation, the EP emphasised the necessity for an EU policy that would extend the system. Adopting the trade unions stance (see: ITF, 1994b), the EP report also called for shipping inspections to be kept under government ownership and control, and demanded EU binding rules and standards to be agreed and then safeguarded by a single pan-European coastguard. Moreover, it challenged the power of IMO in fighting the case against substandard vessels, 'as the IMO has not been adequate to prevent shipping disasters legislative activities are needed by the member states and the EU should become a contracting party to the relevant IMO convention'. It went on to propose that 'in the long term it may be desirable for the Union itself to become a full member of the IMO'.[16]

According to a principal administrator of the DG-VII safety unit, 'the safe seas communication remains 'the Bible' for the Community safety policy' (De Dieu, 1996). Everything that the Commission is doing is in line with it, aiming to implement the concrete programme that is attached to this communication. Endorsed by the EP, the Ecosoc, ('as the Commission initiatives should reflect the views of the social partners that the Ecosoc represents', and especially the Council, 'in a resolution, that agreed to the main principles as they had been foreseen by the Commission, and this means that the 15 member states are ready to do the most to implement the programme attached to that' (ibid.), the Commission began the implementation of the specified framework almost immediately. When the 1996 maritime strategic document reinforced the ideas first expressed in the safe seas document, the EU maritime safety legislation included already two regulations, referring to the tanker industry and the safety management of roll-on/roll-of (ro/ro) ferries respectively. It also included several directives, 'the most significant being the one concerning the minimum level of seafarers' training' (Jones, 1996).

Another noteworthy directive concerned the uniform implementation of the member states' PSC systems.[17] Before its introduction these systems had been voluntarily undertaken under the Paris MOU, so there were no systematic criteria for inspection, or detention, of ships. As within the 'safe seas' document the PSC became a key direction for European policy. Judging that the PSC was the most effective tool the industry has got to force the substandard tonnage out and should therefore be improved (De Dieu, 1996) the Commission submitted a proposal for an EU directive that provides for harmonising member states' inspections and ships' detention by law. Moreover, it includes conditions under which a vessel may be banned from entering into a European port if it has already been detained elsewhere. Notwithstanding its voluntary character, the European (albeit non-EU) MOU had already highlighted the common member states' attitudes in inspecting the application of maritime safety rules. Moreover, in the aftermath of the 'safe seas' document both labour and shipowners supported the strengthening of the PSC system. In this context, the adoption of the EU rule was uncontroversial. As an interviewee observed, the Council discussed and agreed to push the Directive ahead without problems although prior to the 'safe seas' document several member states had the view that if you translate the PSC to European law then there would be a retaliation elsewhere (Orrell, 1996).

Directive on Minimum Level of Training for Seafarers

With human error playing a great role in maritime incidents, the 'safe seas' document provided that EU measures regarding the quality of crews onboard was 'a matter of urgency', more so when the transportation of dangerous goods and passengers is involved. In this vein, the first Commission proposal to follow the 'safe seas' document was an EU directive on the minimum level of training for maritime occupations (CEU, 1993b). The proposal was rationalised on the ineffective implementation of international rules governing working conditions at sea. As member states had adopted the relevant 1978 STCW convention but not always applied it, the Commission was of the view that it had the task to guarantee by means of EU law, the uniform application of the IMO instrument, and that all seafarers employed on EU-flagged ships have received appropriate training in compliance with its standards.

The recommended directive, which would in the future be amended in parallel to any STCW review, provided two additional points of substantial importance. The first one concerned mixed national crews onboard, with the Commission proposing that all seafarers should be 'able to communicate in a common language' with each other. Special requirements for personnel on vessels carrying hazardous goods demanded the knowledge of 'a common working language', while those on passenger-ships should be able to communicate in cases of emergency 'in the languages appropriate to the majority of the passengers carried on a particular route'. The second point concerned the level of training of non-EU nationals. The Commission proposed that seafarers with no training from a member state should be allowed to serve onboard provided a satisfactory agreement ensuring the implementation of the STCW has been concluded between the EU and the third countries of which the seafarers concerned are nationals. Otherwise, ships should be given priority for PSC inspection and detained if seafarers could not prove professional proficiency for the duties assigned to them. To the Commission, the directive would ensure safety and create a level playing field for all EU-flagged vessels. The closer monitoring of third countries' training and education was essential because STCW certificates could no longer be relied upon as evidence of non-EU nationals' professional competence.

The IMO had already embarked on a discussion for a limited review of the STCW provisions since 1992. This was only partially because adjustments to technological developments were essential. From the late 1980s the STCW was gradually losing credibility. Major dissatisfactions were the product of the fact that, although 114 flag states aggregating 95% of the world tonnage had signed this agreement, the level of education, and subsequently the certificates, they provided did not comply with the required standards. The 1978 STCW prescribes a model on which flag-states must necessarily base their crew requirements; auditing of administrative, training, and certification, procedures remains subject to the satisfaction of each country. Thus, despite its global acceptance, the widely varying interpretation of standards dissatisfied several countries, but also employers and employees. The weight of the human element in the chain of events leading to accidents continued to increase, and more than 60% of accident claims by shipowners referred to human error.

Two months after the Commission's proposal, in May 1993, IMO decided to give priority to a comprehensive STCW review. It also accelerated the review process by establishing a small group of consultants sponsored by four EU states, namely Germany, the Netherlands, Spain, the United Kingdom, as well as Mexico, Korea, and the United States, and consulted the ISF and the International Confederation of Free Trade Unions (sponsored by the ITF). The original date for completing the revision at IMO level was 1998, meaning that the revision conference would probably not have been held until 1996. Under the accelerated programme the conference was brought forward to June-July 1995.

Interest Groups Mobilisation

Irrespective of whether they address safety issues, policy measures affecting manning conditions involve, inevitably, a change in employment practices. Table 4.2 displayed the substantial number of non-EU seafarers onboard EU flagged vessels. Most of them are lower decks whose employment is subject to bilateral crew accords that have been entered into force since the late 1970s, and following agreements between shipowner associations with third world seafarers unions. By limiting the employment of non-EU officers and crews to those holding certificates or diplomas meeting STCW related standards most of these seemed certain to be outlawed under a Council directive (Sarlis, 1996). Subsequently, shipowners became outspoken opponents of the proposed draft arguing that it would damage the cheap crewing base on which the fleet had survived in recent years in a very international trade (Richards, 1996). The timing of its submission further perplexed the specific initiative. It happened when the Euros proposal was at a standstill, primarily because of the controversies over the manning rules that should govern it. According to shipowners, the proposed directive 'could unreasonably reduce the essential labour market flexibility applied to the EU-flagged fleet, when there was a recognition in the Euros discussion framework that such reduction would hamper its competitive position'. To them, the absence of such flexibility would lead to the real prospect of EU owners having to flag-out, because EU legislation with limited practical effect in terms of safety and environmental protection would be more burdensome than that applicable to their competitors (Economou, 1996).

On the other hand, ECSA acknowledged that the Commission was correct in identifying the need for better manning standards, and accepted the EU role in facilitating the proper implementation of the international rules. Still, it pointed out that it would not be feasible to apply an EU directive unless it mirrors internationally agreed and ratified standards (Economou, 1996). This is not to say that there were not suggested reservations because the subject was already covered by the STCW. For example, the Greek ownership advocated that, instead of proceeding alone, the EU should support the international standard setting in view also of the fact that the IMO was already proceeding with the revision of the STCW Convention (Peppa, 1996). However, when it was realised that a Council agreement on the principles of this proposal was possible shipowners sought to prevent the adoption of provisions that 'did not reflect the reality and would place unnecessary costs on ships' (UGS, 1995).

These concerted efforts at domestic and EU level referred to the two additional proposals included in the Commission's draft. The precondition of the knowledge of a 'common language' by crews onboard would in practice limit third-world seafarers and increase operating costs. Shipowners argued that these requisites had to be amended in a way that would allow more flexibility in establishing an effective line of communication. Then, they disliked the idea of the Commission assuming responsibility for the verification of training certificates provided from third countries, due to 'the tendency of the EU for higher standards' (Economou, 1996). Shipowners were satisfied by the bilateral, not necessarily associated with the STCW, agreements that national governments had signed with respective third countries. Moreover, more than half of the EU fleet, which is the Greek fleet, operated under national legislation providing that in the absence of capable nationals a post may be covered virtually free of nationality, or training certificate requirements. Finally, shipowners concluded that the employment of third world seafarers is often the product of the shortage of European seafarers, therefore, they called for the EU to introduce funding programmes for training schemes, supply and demand assessment, and R&D.

Organised labour had already argued that if the EU policy is going to enhance safety then attention should be given to manning rules. To them, a coherent implementation of the STCW could have a positive impact, as it would increase market pressures in favour of quality shipping and crews. With contemporary manning practices involving contracts with ship-managers who operate ships and provide manpower the quality of which it is difficult to control, 'the EU was rightly pointed towards that direction' (Tselentis, 1996). The proper monitoring of non-EU countries' certificates was essential in order to detect the actual level of compliance to international standards. Like shipowners, trade unions saw the recommended directive as meaning an end to jobs going to non-EU nationals. It would *de facto* enhance the employment prospects of European seafarers who retain a comparative advantage as far as their qualifications are concerned. Given the likely difficulties by some major non-EU seafarer providing countries to fully comply with the STCW and bring sufficient evidence of compliance if rules would be properly implemented, the EU rule could increase the inducement of EU-flagged shipowners to employ EU certificated seafarers (Orrell, 1996).

However, seafarers strongly criticised the draft directive because 'it did not add but one provision to the STCW convention' (Tselentis, 1996). The 'common language' provision was important for them, as the shipping industry had failed to control the language problems among polyglot multinational crews, jeopardising the maintenance of safe communication and producing an inherent state of continuous danger. But they maintained that, because a reputable and responsible operation represents commercial value, the EU should introduce tight safety standards creating a long-term benefit to the EU-flagged shipping industry. Trade unions also maintained that, instead of offering minimum educational standards to guarantee the safety of vessels, the directive should introduce common guidelines and criteria to upgrade education and secure employment.

In this vein, they offered a list of alternatives, including the introduction of a single educational system, the adoption of common promotional criteria, common rules to train EU maritime instructors, and the same language requirements for all employees in shipping. The EU should focus on training 'because the problem starts by the fact that it is cheaper to train seafarers from the developing world with basic education and language communication problems'. As several national governments continue to neglect their duties in that field organised labour asked for EU sponsored schemes for onboard training prospects to EU seafarers, 'which in the short term are more costly but in the long term secure a safe operation' (Orrell, 1996). Referring to a growing requirement for high quality seafarers, they also focus on the necessity of the EU to encourage sufficient new recruits in their profession.

Policy Makers Reactions

The Council had a first discussion on the initiative in the early stages of the policy-making process (November 1993), when it agreed 'on basic elements of the proposed directive' but incorporated several reservations to the Commission's draft.[18] National administrations agreed to an EU rule for the uniform STCW implementation but rejected the two additional elements. According to an official of the Council secretariat, 'there are seven or eight Council members that usually speak on maritime matters' and none of them was particularly supportive of the Commission's proposed rule for higher crew communication standards onboard EU-flagged vessels (Vermote, 1996). Nonetheless, the Council did not reject the specific notion but would return to it after conclusion of the consultation procedure. As the Greek Minister noted later, there was an agreement that the issue should be solved in a way that would satisfy the scope of the directive to increase maritime safety and prevent losses of life but also in response to the problem with the necessary realism.[19]

The Council also rejected the idea of expanding Commission competency over non-EU seafarers' certificates, preferring the issue to remain the responsibility of individual member states.[20] Several administrations, including the Greek one, pointed out that the logistics involved in a decision to sign bilateral agreements with all third countries were not feasible (Bantias, 1996). The Council agreed, however, to integrate national approaches through the establishment of common criteria. Notably, the comprehensive STCW revision within the IMO mechanism was already underway and two of its main issues were the 'communication' problem, which was recognised as a vital safety problem by both ISF and ITF, and a Norwegian proposal for the minimum education, training, and certification, requirements to be monitored internationally by the IMO.[21] A third major alteration to the draft directive was raised within the Council, however it was not endorsed. The Italian administration demanded, unsuccessfully, the extension of the directive to vessels registered by the offshore registers of the member states, arguing that it is part of the EU responsibility to ensure the safe operation of these vessels.

According to the Rapporteur of the EP Committee on Transport, it was evident that the Council had drawn its own balance and would reject the Commission draft proposal for not meeting its view. Therefore, he suggested an amended directive that was trying to bridge the disagreement between the Council and the Commission in serving the needs of the shipping industry (Sarlis, 1996). His report asked for the 'common languages' requirements to be erased, so as to avoid confusion. However, several members of the Committee were more supportive of the Commission's proposals and following an evenly balanced vote the specific amendment was rejected. Instead, the Committee opted for an alternative that was put forward by the MEPs of the biggest political group (PES).[22] The EP view was that 'crews onboard should have a permanent and effective line of communication, which may include a common language'. As regards passenger-ships, the members of the crew with responsibilities for the operation of life saving equipment should have communication skills that are sufficient for that purpose taking into account an adequate combination of a list of criteria but communication requirements should not be extended, as the Commission had suggested, to include the rest of the crews. On the other hand, agreeing with the Rapporteur the EP demanded the withdrawal of the special requirements for crews on tankers.

The Rapporteur's view regarding the employment of non-EU seafarers was also rejected. The EP suggested that they should be allowed to work on EU-flagged vessels if their competency certificates meet the criteria to be established after a proposal submitted by the Commission in cooperation with the EP, rather than defined by the Council itself. There was a consensus within the EP regarding the rest of the 32 endorsed amendments. All but three responded to technical weaknesses of the draft proposal. The first of these three provided that instead of absorbing future STCW articles to EU law, the directive itself should be referred to as those 'in effect at any given time'. Subsequently, any future IMO modification would automatically come into effect as EU legislation, rather than following discussions, and the ratification of international convention would also be subject to less delays. The second amendment called for an EU action programme for attracting young people into the shipping sector. The third one provided that for a maximum of six months competent authorities should be able to offer a dispensation permitting a specified seafarer to serve without holding the certificate.

The Ecosoc unanimously agreed that a full revision of the draft directive was essential, in a way that would automatically incorporate the comprehensive STCW revision that would take place in 1995, and absorb future STCW provisions (Ecosoc, 1993c). Anyhow, EU regulations should not lay down higher training standards than those agreed by IMO. That said, the Ecosoc opinion emphasised the crucial importance of the directive to stipulate that all the crew can communicate with each other in a common language. It did not, however, support the measure for EU agreements with third countries, as there was no reason to believe that these countries would respect agreements with the EU any more than the provisions of the STCW. So, it stressed the necessity for effective surveillance measures, including operational checks on crew competence, in the context of the PSC.

The Commission had the opportunity, as provided by the Treaty, to revise the proposal in the light of the preceding EP remarks. In this context, not only did it accept most of the EP amendments concerning improvements of a technical nature, but submitted to the Council a substantially altered proposal (CEU, 1994). Firstly, it agreed to the proposed EP system regarding the recognition of third countries certificates. Whereas there was a strong Council objection to the initial proposal, the EP amendment would empower the Commission and the EP to draw up those criteria that member states should apply. The Commission also modified the 'communication' provisions in line with the EP requests. However, it did not accept the deletion of the special provisions for tanker crews. Nor did it accept the EP amendment that referred to education and an action programme to recruit people to a maritime profession. To the Commission, such commitment should be discussed but not as part of the specific directive. As the sole purpose of the latter was to ensure safety, the Commission thought that additional elements would unreasonably weaken this scope.

The reviewed proposals remained unsatisfactory to national administrations. The Council (June 1994) adopted a common position, which retained a different approach regarding the two additional provisions to the implementation of the STCW. There was a consensus among maritime member states that the amended 'communication' proposals were not as flexible as needed. The German administration put forward a counterproposal stating that crews' synthesis should be such that there are at any time means in place related to safety for effective oral communication. The Commission's proposal for passenger-ship crews was endorsed, but for tankers and ships carrying chemical products the Council agreed that crews should be able to communicate in one or several common languages. These criteria gained the accord of the rest of the national administrations, satisfied shipowners (ECSA, 1995) but frustrated trade unions: 'although the initial proposal had some positive elements the directive that was finally adopted was disastrous' (Tselentis, 1996). As regards non-EU training certificates, national administrations agreed that the practice should remain under their auspices, and subject to mutual recognition. Yet, they accepted that common EU criteria would standardise the level of training. Rejecting the specifications of the Commission's proposal, the Council provided that the common system would be defined within one year by itself, 'according to the Treaty'. Moreover, member states undertook the obligation to notify what certificates they recognise. Such decisions would be valid if neither any member state nor the Commission objected; otherwise, a regulatory committee would deliver its opinion by majority vote.

According to the Greek presidency, advancing the regulation to the adoption stage was not an easy task. Therefore, and despite the fact that the main target of this administration had been to gain the Council's commitment to take more action within the IMO rather than unilaterally,[23] the common position was conceived as 'a major presidency success'.[24] This agreement was adopted with the abstention of Italy. As this member state continued to oppose the practice of second and offshore registries,[25] it held that the EU measures should apply to crews under offshore flags. There was not support for this proposal on the ground that these territories and their flags are not considered to be part of the EU. Yet one should recall that these registers based their presence on high manning flexibility to understand the inaction.

The policy-making process led to a directive incorporating the majority of the amendments that the EP had proposed, though those referring to the most disputable point were altered. Assessing all but one of the rejected amendments as of minor importance, the EP found the outcome of the Council satisfactory.[26] During its second reading the EP returned only to the subject of seafarers' education. Referring to its major importance for safety, and the need to maintain a core of maritime know-how, it urged the Council to incorporate in the directive a programme considering the underwriting of the professional maritime education costs. But the Commission continued to oppose the inclusion of that amendment to the directive insisting that this subject should be a matter of more thorough examination. In agreement with this view, the November 1994 Council meeting simply ratified the content of the common position.[27]

Before the common system of recognising non-EU seafarers training could be defined, the STCW review had been finalised in record time (1995). The outcome, which was welcomed by the international associations of both shipowners (ISF) and labour (ITF) as a significant step forward, gave to IMO the powers to control and react to ineffective administrations by refusing to approve their certificates. So, when the Commission proposed in October 1996 the amendment of the directive to come in line with the provisions of the 1995 STCW it endorsed the recognition system of the STCW leaving no scope for a different EU system to develop (CEU, 1996c). Since the adoption of this amendment in May 1998,[28] the national systems of recognition are harmonised through the rules of the international convention. Meanwhile, IMO had asked the EU to assist its work in the implementation of the STCW amendments by providing financial assistance to IMO to hold seminars and workshops in different parts of the world.[29]

Regulation on Segregated Ballast Tankers

A second Commission initiative made a step towards the translation of voluntary IMO instruments to compulsory EU legislation. Specifically, the Commission proposed the adoption of a Regulation that would make mandatory the implementation of an IMO Resolution laying down technical procedures for tonnage measurement of oil tankers carrying segregated ballast tanks (SBT) (CEU, 1993c). In contrast with conventional tankers, which must carry part of their ballast in cargo tanks, modern tankers are equipped with SBT that are completely separate from the cargo, oil, and fuel, system, thus ensuring safer operational conditions at sea. An IMO Resolution had already recommended that the tonnage corresponding to this space should be exempted from port dues. However, member states and port authorities continued to charge similar dues for both conventional and SBT tankers, or else made a small deduction from the total tonnage. The Commission responded to the situation by putting forward a proposal that would make it mandatory for all European ports to offer a rebate to all SBT tankers irrespective of their flags.

The specific initiative, the potential of which had been mentioned in the 'safe seas' document, was grounded on the Jumbo Council conclusion that the EU should support the IMO actions on the reduction of the safety gap between new and existing ships, paying particular attention to oil tankers. By putting forward a regulation that would be directly applicable to all the EU ports, 'the Commission did not only provide a measure that would encourage operators to use environmentally friendly tankers, but also promoted an instrument utilising the responsibility of the member states as contracting parties to IMO'. Due to the latter, the proposed regulation 'emphasised a commitment to the IMO and prevented its turn to a paper machine of voluntary resolutions that are never implemented' (De Dieu, 1996).

Interest Groups Mobilisation

Not surprisingly, shipowners had been supporters of the IMO resolution and of its implementation around Europe as a measure towards environmental protection. Their argument was that SBT tankers had been ordered for the benefit of the marine environment but, by charging dues equal to the volumes that conventional vessels were charged, ports created an operational disadvantage. As an SBT tanker has a space which cannot be used for cargo, they had proposed that lower pilot and port fees were necessary to reward operators of environmentally friendly tankers. Apart from rectifying an ethical anomaly, it would act as an incentive to replace conventional style tankers with new safer and more environmentally friendly ones (Southorn, 1996).

Notwithstanding that, regulating the issue at an EU level was a second best option. For European shipowners it was a matter of principle that such decision should be taken at the IMO (Peppa, 1996). The major part of the tanker industry advocated that the initiative was misplaced and represented one more case that the IMO should be the level where compulsory or obligatory decisions should be taken. A collective member states' decision to press for the international mandatory implementation of the IMO resolution would be the best option as it would oblige more countries than the EU member states to ratify and implement the decision. Still, when the Commission made known its intention to draft the proposal, shipowners actively supported the initiative because 'it was designed to take away apparent financial penalties' (Mavrommati, 1996). The timing was important, as this was a period of great concern on the direction of the EU initiatives and, particularly, the possibility of tough measures against the tanker industry.

On the other hand, the regulatory proposal was strongly opposed by port authorities and became a central theme of their European campaign. Their newly established Euro-federation, ESPO, opposed the proposal on two grounds. First, it would influence the level of ports revenues and, hence, affect their economic position. Second, as a matter of principle, the Commission should not interfere in the settlement of port dues that is the main commercial decision of port authorities. Notably, the evidence of such interference was one of the main reasons for the formation of ESPO. To port authorities the decision of the Commission to treat ports as its agents and offer an inducement to owners to build vessels equipped with SBT was a disturbing sign of the emerging trend to use ports to resolve problems between member states and the shipping industry. The implementation of the rule should remain voluntary and the Commission should follow the principle of subsidiarity allowing ports to charge those dues they wish. In any case, the port industry argued that 'the actions of various ports do not authorise the Commission to act' (Suykens and Le Garrec, 1996).

The latter is linked to the fact that, because of the remarkable diversities of European ports, the intensity of opposition to the rule varied (Pallis 1997). Several ports in the North are entirely private commercial enterprises (i.e. the UK), but local and municipal management represents a tradition in Scandinavia, the Netherlands, and Germany. The typical structure of ports in the Mediterranean countries incorporates a certain, though varying, influence of central government. Private ports felt most strongly about the proposal, with British ports associations leading the opposition. To them, this 'was an intervention on what we charge and how we should charge; and because all the funding is coming from the users, the EU was imposing restrictions on how ports might compete' (Jeffery, 1996). Whilst the objective was assessed to be 'fair enough', 'the rule would distort competition in benefit of European ports that are getting assistance from their government' (Jonston, 1996). Therefore, the British associations representing small and big size ports (BPA and UKMPG, respectively) urged, albeit unsuccessfully, their government to reject the EU initiative.

Ports having a very strong state ownership involvement were more prepared to accept the regulation. According to a British interviewee, ports like Rotterdam and Hamburg were pressurised by the governments, or instructed by the municipal authorities, to do so (Jeffery, 1996). In fact, Rotterdam (the biggest European port) introduced unilaterally a preferential rate for ships meeting certain environmental criteria, aiming to see the scheme developed to a pan-European measure. The issue was less important for the entirely state-owned Greek ports. The only consequence of the potential EU regulation would be the re-routing of the financial inducements offered to shipowners through taxation and other means targeting further investments in environmental friendly vessels (Hatsakos, 1996). Finally, geographical characteristics also played a role, as in the Mediterranean area competition between ports is considerably less important than in the rest of the EU.

These national, or local, variations did not encumber the achievement of a collective port authorities' stance. This stance took into account that the shipowners' movement to reduce their costs was assisted by the political momentum. It was estimated that, 'although this regulation would distort competition and was against the EU law, it would be very difficult to be challenged because of its environmental dimension' (Suykens and Le Garrec, 1996). Consequently, ESPO recommended a different rebate system that would not be based on a different calculation of the SBT tankers dues, but on a 10% flat-rate difference between SBT and non-SBT vessels. This modification would allow any ports that wished to raise tariffs and then offer rebates to SBT tankers. It would also allow them to continue charging vessels using their preferable system.[30] Even though changes were made in the light of these counterproposals, the industry remained disappointed by the failure of DG-VII to consult them before the publication of the draft proposal. It was acknowledged, however, as ESPO was a new organisation the industry was perhaps not equipped to be consulted (Jonston, 1996). But with ESPO not being formatted earlier in 1993, the port industry had not reacted in time neither to the 'safe seas' communication, nor to the preparation of the specific rule.

An interest group of a different nature also tried to influence the final decision. AMRIE, which is an attempt to promote the various interests of European maritime regions, expressed a favourable view for the initiative. With its members being particularly interested in the protection of the marine environment, AMRIE supported the idea of financial incentives, like discounts on pilotage, transit, and port dues, for ships that are designed to avoid pollution. Arguing that such initiatives would help the self-regulation of the shipping industry, it lobbied the Commission and the EP for the adoption of measures that would help the operation of 'green' vessels. As regards the details of the regulation, AMRIE was of the view that it was up to the European institutions to find the balance between the industries involved and finalise the appropriate EU measure (Seidel, 1996).

Policy Makers Reactions

As port authorities had not expressed their critical views before the publication of the proposal, the EP Transport Committee became the focal point of their lobbying activities. With shipowners also closely following the work of this Committee, the latter arrived 'at the point where the Council or the Commission should be trying to find the best balance between the various interests' (Economou, 1996). Enthusiastic to the idea of the Commission's programme being implemented, the EP accepted the proposal, as the right policy to cancel out operational imbalances, but endorsed significant amendments that would satisfy the port industry.[31] Specifically, it suggested that the aim of the rule could be ensured either when ports calculate their charges by deducting the tonnage of the SBT from the total ship tonnage, as the Commission had suggested, or alternatively when the fee for SBT oil tankers is at least 20% lower than the fee for a conventional tanker of the same gross tonnage. The EP also agreed that ports could assess their fees on a basis other than that of gross tonnage, provided that SBT tankers receive treatment no less favourable than when fees are calculated in accordance with the above method. Finally, it proposed a one-year transition period for the implementation of the Regulation. Although adopting its essence, the EP rewrote the initiative in a manner that endorsed some ports demands but still provided SBT tankers owners with a considerably more satisfactory operating regime.

On the other hand, the Ecosoc opinion provided a more general support for 'a regulation that would have beneficial effects for the protection of the marine environment and ensure fairer competition between ports and between SBT and non-SBT tankers', incorporating only minor amendments to the initial draft (Ecosoc, 1994). With this background, ports continued to lobby for a better solution, insisting that any rebate higher than 10% was unacceptable (Whitehead, 1996). Considering the different approaches that had been expressed between the EP and the Commission both ports and shipowners were ready to redirect the pressures that had been exercised by the EP to the Council. But the Commission accepted the compromise solution provided by the EP and, as a representative of ECSA remarks, 'facilitated the Council to reach a conclusion' (Economou, 1996).

In June 1994 the Council agreed to an EU regulation according to the system that had been proposed by the EP and accepted by the Commission. Its common position did not however endorse the 20% flat rate rebate recommendation. Influenced by the considerable loss of revenue for ports dependent on tanker traffic, it agreed to reduce the rate to 17%. This position was objected to during the discussion by two member states. Germany did not want to see a regulation allowing the recommended flexibility, preferring one closer to the initial proposal.[32] On the other hand, the British administration argued that if the rebate was meant to reflect the amount of cargo space given over to ballast, it should be 20%. These two member states finally agreed to the views of the majority, hence, the common position was unanimous. Judging the different approach on the level of the rebate as a minor theme, the EP approved the Council position as it stood,[33] and the Regulation was formally adopted in November 1994 scheduled to enter into force on 1 January 1996.[34]

Regulating Safety of Roll-on Roll-off Ferries

Among the issues dominating the EU maritime agenda in recent years are the risks associated with roll-on roll-off passenger ferries (ro/ro). Due to the casualty record of such vessels, their safety requirements have been a very controversial topic, with IMO for many years trying to develop international rules. SOLAS 74 achieved an agreement on cargo loading conditions but doubts about other aspects remained. Following the *Herald of Free Enterprise* incident (1987) several amendments were suggested, the best known concerned a higher 'stability' standard and became known as SOLAS 90. In technical terms, the ruling aims to give vessels an 'adequate standard' of construction stability and protection following accidents in waves up to 1.5 metre and assumes that damage occurs below the waterline. However, there was considerable reluctance to introduce the amendments because of the reconstruction involved to existing vessels and a desire not to interfere with the convenience of the ro/ro ferry design. The majority of IMO members opted for a lower standard version that would be voluntarily implemented.

Regulating Safety Management

At the beginning of 1993, the agreed IMO standard was mandatory only for ships operating between the UK, Ireland and continental Europe. Having the support of British shipowners, the UK government made ro/ro stability a priority of its 1992 Council presidency programme (BSC, 1993). However, the search for an agreement which would made SOLAS 90, and if possible higher standards, mandatory to Europe was unsuccessful. On the grounds that operating conditions in the Mediterranean are less dangerous than in the North Seas, all southern member states were keen to see any ro/ro construction standards agreed internationally and their application to remain voluntary allowing the essential flexibility (Bantias, 1996).

The 'safe seas' document underlined problems related to ro/ro vessels and the need of an EU policy for the convergent implementation of the relevant IMO resolutions. Yet, the Commission focused primarily on operational issues, explicitly on the examination of the expediency of making relevant provisions of the International Safety Management (ISM) Code, at that point of time a non-binding IMO instrument, mandatory for all those operating ro/ro vessels to and from EU ports. As regards 'stability', the first Commission move took place in July 1993, when it participated in a special meeting of the national administrations from nine EU member states (all but Italy, Portugal and Luxembourg), Sweden, and Norway. The meeting reached a non-binding 'agreement in principle' that SOLAS 90 standards would progressively be fully established for all ro/ro ferries operating in European waters by the end of 2007. To the British administration this was a significant step forward, although it would have preferred to reach an IMO agreement.[35]

Policy developments accelerated remarkably in the aftermath of the notorious *Estonia* incident in September 1994. A barrage of media questions followed this incident, which cost more than 900 lives, on the effectiveness of the rule making authorities.[36] The Commission indicated that if IMO failed to secure support for more stringent rules it would introduce and enforce its own legislation, which would not only look at stability but possibly an overall safety assessment of these vessels. It acknowledged, however, that any of these changes should be the outcome of a lengthy procedure, not least because they should allow time for shipowners to adapt. Therefore, it decided to propose short term initiatives, notably the use of the PSC legislation to tighten ro/ro monitoring and prevent poor shipboard operation and management. These proposals were prepared in an extremely short time. The Commission had to act quickly, ahead of the forthcoming Council meeting where it was likely that some countries would demand an increase in safety (De Dieu, 1996). The EP Transport Committee put forward a resolution that was in line with the Commission's ideas, but also supported the development of further 'urgent' policy measures. Specifically, it suggested that given the already proposed EU directive for the effective implementation of PSC, the Council should support tougher PSC on ro/ro vessels, including those on short and cabotage routes, as IMO is not involved in such cases.[37]

North European governments were supportive of the development of an EU policy. Denmark, Finland, and Sweden ordered the immediate inspections of all the ro/ro vessels visiting their ports, while a special conference was organised to discuss the possibility of a common Nordic countries position for higher stability rules including the involvement of the UK.[38] Germany had assumed the Council presidency (second half of 1994) declaring that the development of tough actions in the field of maritime safety would be its major priority, though measures regarding ro/ro vessels were not an explicit part of the agenda.[39] Antithetically, neither a tough regulatory regime nor EU-level action was considered as necessary by southern states. In particular France, Greece, and Italy remained focused on the excellent safety record that ro/ro vessels have in the Mediterranean area. Despite these objections, DG-VII was confident enough that it 'would be told' by the Council meeting to set up a licensing regime for the operation and inspection of ro/ro ships that are operating and regularly visiting EU ports.[40] Under the terms of this move these ships would be subject to expanded PSC inspection and, most notably, owners would have to comply with the terms of the ISM Code, which would become mandatory.

Indeed, when the Council agreed 'to put pressure on the IMO for tougher action over ro/ro safety', it also adopted a resolution for the application of the ISM Code by July 1996.[41] The Council also 'took note' of the Commission's intention to submit more policy proposals. It responded by 'instructing' the Commission to design measures for a mandatory regime that would include operational inspections before the start of new services, and at regular intervals. Neither the possibility of mandatory application of non-binding IMO resolutions regarding working hours, nor that of regulating the conditions of crews onboard and safety rules for passenger vessels engaged in cabotage (and not covered by the STCW) was objected to. With the British administration objecting to any direct or indirect implementation of the TEU Social Chapter, and the Mediterranean states in the process of opening their cabotage markets (Chapter 8), the contrary would have been expected.

However, 'stability' remained the controversial point. The absence of progress on this issue dissatisfied Scandinavian states, which expressed the intention for a regional accord, and the British government, which also decided to discuss the possibility of a North Sea agreement[42] against its earlier maintained stance against unilateral actions.[43] Notably, the day of the Council meeting, the Commission announced that it would stimulate the British efforts to research the need for higher stability standards. The

British DoT and the Commission would co-operate in a joint venture to test the safety criteria of integral aspects of ro/ro design, an initially British idea aiming to determine the necessary policy initiatives.

In February 1995, the Commission proposed a Regulation that would provide for the mandatory implementation of the ISM Code to all ro/ro operators in the EU from 1 July 1996 (CEU, 1995b). This Code requires the shipowner, manager, or bareboat charterer, to establish a safety management system designated to ensure compliance with all standards recommended by IMO and subject to periodical validation. It was initially conceived as a simple recommendation, and remained so when the Commission had first discussed the possibility of translating it into EU legislation. But four months before the Estonia incident the Code had become part of the SOLAS convention and would be mandatory implemented by ro/ro ferries engaged in international trade from 1 July 1998. The EU regulation would only advance its implementation by two years. Still, the Commission was keen to promote it, because the transposition of the relative IMO rules into the national law of each member state would be a long and complicated operation, when the regulation would be applicable immediately throughout the Community as soon as the Council would approve it (De Dieu, 1996). The Regulation was conceived as an instrument that would bring the code into mandatory effect two years earlier but also ensure effectively and uniformly controlled implementation.

Interest Groups Mobilisation

European shipowners continued to advocate that the priority should be the achievement of internationally agreed rules but recognised that the Estonia incident was one of the particular situations that the political determination to take actions in the European context reflected understandable concerns. Against this background, ECSA responded as early as the Commission's intentions became known, agreeing to the early mandatory application of the ISM Code but objecting the recommended July 1996 date. Arguing that there would not be sufficient time for arrangements to be in place and the measure to operate, they demanded a flexible regime, which would take into account special conditions.

ECSA was more critical of the other Commission initiatives that were notified as being in the early stage of preparation, though it did not categorically reject the possibility of future EU rules. Specifically, it questioned the logic of the Commission's intention to bring forward separate proposals for working hours on ro/ro ships when the organisation of working time in maritime transport had been excluded from the parent directive. Nevertheless, ECSA would seek to agree with the unions and the Commission on consistency with the contemporary work undertaken in the IMO and ILO workable regime. Then, it warned of the emerging danger of translating IMO Resolutions to EU legislation and expanding them at a national level, not least because they would be counterproductive in terms of safety through the proliferation of regional regimes worldwide. Still, it agreed to a thorough examination of these issues. In this vein, it began discussions with the Commission on the measures envisaged, suggesting that the expertise of the ECSA Technical Committee can contribute to finding practical solutions.

Even though IMO had already agreed to a mandatory ISM Code, neither the unified, nor the unqualified, approval of the proposed initiative by European shipowners was easy. The maritime industry had never had a common set of detailed safety management procedures covering everything, from shore based management practices and communications to emergency procedures. In this respect this was a major breakthrough that had divided European shipowners, who follow heterogeneous operation and organisation practices. At the one end of the spectrum, British, but also German and Scandinavian, shipowners had consistently supported the development of a mandatory code since a voluntary implementation was likely to be ignored by the very companies that were most in need of its application. So, they welcomed the Commission's proposal for passenger ships being in favour of a harmonised EU implementation.

At the other end of the spectrum, Greek shipowners had argued that the ISM Code was impossible to justify due to the efforts and expenses the shipping industry would be subject to. To them, 'traditional' ownership survives because it is voluntarily committed to quality management and effectively responds to the demands of the complex regulatory framework (Peppa, 1996). The ISM Code simply provided an additional bureaucratic instrument drafted with the development of large corporations in mind and supported by very different market actors. These are classification societies, who would have to provide certificates of compliance, shipowners whose property was operated by management companies, and shipmanagement companies themselves, which need to certify their compliance with international regulations to enhance their business. Thus, the traditionally structured Greek shipping industry was seeking the best possible national interpretation to the IMO agreement: 'because the decision to apply the ISM still leaves various important issues unresolved and places a formidable task in many administrations who must make arrangement for the inspection of vast numbers of ships and shipping companies, it is to be hoped that these issues can be resolved in a practical manner, in order to avoid the undesirable adoption of an unworkable mandatory regime' (UGS, 1995). With an EU regulation limiting national level interpretations, Greek ownership suggested several amendments, in particular a derogation from unachievable advancement of the code's application, and a regulation that would apply neither to cabotage, nor to companies managing ships of less than 10000 grt. Yet, they supported the decision that flag-state administrations would directly audit companies and vessels flying their flag rather than through recognised organisations.

Shipowners remained overtly divided over the 'stability' issue. To northern shipowners it was unfortunate that the EU was unable to intervene and ratify the amendments of SOLAS 90. To Mediterranean shipowners the continuous row could be solved only if regional (non-EU) accords were promoted, as neither the weather nor the trading conditions for ro/ro ships are the same in every part of Europe. They claimed that the cost of compliance to higher stability rules would range from $7 to $8 millions, an unjustifiable expense on two grounds. First, the Mediterranean Sea is not subject to similar weather conditions and, second, costly technical improvement on ferries will not reduce the likelihood of human error that is responsible for 80% of all accidents.[44] Suggesting that the focus should be on prevention measures, i.e. sailing restrictions in case of adverse weather conditions, than construction standards, they objected to any EU-level harmonisation.

Trade unions were more enthusiastic and with less divisions over the proposed measure. After the *Estonia* incident they urged European institutions to act 'so that maritime safety will no longer be subject to overriding economic interests or to the ineffectiveness of public authorities'. ITF formed a working group on European ferry safety, which called for the EU to develop ro/ro safety measures because governments were persistently ignoring the union's proposals and creating a situation that would result in further disasters. The mandatory application of the ISM Code was one of the demanded initiatives. With several shipowners using foreign crews and further disputes over relaxation of nationality requirements being developed,[45] organised labour focused on the link of safety management to employment partners. The ISM Code would eventually bring some of the necessary control over the use and quality of non-EU crews on ro/ro ferries (Steinvorth, 1996).

Still, the proposed regulation was conceived as an instrument likely to rid the seas of some substandard ships but not one to tackle the root of the industry's problem, namely the lack of qualified experienced seafarers or the employment of cheap and incompetent crews (Tselentis, 1996). Therefore, trade unions, through the work of the ITF panel, demanded more action on the ownership front. Associating safety with FoC shipping, they asked for the establishment of a genuine link between the owner of a passenger ferry and country of registration. Moreover, they asked for EU measures that would limit working hours and tackle the critical fatigue factor, ensure the employment of competent personnel, and seafarers pre-sea training, as well as the setting of a technical working group with the participation of the Commission and the social partners to examine possible initiatives. Notably, they also agreed to the necessity for stability requirements to be reviewed and unsafe ferries removed. Trade unions did not however have to specify stability standards that would be acceptable to them and this facilitated their common stance.

Policy Makers Reactions

The EP Transport Committee endorsed the Commission's proposal but put forward several amendments.[46] A first set aimed to guarantee that the regulation represented only the first of continuing EU measures. The second set referred to the content of the Regulation, calling for an exemption of small companies operating in cabotage trade, and for a 18 months derogation applied to Greek maritime companies that register their ships under the Greek flag and operate in cabotage. The EP also demanded the establishment of an implementation monitoring process within which the Commission would propose the measures it deems appropriate. Similarly, the Ecosoc 'unreservedly' supported the initiative as a step in the overall maritime safety programme. However, it suggested that, despite the queries, derogations to the July 1996 deadline should be kept at a minimum and limited to small companies and at cabotage trade (Ecosoc, 1995). This opinion gave special attention to the parts of the ISM Code concerning resources and personnel, specifically the quality of ships crewed by non-EU seafarers. Finally, it argued that the recognition of the documents of compliance issued by non-EU flag states should be permissive and not mandatory, as the latter case would jeopardise the recognition of substandard operations.

The Commission adopted the EP proposed amendments that had a reference to the content of the Regulation, on the ground that they aimed to strengthen the initiative (CEU, 1995c). A twelve-month derogation to mandatory ISM code compliance was granted for companies operating ro/ro ferries in protected waters or exclusively in cabotage trade and until 31 December 1997 for Greek companies regularly serving ports located in Greece. However, the Commission did not take on board the 'irrelevant to the Regulation' demands for a clear commitment to 'more' and 'urgent' measures concerning either the operation or the construction of ro/ro vessels.

The Council accepted the amended proposal, announcing symbolically its common position on the first anniversary of the Estonia tragedy. In fact, transport ministers had came to a political, albeit non-binding, agreement in March 1995.[47] The common position had, however, a difference from the submitted initiative, regarding the process that would govern the future amendments of the regulation. Whilst the Council agreed on the role of the Commission in monitoring the implementation, it provided for a regulatory committee that the Commission would rely on for future proposals. The same day the Transport Commissioner, N. Kinnock, announced that the Commission would table a series of new EU measures to step up safety of ro/ro vessels. The Commission would follow the work of IMO regarding construction and operation rules. With a special IMO meeting only a month later, the Transport Commissioner left the option for further EU actions open. He did so by stating that in the absence of an agreement, or if the Commision would feel that the new rules are insufficient or unsatisfactory then he was ready to table proposals for EU rules to apply to all ro/ro ferries in EU waters regardless of their flag or home port. He would do so because 'general EU application of effective rules has particular advantage for all who use ferries in any part of the Union' therefore he was hoping 'for firm cooperation from all member states'.[48]

The EP continued to urge the advancement of further but also stricter EU rules. When the tripartite committee that France, Sweden and Estonia had set up to examine the *Estonia* event published its preliminary report,

MEPs expressed the view that the Commission should have a greater role in issues of ro/ro safety and should have participated in the investigation, prompting the Commissioner's response that its role is to follow the IMO work and intervene only in case of failure.[49] The pressures became more evident when the EP Transport Committee unanimously reported on the Council's common position on the ISM Code proposing two major amendments. First, more regular verifications of the conditions required for obtaining the safety management certificate, specifically inspections of ro/ro vessels at least once a year, whilst the Council position considered a 30 months provision as sufficient. Second, the Commission should rely upon a consultative committee rather than one of a regulatory nature as the Council was suggesting.

Both amendments were rejected by the Commission, which preferred to stick to the initial decision. The compliance verification process would be amended once the Commission had monitored the implementation of the regulation and considered that this was appropriate. Then, though the consultative committee would facilitate the Commission's ability to introduce future initiatives, the Commission rejected the EP amendment, chose not to open the discussion again and adopted the Council's common position as it was (CEU, 1995d). In this context, the Council simply confirmed the adoption of the EU Regulation.[50]

Meanwhile, in November 1995, a special IMO conference was attended by flag-states that were parties to SOLAS and discussed the establishment of international ro/ro safety rules. Several measures were adopted but the meeting was marked by a conflict between European countries over 'stability'. Scandinavian countries, the UK, Germany, and Ireland, demanded the immediate decision and mandatory implementation of higher standards than SOLAS 90. The move was backed by Belgium, Netherlands, and Spain, whereas Norway continued to ask for a North sea pledge. On the other hand, French, Italian, and Greek, representatives supported the adoption of higher standards, as long as they would not apply to the Mediterranean trades. The cautious French government argued that IMO should allow a two years period before a final decision be reached. The IMO meeting concluded with a compromise that allowed those countries who wished to require higher standards, but they could not impose them on other nations. With the IMO secretary-general remaining unconvinced that this outcome would be enough to secure a long-term safety standard, the two-tier regime was a further blow to the organisation's credibility and efficiency.[51]

The dichotomy remained apparent during the December 1995 Council, though the latter welcomed the result of the IMO conference. A Swedish initiative for stricter EU rules was opposed by the southern member states. Having the IMO approval for a regional agreement, Northern states responded by accepting the Swedish invitation to a regional conference. The Commission reacted to these developments by announcing that it would work towards a common EU stance rather than a regional accord spanning the whole of the EU.[52] In this vein, it would be involved in the Swedish initiative to ensure that a barrier to trade was not created between the two parts of the EU. The EP added its concerns at the continuation of this split. Each year, during the first EP Plenary session in Brussels the Commission answers questions on 'urgent political problems of major importance'. In 1996 MEPs selected safety at seas and in particular of ro/ro ferries to be one of the three topics on the agenda.[53]

The Swedish initiative produced a northwest European agreement for higher stability rules to be established until October 2002 for all ro/ro vessels operating in international trade in this area. To the Commission the 'Stockholm agreement' was an undesirable development as 'the aim of the EU should be to minimise the number of bilateral and multilateral agreements' and 'ideally a single agreement should be concluded and all member states adhered to the same ferry safety rules' (De Dieu, 1996). This agreement provided the background to begin immediate investigations aiming to bring all EU states within its scope. In the spring of 1996, DG-VII formed a group of experts to study the different national legislation regarding ro/ro stability and suggest ways of harmonisation. They aimed to examine several criteria, including types and size of vessels, extent of traffic, sea and weather conditions in the Mediterranean as well as the Atlantic coast, and to conclude following the pattern of the Stockholm agreement.

Meanwhile, the IMO SOLAS 90 Convention was amended in 1997, providing new ro/ro ship configuration, construction and operation standards for all existing ferries. The dates of compliance ranging from 1998 to 2010 depending on a combination of a probabilistic damage stability calculation of ships that was adopted by IMO (as a means of trying to compare the survivability of one vessel against another and achieve a hierarchy for phasing-in purposes), the number of persons carried and age.

However, since the great majority of ro/ro passenger ferries were designed and built prior to the coming-into-force of SOLAS 90, few of them comply with the new requirements. Moreover, the European North-South divide, continues to cause unrest, particularly at European level. At the same time, the impact of the Stockholm agreement on the existing fleet of northwest Europe has been much more positive than most people feared. Shipowners have either found a cost-effective way to compliance through performance-based approaches (numerical simulations and model experiments), raising the safety of their fleet, or cut their losses and opted for new, modern, safer, more efficient ship designs (Papanikolaou and Vassalos, 2001). Efforts to assess the status quo in northwest Europe and use this information as a means to predict the potential impact of introducing the Stockholm agreement in the South, led the Commission to initiate a dedicated study aiming to provide an introspective look at the Stockholm agreement, and to look into the prospects of extending its application to South Europe in due time.[54]

The results of this study, to be released in public at a later stage, are currently under review by the Commission and might prove invaluable in paving the way forward The ultimate target is to provide a proposal for a solution that would minimise bilateral and regional agreements in the EU, and allow the Commission to submit a feasible proposal to IMO for its extension.

As regards the safety management of ro/ro passenger ferries, on 15 September 2000 the Commission put forward a proposal for a regulation amending Regulation No 3051/95 on (CEU, 2000b). The amendments made consist of deleting the terms referring to the date on which the regulation was adopted and of replacing the committee set up under Directive 93/75 by the Sea Safety Committee. Parliament approved the proposal from the Commission, subject to certain technical amendments on first reading on 13 February 2001, with the Commission expected to approve most of those amendments.

Following up Initiatives

The Commission submitted further proposals concerning the safety of ro/ro vessels, the first one refereeing to the harmonisation of rules for ro/ro ships operating in the internal maritime market (CEU, 1996d). As international conventions do not apply to domestic routes, and SOLAS gives exemptions to short international voyages (within 20 miles from the coast) these trades are covered by national rules. Grounded on the ongoing market liberalisation, the Commission suggested that a substantially similar level of safety should be established throughout the EU. Therefore, it proposed that SOLAS should apply to EU cabotage trade, encompassing the developments of the November 1995 IMO conference. Still, because of the variety of geographical characteristics and operational demands, the application of these rules would be neither homogeneous nor immediate. But different standards, or exceptions from full compliance, would become subject to submission to the Commission, with the latter having the right to object, require amendments, or revoke the proposed measures. Interestingly, this directive would not apply to short international routes. Such measure would apply only to ships under the EU flag, thus leading to the operation of the same ships under a third flag, This is not possible in cabotage services, given that it has already been decided that these services should remain open only to ships operating under the flag of a member state. So, the Commission asked the Council to work within the IMO for a mandatory arrangement regarding these services.

The EP reacted by demanding the directive to be changed to a 'minimum-standards directive', and a commitment for future higher EU safety standards. Moreover, it suggested several time derogations and specific exceptions from the technical requirements of the stability rule. In November 1996 the Commission accommodated 'with reservations' those amendments regarding the postponement of the implementation date and stability. It did not however accept the demands for higher standards, as 'such acceptance would weaken the provisions of the proposal' (CEU, 1996e).

The Directive was finally adopted in 1998 and provides an harmonised set of safety rules and standards for passenger ships engaged on domestic voyages that applies to new passenger ships; existing passenger ships of 24 metres in length and above; and high-speed passenger craft, regardless of their flag, when engaged on domestic voyages.[55] Member states, in their capacity as host state, inspect ships and craft engaged on domestic voyages and may audit their documentation, in accordance with the PSC Directive.

Following further initiatives, in the beginning of 2001, the EU policy record is substantial and with reference to various aspects (Table 5.1). Measures aiming to make passenger ships safer include the security and the administration of ro/ro transporters of passengers, the conditions for the operation of regular ro/ro ferry and high speed passenger craft services, safety rules and standards for passenger ships, and the registration of persons on board.

Table 5.1 The Common EU Policy on Safe Seas in 2001

Transfer of ships from one register to another within the Community	Council Regulation (EC) 613/91 of 4.03.1991
Radionavigation systems for Europe	Council Decision of 25.02.1992
Requirements for vessels carrying dangerous or polluting goods	Council Directive 93/75/EEC of 13.09.1993
Implementation of IMO Resolution A.747(18) on the tonnage measurement of ballast spaces in SBT	Council Regulation (EC) No 2978/94 of 21.11.1994
Ship inspection and survey organisations	Council Directive 94/57/EC of 22.11.1994
Minimum level of training of seafarers	Council Directive 94/58/EC of 22.11.1994
Enforcement of international standards for ship safety, pollution prevention and onboard living and working conditions (PSC)	Council Directive 95/21/EC of 19.06.1995
Safety of roll-on roll-off passenger ferries	Council Resolution of 22.12.1994
Safety management of roll-on roll-off passenger vessels	Council Regulation (EC) No 3051/95 of 8.12.1995
Marine equipment	Council Directive 96/98/EC of 20.12.1996
Safety rules and standards for passenger ships	Council Directive 98/18/EC of 17.03 1998
Setting up a harmonised safety regime for fishing vessels of 24 metres in length and above	Council Directive 97/70/EC of 11.12.1997.
Registration of persons on board passenger ships	Council Directive 98/41/EC of 18.06.1998
Mandatory surveys for the safe operation of regular ro-ro ferry and high-speed passenger craft services	Council Directive 99/35/EC of 29.04.1999.

Still these are only part of the current picture of the EU Maritime Safety Policy records. Other issues are also under consideration (i.e. port reception facilities for ship generated waste and cargo residues; requirements and harmonised procedures for the safe loading and unloading of bulk carriers), with the bulk of them referring to the safety of seaborne oil trade (i.e. accelerated phasing-in of double hull or equivalent design requirements for single hull oil tankers, amendments to the rules for ship inspection and survey organisations, and for PSC). The latter are part of the so-called Erica Communication, a Commission initiative undertaken in the aftermath of a major accident, when the oil tanker Erika broke in two 40 miles off the coast of Brittany. More than 10000 tonnes of heavy fuel oil were spilt and the pressure of public opinion has prompted the Commission to propose action at Community level. According to the Commission, this action is designed to bring about a change in the prevailing mentality in the seaborne oil trade and has been undertaken because 'action on maritime safety under the auspices of the IMO falls short of what is needed to tackle the causes of such disasters effectively....(and) is severely handicapped by the absence of adequate control mechanisms governing the way the rules are applied throughout the world' (CEU, 2000c).

Summary

This Chapter examined the progress towards the establishment of a common EU policy concerning the safety of persons at sea, of ships, and the prevention of environmental pollution by maritime transport operations. In the beginning of the 1990s the concerns over these issues were accompanied by a minimal policy output of policy recommendations. Following a long-standing tradition, maritime safety continued to be governed by an internationally developed regulatory framework. Nonetheless, several EU regulations and directives followed the publication of a policy framework in 1992. This analysis examined the interaction of the actionable factors during the transformation of this issue-area to one of the four pillars of the 1996 re-assessment of the CMTP strategy, and the economic context within which these developments took place. When this reassessment took place the safety management of ro/ro ferries, and EU instruments regulated the port dues of modern 'environmentally friendly' SBT tanker. The minimum training requirements for crews on EU-flagged ships, and the PSC systems of the fifteen EU member states were subject to respective EU directives. The possibility of an EU rule on the most controversial ro/ro stability standards and other EU measures were already under discussion. In the forthcoming chapter the findings and conclusions of this case study are detailed.

Notes

1   The only figures available (published by Lloyd's Register) are actually limited to those reported when the ships are *totally lost*. Research has suggested that to estimate the actual number one should multiply these figures by something in the region of 10 (Goss *et al*, 1991).

2   When the tankers *Aragon* and *Khark-V* discharged more than 100,000 tonnes of oil in European seaways.

3   Council Resolution on the prevention of accident causing marine pollution, of 11.5.1990.

4   Most notably the losses of the *Herald of Free Enterprise* in 1987 and the *Scandinavian Star* in 1990.

5   Council Resolution on improving passenger ferry safety, of 19.6.1990.

6   See: OJ C258/93, p. 21: and OJ C283/93, p. 11.

7   Hellenic Chamber of Shipping, *Shipping Report No 127*, October -December 1992.

8   The *Aegean Sea* spilled 79000 tonnes of oil off the coast of La Coruña in December 1992, and *Braer* was involved in a serious incident in January 1993 off the Shetland Islands.

9   *Seatrade Week Newsfront*, Braer effect, Vol. XII, 15-21 January 1993.

10 *Agence Europe*, 26.1.1993.

11 Hellenic Chamber of Shipping, *Shipping Report No 128*, January-March 1993.

12 Noteworthy, whilst the 1992 annual report of these two major shipowning association had no reference to EU actions regarding safety the picture was different at all the respective reports since 1993.

13 Views presented by the CTWUEC at the 'Safer Ships Cleaner Seas' Conference organised by the Socialist Group of the EP, Brussels, March 1994 (see: *Lloyd's List*, System blamed for Ships Losses, 7.3.1994).

14 *Agence Europe*, 15.3.1993.

15 Council Resolution on a common policy on safe seas, of 8.6.1993.

16 EP Doc A3-68/94. Rapporteur: K. Stewart, PES, UK.

17 Council Directive 95/21, of 19.06.95.

18 *Agence Europe*, 30.11.1993.

19 G. Katsifaras in: *Naftemporiki*, Significant decisions for the protection of the environment and safety, 15.7.1994.

20 *Lloyd's List*, EU ministers 'steal a march', 21.2.1994.

21 IMO Maritime Safety Committee, Training and watchkeeping-Maritime education, training, and certification. Introduction in quality assurance principles. Doc 62/INF 9, of 25.3.1993.

22 For the first EP reading see: EP Doc A3-83/94. Rapporteur: P. Sarlis, PPE, Gr; and OJ C91, of 28.3.1994.

23 *Mesimvrini*, Shipping and the Greek Presidency, 23.1.1994.

24 See the interview of the then Greek Minister for Mercantile Marine, G. Katsifaras, in: *Lloyd's List Focus Magazine*: Greece, June 1994.

25 *Seatrade Week*, Fiori rejects second registry, 8-14 July 1994.

26 EP Doc. A4-42/94. Rapporteur: P. Sarlis, PPE, Gr.

27 Council Directive 94/58, of 22.11.1994.

28 Council Directive 98/35 of 25.05.1998.

29 *Lloyd's List*, STCW amendment have added teeth, 2.11.1995.

30 At the moment, some of them, i.e. Dutch ports, use the gross and others, i.e. Italian ports,

the net tonnes system.

31   EP Doc. A3-221/94. Rapporteur: P. Sarlis, PPE, Gr.

32   *Lloyd's List*, EU agrees rebate plan, 14.6.1994.

33   EP Doc A 4-41/94. Rapporteur: P. Sarlis, PPE, Gr.

34   Council Regulation 2978/94, of 21.11.1994.

35   Lord Caithness, in: *Maritime Engineers Review*, Europe unites on ro/ro ferry safety standards, August 1993.

36   See the coverage of the incident by the daily press: October 1994.

37   EP Doc B 236/94.

38   *Lloyd's List*, Norway plans to stabilise ro-ros, 13.10.1994

39   *Lloyd's List*, Ship safety will top EU agenda, 17.6.1994.

40   R. Salvarani, Head of the DG-VII Maritime Safety Unit, interviewed in: *Lloyd's List*, EC Plans tough safety rules for passenger ro/ros, 11.11.1994.

41   Council Resolution on the safety management of ro/ro passenger ferries, of 22.12.1994

42   *Lloyd's List*, UK Agency opens ro/ro safety talks with Norway, 10.12.1995.

43   *Lloyd's List*, UK warns of danger of unilateral role, 26.10.1993.

44   Hellenic Chamber of Shipping (1995), Modern Passenger shipping: Ro-Ro Ferries, in: *Shipping Review*, No 135, November-December 1995, pp. 6-7.

45   For example the changes of the British law over the rules governing ro/ro operation in the Channel route and the objections raised by both French and British unions (Lloyd's List, UK seafarer rules fuel confusion, 14.10.1995).

46   EP Doc. A4-115/95. Rapporteur: K. Watts, PES, UK.

47   *Agence Europe*, 10.3.1995.

48   *Agence Europe*, 29.9.1995, p. 9.

49   *Lloyd's List*, MEP attacks Estonia preliminary report, 25.9.1995.

50   Council Regulation 3051/95, of 8.12.1995.

51   See: *Lloyd's List*, IMO in ro/ro compromise, 30.11.1995; IMO disappointment, 1.12.1995.

52   *Lloyd's List*, EC to seek united ferry safety policy, 7.12.1995.

53   *Agence Europe*, 25.1.1996.

54   A contract awarded to two closely collaborating teams, namely the Ship Stability Research Centre of the University of Strathclyde, UK and the Ship Design Laboratory of the National Technical University of Athens, Greece, herein practically representing the North and South of Europe, respectively.

55   Council Directive 98/18/EC of 17.03.1998.

6 Safe Seas: Developing a Common Policy Against all Odds

The previous chapters concentrated on the contemporary economic environment, and the policy preferences of, and interaction between, policy actors involved in the establishment and progress of the common EU policy concerning the safety of persons, ships, and the environment, by maritime transport operations. The intention was to generate knowledge regarding the role of these factors in deciding what this policy is about and in determining the content of the rules now in place. This chapter discusses the findings and concludes on how has the EU developed a substantial policy record in a 'no-go', internationally regulated, issue-area since the beginning of the 1990s.

Economic Environment

The state of the contemporary economic environment of shipping and its implications for maritime safety provided the critical background. Changes that emerged in the post-oil crises period turn to permanent industrial characteristics with critical consequences on market organisation, policy-making powers, and maritime safety. Primarily, they produce structural market deficiencies jeopardising the safety of maritime transportation. Despite favourable demand conditions the levels of prosperity that the sector experienced in the past seem to be unachievable. An inherent fleet oversupply stabilises freight rates at low levels, leading to the absence of the financial resources to replace operating assets. The maritime fleet is characterised by over-ageing and an unprecedented exploitation of the most negative, in safety terms, aspects of the contemporary registration patterns. To express it more poignantly, the new economic environment allows the operation of high-risk 'third-age' ships of unknown owners that may not comply with basic international rules and/or are manned with incompetent low cost crews. The scale of these phenomena has generated a necessity for regulatory realignments in the area of maritime safety.

Simultaneously, this environment challenges the effectiveness of the pre-existing non-EU policy-making frameworks. During the years that personalised shipowning ruled the waves, self-regulation played an important role in promoting maritime safety. Antithetically, in the golden era of FoC, shipmanagement, and 'straw' companies, the remarkably different regulatory frameworks and market principles restricted the promotion of common industrial practices. The modification of the relationships between the social partners impedes further the achievement of self-regulatory agreements. There is an increasing confrontation between confidently negotiating shipowners, who are empowered by both flagging-out and operational reorganisation opportunities, and labour, the more organised part of which is historically located in western maritime nations and has seen its employment opportunities, and eventually its negotiating powers, reduced.

Most importantly, the response of the principle international policy making machinery to the new context has been ineffectual. In the past, IMO established consequential rules on the grounds of a traditional hierarchy, detailed as flag-state decision making consensus and reciprocal effective implementation. This mechanism functioned satisfactorily, and was monitored adequately, over the years that the ownership and registration of world tonnage were largely concentrated in countries sharing similar principles. This is not the case anymore. The rise of new flag-states with different market priorities and social values restrains the achievement, coming into effect, and proper implementation, of international agreements. The IMO deficiencies have concerned several nations and market actors. Events suggest (and all the interviews conducted by this researcher confirm) that whilst the work of IMO remains highly respected, it is acknowledged that in recent years the organisation has not produced the results that it expected to.

On the other hand, the transboundary dimension of the problem disinclines member states to develop national policy responses. They would increase registration costs and proliferate flagging-out, when, new registration forms and other deregulatory or financial incentives attempt to persuade European shipowners to operate under their national flags. The fact that the shipping industry uses extensively the opportunities to re-register its assets under FoC, in order to avoid or pressure for changes of undesirable highly regulated frameworks, profoundly restricts the effectiveness of national policies. Unilateral flag-state rules cannot alter the safety performance of maritime operations. They would lead to the operation of the same ships in the same routes under third, more convenient, flags. This disinclination is not, however, a recent phenomenon. Unlike other industries, the internationalisation of maritime transport is not contemporary but is as old as the industry itself. True, in the adverse conditions of the recent past the use of FoC has been remarkable in quantitative terms and different from the past in qualitative. But the power of any flag-state to regulate maritime safety unilaterally has historically been limited.

Notwithstanding that, the extent of the contemporary internationalisation of registration and employment partners affects the policy attempts to address safety problems. The development of the PSC system in Europe, and more recently in Asia and Latin America, is closely related to a search for alternatives that would not be limited by the 'routes to escape'. As endemic mobile shipping capital and seagoing labour offer transportation services that are *per se* localised, there is a redirection towards policy actions based on 'port traffic' and more effective enforcement of rules, than 'ship registration'. Yet, precisely like flag-state actions, the second best (due to their reactive rather than preventative nature) port-state practices cannot be imposed unilaterally. They would increase the cost of visiting ports under a state's jurisdiction, redirecting traffic to nearby ports, or disadvantaging the competitive position of the port industry. The origin and destination areas of trade are defined irrespective of national boundaries.

Policy Actors, Process, Outcome

The Commission has taken advantage of the windows of opportunity that the economic structures produced to develop an EU policy agenda, and has led the way to progress it. National administrations and stakeholders are dissatisfied by the current operating and regulatory *status quo*, not least because, in the long-term, it encumbers the economic position of the sector. The effects of maritime incidents on employees, passengers, or the ecosystem, create enormous public attention. All these happened, in the 'green' years that the integration of environmental and safety targets to sectoral EU policies forms a general commitment, explicitly reaffirmed in the TEU and succeeding policy statements. This background created a 'policy gap' and in an expedient move the Commission effectively used it to ground the development of an EU policy framework within a very unlikely issue-area. The dominant view is still that safety should be subject to international instruments. Although the Commission continues to adhere to this conception it moved decisively to 'fill the gap' and promote policy integration, which nonetheless is the very scope of its existence.

The timing and the content of the 'safe seas' document were parameters that managed to pre-empt the following debate and provide the foundations of the common policy. Although there had been earlier indications of a possible EU policy framework, DG-VII and the Transport Commissioner himself used the rising public concerns to precipitate it. Against little support by organised interests, as 'proactive' shipowners were opposing the development of any EU initiative and supportive labour remained 'reactive' to such initiatives, public concerns provided legitimacy to the Commission to exercise its initiating role. This legitimacy was stimulated by the intensification of the EP, as well as the Ecosoc, demands for concrete EU actions.

Authorisation to act was enhanced, however, by the non-binding Council reactions to maritime incidents and their subsequent public awareness. More precisely, it was enhanced by the preparedness of member states assessing differently the content, or even the necessity of a future EU policy to agree within the Council to resolutions and, seemingly vague, political statements favouring EU actions. Notably, such Council moves took place in the aftermath of major accidents, when the commitment to the EU empowered national governments to become more autonomous from the pressures of powerful interests (shipowners) and declare their willingness to satisfy public concerns. In the field of maritime safety, what Grande (1996, p. 328) has termed the 'paradox of weakness', that 'public actors purposefully use the 'internal' ties and commitments produced by joint-decision making to strengthen their bargaining position *vis-à-vis* 'external' private actors and interest groups', has been more than a speculative possibility.

The chosen content of the policy framework permitted the Commission to work as a 'consensus-builder'. It was a coherent framework not hesitating to discuss the potential of a wide range of common measures based on the capacity of the EU members as both 'flag' and 'port' states, and frame EU actions in the international arena. But it was also a 'problem solving' framework segregated from the most controversial ideas that had been tabled either by the Commission itself (Euros) or national administrations (OPA 90, higher European standards), than an 'ideology (or principle) driven' framework that would confront the most sceptical to the development of a common policy amongst member states (Gr, UK) or stakeholders (shipowners). This facilitated the debate to conclude with all public and private policy actors adopting a more supportive stance for the development of a common policy than before. Securing positive institutional reactions, foremost a positive Council commitment enabled the Commission to accelerate its policy-initiating role.

The Council provided the mechanism within which disagreeing member states committed to a common policy, notably surpassing the normal EU decision-making procedures. Member states departed from different positions, informed by the degrees or kinds of sectoral interests, domestic policies, and not least geographical morphology. Several states have no interest in the sector at all; others are maritime states without, for instance, any interest in the tanker market, which in turn is a priority field to the rest. Subsequently, some prioritised the environmental dimension and higher EU safety standards, others were mostly interested in the industrial dimension and the cost effects that a regional EU policy would have. Within the Council, however, administrations positioned at the two ends of the spectrum did not sustain for long their initial positions. Greece and the UK dropped the 'non-integration' demands, Germany abandoned its requirements for tough actions, and the support that the stance of the latter administration had generated for higher standards evaporated. The 'edge effect', the fact that the carriers of those national views standing at the edges of the Council realised their no-win position and reluctantly abandoned it sooner rather than later in order to have a more substantial contribution to the content of the agreed policy (for a similar argument in a general context: Garret and Tsebelis, 1996), eased the EU involvement in this policy area.

The assignment of legislation to a particular sectoral Council, introduced a bias into the process, favouring the need to prioritise the industrial implications of the policy at the expense of higher environmental standards. The Environmental ministries that had an interest in this subject matter had been isolated and needed to channel their views indirectly through coordination in the national arenas. As the domestic procedures of member states probably exacerbated the isolation within the 'technical' Transport Council of these policy developments (Bulmer, 1994a), this organisational fragmentation generated certain industry sensitivity, which helped an agreement on the direction of the common policy.

Thereafter, the pattern of the Commission's actions was to develop initiatives whenever inappropriate and dissimilar implementation of international rules within the EU was apparent. This practice was rationalised on both institutional and contextual features. The former were the obligations deriving from the Treaties, and the fact that, by superseding national legislation, the EU law provides a means of speeding the harmonised accomplishment of member states international commitments. The latter were the needs for effective responses to the loopholes of international rules. The product was the transformation of both mandatory and non-mandatory international instruments to EU rules and consequentially to national laws. While the constraints of the economic context made the idea of a fortress high-standard Europe unacceptable, the EU-level activities assumed a dominant role in the convergent and uniform enforcement of the international rules by its membership. These developments were not entirely intended by, at least some of, the national administrations when they agreed to a common policy. For instance, the preference of the British and Greek administrations was for this role to remain an issue between them and the IMO.

The dynamic generated by the discussion of the 'safe seas' document reflected in the untroubled adoption of the PSC directive a measure that had been unsuccessfully discussed a decade earlier. It was only in the aftermath of the presentation of a policy framework that shipowners did not object to a role for the EU in the strengthening of the PSC system, though their self-interests against the lax implementation of existing rules should not be underestimated. Before that point of time a mandatory PSC had been a development supported only by seafarers. Moreover, the geographical scope of the EU is considerably wider than 15 years ago and includes all the European states subscribing to the MOU principles except Poland. Hence, membership limitation does not represent a major impediment as it did in the early 1980s. All these factors contributed to the dilution of the emphasis that had been given by national administrations during the very first years of the CMTP (but also the age of Eurosclerosis) to strictly hold this system under their exclusive regulatory competence and voluntarily implementation.

The selective agenda setting by the Commission impelled policy developments. Instead of passively waiting for the pending IMO discussion to conclude, as member states and stakeholders preferred, the Commission utilised the need for regulatory adjustments, and the presence of a lengthy international policy-making process of an unknown outcome, to promote the minimum training directive. Member states supported the IMO proceeding to amend the relative STCW convention in a record time; shipowners and seafarers devoted efforts towards the same direction, yet the Commission had already set in motion an EU decision. By introducing the SBT Regulation the Commission gained the support of the most sceptical part of the shipping industry, the tanker owners. Although an 'authority building' element was detected, they had no reason to reject a financially beneficial rule that had been strongly promoted in the IMO context. In the early days of the common policy shipowners found themselves eventually standing by the Commission, despite their long advocacy of the necessity to keep the EU disengaged from the development of such policy at all. In the case of ro/ro ferries safety the Commission focused on the less (but still) controversial operational matters to establish an EU role and assess the potential of further policy integration. Insisting on the regulation of operational conditions, even though before translating its thoughts to a policy initiative the respective international instrument (ISM Code) had become mandatory, reinforced the Commission's desire to become more actively involved in other initiatives concerning this market segment.

The Commission also tried to promote its competencies at the expense of national administrations and occasionally introduce higher European standards without the same level of success. It 'tested' the breakthrough proposal of an *en bloc* EU IMO membership albeit the proposal was negatively received by all national administrations and private actors. It appears that even the Commission itself detected limited scope in such move. Yet, the absence of support poses as an insuperable constraint to the progress of the Commission's favourable idea of becoming a contracting party of IMO decisions, and consequentially assuming a greater role within the organisation. Nowadays, the priority is to become a contracting party to the IMO conventions, not in place of the member states but together with the member states. An en bloc IMO membership is considered 'a little premature' (De Dieu, 1996).

More emphatically, the Commission tried to exploit the widespread dissatisfaction from the STCW convention suggesting higher European manning standards in certain operations and the transferring of substantial monitoring competencies to the EU. The specific proposals were eventually amended in a way underlining that the Commission has the capacity to shape and promote its agenda but this does not imply that it can necessarily impose its views. As the draft initiative for a minimum training directive gained little support by the other policy actors its chances of being adopted diminished. Shipowners emphasised its potential flagging out consequences and, in a different vein, organised labour reacted strongly to the limited progress of higher standards. In line with domestic policy choices, and assessing differently than the Commission the regulatory constraints imposed by the economic environment, member states were supportive of the more 'flexible' manning rules demanded by shipowners. However, this did not imply the demise of the proposal but a search for an alternative common denominator. Moreover, as all national administrations are zealous in maintaining their powers, a categorical opposition was expressed to the passing of powers to the Commission regarding non-EU training and education certificates. Once more, the question was not whether to integrate the national systems, but a struggle over the balance of authorities in the design, implementation, and administration of, this policy within the EU framework.

In the presence of diverse views the policy-making process became remarkably meaningful in the course of the final outcome. Policy actors took into account the stances of each other and altered their initial positions. Organised labour was the exception, as it continued to demand higher standards that would compensate for inefficient national employment policies. Retaining a view with little support by the other policy actors, they had a minimal impact in the process. On the other hand, shipowners withdrew from their initial rejecting stance trying to exploit the variation of the institutional views in a favourable way. The knowledge of interest groups and member states positions informed the actions of the Commission, which adjusted its approach. Being attentive to the concerns and the likely balance of the Council, the Commission did not insist on the maximisation of its targets but endorsed the EP proposals, rewriting the directive in an attempt to increase the possibility of it becoming acceptable to the Council.

Still, the policy outcome was different from the reviewed proposal. Member states have the power to agree collectively on a different direction than that preferred by the Commission or the EP, and did so over both controversial rulings. That said, the Council represented an apparatus that handicapped those national voices that did not favour the proposal submitted for adoption. The presence of a non-active body consisting of seven-eight 'quiet' member states, which have little interest in maritime affairs, increased the actual power of the Commission proposals making a Council differentiation difficult (according to a Council official) (Vermote, 1996). 'Those are votes for the Commission. You get the proposal by the Commission and we have these non-active delegations, which say 'we don't object'). Therefore, despite the willingness of the major EU maritime nations for a different balance, the Greek presidency had to work hard to ensure a rallying around a compromise German proposal, which in turn was searching for a common denominator between the Council and the Commission. The Greek administration did so although its own national policy choices were different; it preferred the issue to be retained under the rule of the IMO. Holding the presidency was conceived as a means to ensure that the second-best EU policy would be closer to its national priorities, but also generated a bureaucratic interest in successfully fulfilling the 'presidency role'.

The retention of national powers in recognising non-EU certificates progressed easily within the Council. Yet, the decision replaced the *status quo* by a common 'mutual recognition' system of rules defined by member states, and monitored in association with the Commission. A comparison of policy outputs in different occasions is constructive. During the discussions of the 'safe seas' document, member states explicitly preferred to coordinate their actions via the vertical axis of the Council but agreed to the replacement of the existing Council working group by a committee with the participation of the Commission. Later, they would reject the idea of the Commission monitoring the ISM Code Regulation but would agree to a regulatory committee chaired by the Commission. In general, the policy making process institutionalised a more integrated policy-making framework wherein the Commission shares some responsibility in the making, implementing, or amending, of agreed EU rules, irrespective of whether member states had forcefully refused a direct transfer of substantial powers to the EU. As regards the specific rule, the intense disagreement between the Commission-EP coalition and the Council watered down the directive according to the preferences of the latter, nevertheless it produced a different outcome that the maritime states would prefer.

The EP consistently attempted to promote the development of an EU policy. By pronouncing maritime safety as an 'urgent political problem of major importance', demanding the alteration of EU policy initiatives to rules that would automatically incorporate future amendments of international rules and suggesting relative amendments to the draft proposals, the EP tried to commit the Commission and the Council to 'more' and 'long term' policy programmes. Although ineffective for achieving such explicit commitments, the EP had a distinctive influence on the content and progress of the EU policy measures that were examined. Formally entering the decision making process when the views of member states and those of interest groups are well documented has enabled the EP to amend draft proposals and play a pivotal role in the promotion of the EU measures.

The extent and, in most cases, the substance of the EP actions were upgraded whenever the draft initiative was seriously challenged after its publication, either by national administrations or stakeholders, or was not well drafted in technical terms. In the light of different views between the Council and the Commission, the conflict between the social partners, and the technical weaknesses of the drafted proposal, the EP virtually rewrote the minimum training directive aiming to increase its chances of becoming an EU rule. As the debate centred on the transfer of policy making and implementation monitoring competencies, the EP also tried to achieve a new regime that would provide a more influential role for itself. The partiality of the initial draft Regulation on SBT tankers, notably the absence of consideration of the port industry's objections, gave to the EP a major role. Proceeding to its first report after the contending interest groups had made explicit their views, the EP amended core elements of the draft proposal, aiming to a more balanced representation of the shipowners and ports approaches. In the case of the ISM Code Regulation the EP had the opportunity to accommodate the calls of small shipowning companies and the Greek shipping industry for time derogations. Either due to organisational capacity, which was the case of the port industry when the SBT tankers regulation was in discussion, or because of choice, which is the case of the trade unions, some interest groups continue to be 'late comers' in the EU policy-making process. Thus, they shift their attention to the EP, with the latter endorsing some of their favourable amendments always under the precondition that they do not challenge but propel the pro-integration considerations of the institution.

The policy preferences and ideological stance of the Transport Committee Rapporteur had an influence on the final content of the EP report. The socialist Rapporteur on the 'safe seas' document incorporated several points that trade unions had expressed and it is worth recalling that the same MEP had drafted an initial Transport Committee report during the making of the 1986 Regulations that maintained a similar stance. Having neo-liberal deregulatory views that matched the shipowners' conceptions dominating his national constituency, the Greek MEP that reported on the training directive was keen to propose the withdrawal of regulations on manning conditions. Party politics are not however the deterministic variable of the final EP stances. Analysis suggests this variable to be the relationship of these views to the Commission's approach. As history relates, reports on CMTP initiatives have been overturned, either in total or in essence, and elements of ideological conflicts or party politics being notified, only when the Rapporteur was opposed to Commission's stance. Apart from the training directive this had been the case of the initial report on the 1986 Regulations. In the search for a common policy, the EP is reluctant to agree on reports that reject the Commission approach because the indefinite delay of the proposal is not what it wants to see. It may proceed to a critical reading of the draft proposals, but it has an interest to see policy initiatives developed and integration progress.

The EP moves would have been less meaningful if the Commission had not endorsed them. In fact, 'the tendency of the Council is to look only to those things of the EP that have been taken over by the Commission and this is the case everywhere in the Community' (Vermote, 1996). But in all cases examined the Commission consented to take onboard a great part of the EP suggestions, even when they resulted in substantial changes of its initial proposals. They assisted the Commission in overcoming technical weaknesses, absorbing demands and gaining the support of interest groups, or adjusting its proposals to the views expressed during the preliminary Council discussions.

True, the rewriting of the minimum training directive in the light of the EP amendments did not determine the final outcome. However, it was the acceptance of the EP reading that enabled the SBT Regulation to progress and the troublesome relationship of DG-VII with the 'outrageous' port industry to improve. Of equal importance has been the utilisation of the EP reports as a means to accommodate stakeholders' demands expressed in the domestic arenas after the submission of the initiatives and facilitate national administrations to agree within the Council without facing domestic pressures. The endorsement of the EP amendments on the SBT and ISM

Code Regulations in line with the demands of the British port and Greek shipping industries facilitated the respective national administration to support the adoption of these measures. Both regulations arrived at the Council for confirmation rather than for detailed discussion. In that sense, the Commission has been keen to develop a relationship with the EP that goes beyond the juridicial logic as much as the EP itself. This relationship has ironed out the notified disagreements and, by downgrading the substance of the debate that took place within the Council, increased the role that both institutions have played in the policy making process.

This did not mean however that there is a consistent institutional partnership. Both institutions, but primarily the Commission, pay attention to Council balance. Once a common Council position is achieved, the Commission is reluctant to reopen the discussions, preferring to see the political agreement sustained. This left the EP to champion the demands for policy integration. Oxymoron as it may seem, when the second EP reading of the ISM Code Regulation attempted to safeguard more competencies for the Commission the latter resisted translating these calls into proposals to the Council. Then, whilst the Commission assented to modify determining provisions of its other initiatives, it did not subscribe to explicit commitments to more initiatives. The selective endorsement of the EP amendments aimed to help the durability of the Council balance and the incremental promotion of policy Europeanisation. In turn, the EP choices of issues to put forward during its first reading and the noticeable limited number of issues to which the EP returned during its second reading, suggest that the EP is cautious of this Commission practice, as well as the unwillingness of the Council to discuss EP amendments not endorsed by the Commission.

Perhaps unsurprisingly, within the decision making process each member state needed to gain a critical level of support from the other participating policy actors in order to promote its policy preferences. What is important though, this fact has affected the stance maintained by them during the process. Since 1979 an ideologically driven British administration had consistently favoured the deregulation of the port industry (cf. Thomas, 1994). Calls by British shipowners for the implementation of the non-binding IMO rule on SBT tankers had been rejected on the grounds of minimum market interference (Richards, 1996). Yet, this administration did not oppose the respective EU proposal, although the intense pressures by the British port industry offered such opportunities. The Greek administration did not oppose any of the policy initiatives jeopardising its long-term relationship with the shipping industry in the domestic arena. Then, the attempts of the German administration to promote the initial SBT regulation draft were unsuccessful. The dynamic of the interaction between Commission-EP-interest groups had altered the Commission's approach and a refined proposal finally arrived at the Council. The outcome of the bargaining process saw some of the major, commonly conceived as 'powerful', EU member states accept policy developments that they would have preferred not to be adopted, or have seen progress on different terms. Bearing in mind that the unilateral Italian attempts to expand the minimum training directive to offshore registries also failed, it is apparent that in spite of their collective powers to redirect or determine the rate of policy integration, the unilateral ability of member states to impose their views is limited, irrespective of whether they favour more or less integration.

The safety of ro/ro ferries represents a case when a national administration (the UK) was incapable of bringing an issue (stability) to the EU agenda even when it held the Council presidency and had the support of domestic interests (shipowners). On the other hand, the potential to build this support leads member states to turn to the EU when the non-EU policy-making levels (IMO) fail to reach satisfactory agreements. Though in the case examined the IMO failure was precisely the outcome of EU member states' discords, some of these states insisted on an EU rule, and coordinated non-legislative activities with the Commission (i.e. scientific research on very technical issues) to promote it. This helped the Commission to accumulate competence and confidently put forward initiatives despite the unease of several maritime member states with such a development.

Similar help was offered by the fact that the EU has developed an authoritative status as the framework identified with international European policy cooperation. All policy actors and the media reacted to the *Estonia* incident, and more recently to the *Erica* incident, with a reference to the EU, though claiming different responses. In this context, a regional European but not EU agreement symbolises a less satisfactory solution enough to be termed by the EP as 'an urgent political problem'. Although in line with the IMO decisions, the 1996 Stockholm agreement of north European states is conceived as an undesirable development. The agenda did not progress solely because the Commission acted as a policy entrepreneur, but also because in the aftermath of maritime incidents this entrepreneurship was combined with specific problems to prominence and the right political climate to submit EU policy proposals. Still, it was the organisational capacity and the focus of the Commission that enabled rules to be prepared and developed before those circumstances eroded.

The ISM Code Regulation seems a simple bureaucratic decision to translate a nonetheless mandatory international rule to EU law, or an advance implementation that finally became subject to derogations. Judging by the ease of its endorsement, it was perceived by national administrations as such. The Council's favourable resolution remained preoccupied by the symbolism of the EU rule. However, by integrating national policies and putting the monitor of this implementation under common rules the considerable potential for national interpretations has been minimised. For several national administrations the latter represented an important power allowing a reflection of domestic 'elite' pressures. At least half of the EU shipping industry (i.e. Greek shipowners) was already looking forward to making the most of that potential, especially given its relationships with the respective national authority. The member states 'instruction' for an EU instrument pushed the evolution of an EU regulatory competency that would not allow them to activate national interpretations even if in the future they wished to do so.

Moreover, the 'short-term' approach of national administrations and stakeholders pushed further unintended policy developments. When the Commission seized the opportunity and indicated that other policy measures were under preparation, member states and stakeholders remained preoccupied with the controversial 'stability' rule. It was only when these measures were brought forward that several objections regarding their necessity became apparent. Echoing the comment of an interviewee, 'the Commission has shown the capacity to take advantage of the absence of a long term strategy' (Bantias, 1996).

The latter is not however a one-way process. The Commission has also been affected by the preconception of the other actionable factors. A great part of the scepticism and negative stances to EU policy integration has a reference in the heterogeneity of the intra-EU industrial structures or operational demands deriving from the unchangeable geographical characteristics of the EU membership. This guided the Commission to reshape its strategy and promote rules, or implementation procedures, which explicitly differentiate between kinds of maritime operations. An example is the currently under discussion measure for the expansion of SOLAS to cabotage trades. Whenever such differentiation was part of earlier CMTP developments it was conceived as 'derogation' and was the outcome of accommodating demands expressed during the policy making process rather than a component of the initial draft proposal. This time the Commission endorsed this practice to make the submission of the specific rule feasible. The same adjustment is critical in the persistence of the EU involvement over the stability issue. An agenda acknowledging the insurmountable operational heterogeneity enables the Commission to search within a wider realm of alternatives and, foremost, in a consensual climate. Even if some member states become hesitant in the future, the pending investigation of the issue by a committee of experts stands as a perfectly legitimate Commission move endorsed by all of them.

While the role of the institutional triangle Commission-EP-Council has been vital, there was no evidence that the consultative Ecosoc had any real influence in policy elaboration. That the opinions of this tripartite committee were unanimously adopted, when the social partners disagreed over the Commission initiatives, is not irrelevant to this fact. Especially as the balance of each final Ecosoc opinion reflects to a certain extent the views of the appointed Rapporteur. As the Rapporteur on the 'safe seas' document was a consultant of the most sceptical Greek shipowners association, the endorsement of the initiative was more critical than that of the EP, or the Council. On the other hand its opinion on the ISM Code mirrored the emphasis given by organised labour on issues of personnel and working conditions. Those who were able to contribute to the draft at an early stage were satisfied by the presence of their concerns (Peppa, 1996), nevertheless, this study did not detect a real influence of the Ecosoc on the policy making process. Interviewees from other EU institutions confirmed the marginalisation of the Ecosoc. To the Commission 'a positive view from Ecosoc is a very good signal that we have made a good proposal ... having a negative view is simply not pleasant' (De Dieu, 1996). The Council 'takes note ... but there is seldom a formal examination of what the opinion of the Ecosoc was' (Vermote, 1996). The juxtaposition of the non-binding Ecosoc status and the direct representation of the social partners' interests by respective Euro-groups have minimised its influence.

Contending Interest Groups

Interest groups representing shipowners, organised labour, and port authorities, have contended to influence the preceding exchanges of the political institutions. A prestigious national elite empowered by the continuous demonstration of a capability to avoid regulatory measures imposed at any policy level, even internationally, shipowners had a substantial input in the process. That domestic policy revisions and a great part of the previous and parallel CMTP developments aim to discourage disinvestment (Chapter 3), restricted the Commission from a race towards higher standards that would confront the shipping industry. The consciousness of national administrations over the safety manning requirements that the Commission and the EP had proposed were expressions of long term intrastate industry/administrations relationships (see the domestic policy changes). Both the northern states insistence and Mediterranean states rejections of a higher EU 'stability' rule, even the unilateral attempt of the 1992 British presidency to promote the issue in the EU agenda, were rooted to coalitions already developed in the domestic arenas.

Notwithstanding that, the momentum created by the decisions of the EU political institutions, institutional configurations (the EU/national law relationship), and the fact that in the process national administrations converged over a common policy framework, induced a change of the industry's standpoint. Despite their interest in a regulatory realignment, shipowners had forcefully rejected any EU level activity. However, since the potential of an EU framework became apparent, they abandoned this opposition and adopted a critical, albeit not rejective position towards the new agenda. Besides, loyal shipowners' decision to operate traditional flags is driven by economic benefits. As FoC had not tempted them in the 'lean' 1970s and 1980s, they prefer to see the regulatory framework under which they operate not to be unfavourably modified rather than simply flag-out in relatively more prosperous times.

Shipowners strive to build cooperative relationships and acquire powers in the progress of the common policy having a twofold intention: to minimise negative but also to extract favourable initiatives. In this vein, they detected potential gains even from rules that they had initially opposed. The change of strategy to achieve their non-integration preferences has been accompanied by the identification of a positive role for the emerging policy framework. Recognising that concrete measures would follow, they supported the strengthening of PSC through EU actions aiming, *inter alia*, to redirect the EU policy away from 'flag-state' actions. Though the EU assumed power over PSC, the dynamic of the process proved to be such that there is not a case of what the shipowners want and what they do not want to discuss: 'the case is what the Commission would like to discuss' (Peppa, 1996). Then, they tried to elevate the minimum training directive from a safety initiative to one that would respond in favourable ways to their needs to employ trained but expensive EU-seafarers. Yet, although both social partners and the EP worked towards the same direction, the objections of the agenda-setter Commission were able to limit the issue for future discussion.

This decision was not marked by a 'one-off' decision but expressed through the persistent interest representation at any, and the earliest, possible stage including the supply of technical expertise. Substantial lobbying resources and the adjustment of the industry's approach even within the ongoing policy making process in order to remain part of the bargaining game between 'interested to be lobbied' policy makers was fruitful. Shipowners did not secure the withdrawal of the minimum training directive or its most unwanted provisions. But the advocacy of an amended rule, which would not confront domestic policy priorities, deployed relationships with maritime states that secured more (though still not entirely) satisfactory outcomes. Whilst economic power and lobbying capacities were important, shipowners had neither the power to set the agenda, nor the power to control policy outcomes and promote integration according to their, initial or adjusted in the process, preferences. The analysis of the SBT regulation is revealing. The industry initially offered reluctant support to its second-best solution. However, as representatives of port authorities entered the process contending for a different outcome, this support took the form of an active promotion of the Commission's proposal. Still, while the contribution of their well-organised Euro-federation at the early stages of the process proved valuable, shipowners were not able to determine the policy outcome.

Domestic policies and politics, commercial interests and traditions, even geographical features have led shipowners to a noticeable variation of national preferences throughout the policy making process. Occasionally (i.e. stability issue) the achievement of a collective stand was impossible. This industrial heterogeneity created lobbying activities that aimed to create national patterns of preferences that would influence the direction of the common policy. A part of the industry, not necessarily always the same, has been systematically more positive to the EU initiatives. This became vital, especially as the stance of the Euro-federation has been consistently closer to the more 'pro-integration' views, though the more sceptical national associations have constantly included the Greek union, which represents half the industry. A comparison of the ECSA views and those of the British, Greek, or Danish, associations during the discussions of the 'safe seas' document is characteristic. Neither did ECSA expressly oppose the minimum training directive, nor did it maintain that port charges of tankers should remain part of the IMO regulating responsibilities, stances that the Greek association held. ECSA was more inclined to be engaged in a constructive dialogue than rejecting altogether the EU initiatives. In this context, policies that seemed to be unacceptable to some parts of the industry were transformed by its Euro-federation to a search for a 'workable regime'. The decision of ECSA to co-operate with the Commission in the preparation of measures concerning ro/ro safety is an illustrative example. The Europeanised format of interest representation, in turn a response to the creation of a new institutional framework and the willingness of the EU institutions to deal with one group representing the whole industry, has filtered policy demands.

When port authorities attempted to influence those developments directly impinging upon their activities they managed to achieve a partial accommodation of their demands. The EU institutions and most of the member states were interested to make a balance between conflicting preferences of the various stakeholders. Still, the format and the stage that advocacy by interests was expressed were decisive factors to the effectiveness of the industry's campaign. The fact that in the early stages of policy design port authorities had only been organised in an informal group proved to be counterproductive. The policy framework, which agreed in their absentia, created undesirable, to them, potential developments.

Then, entering the policy making process after the Commission had formally drafted the SBT rule proved an insurmountable obstacle to their negotiating powers. The presence of multiple points to influence allowed them to be part of the process but their positioning had already been handicapped. Along with the advantageous position that the competing interests had gained, they had to acknowledge another parameter that has worked against those opposing EU initiatives: the 'momentum' generated in the early stages of the policy-making process. Port authorities fought for amending rather than dropping an 'environmentally sensitive' rule which was believed to distort competition against the TEU provisions. On the other hand, the realisation that the more organised shipping industry had gained a more influential position contributed substantially to the formation of a Euro-federation. Finally, the divergent characteristics of the industry led those ports strongly opposing the EU initiative rule to fight 'alone'. Even though a collective stand was achieved, private interests positioned negatively *vis-à-vis* policy makers weakened as, like in the case of shipowners, different parts of the industry advocated different policy outcomes.

Organised labour had a limited input to the actual developments, although it had been the first to support the idea of a common policy. Features of the economic context, notably the growing internationalisation of the employment partners, had already undermined trade unions negotiating powers in the domestic and international arenas, and did so in the EU context as well. This was not least because it informed labour positioning *vis-à-vis* the meaningful policy making process. Given the employment pressures to its declining membership, trade unions saw the safety measures as an opportunity to demand regulatory initiatives that would replace the trend towards domestic deregulation and the employment of non-EU nationals. Despite their united approach, insisting almost dogmatically to associating that the framework to the wider issue of employment minimised its negotiating power. For instance, they had championed the scope for higher standards but remained sceptical *vis-à-vis* the Commission's proposal for a minimum training directive as it was 'only a step forward'. By suggesting a list of alternative proposals and ignoring the absence of support by any other actor, labour was isolated and did not manage to secure even the provisions of the initial draft directive. Trade unions underplayed their positive reaction to the ISM Regulation, or their support for an EU review of the ro/ro stability requirements; these were rules tackling shipowners' problems rather than 'their own'. But keeping focused on their own agenda, i.e. FoC shipping, limited their contribution to the specific decisions. To some extent, organisational choices of interest representation also contributed to its political inefficacy. Choosing to maintain a reactive approach to policy developments proved to be another handicap. Dissatisfactions from domestic national policies led to a greater advocacy of EU developments aiming to achieve better outcomes than in the domestic arenas. But the choice of simply reacting to the drafted proposals (according to the CTWUEC secretary (De Villele, 1996) 'trade unions are not policy makers ... we are a reactive organisation and we do not provide policy proposals') resulted in less influence on the details of these initiatives.

Research found no evidence of any other groups positioning *vis-à-vis* the EU policy developments. Shippers were not interested in the details of a process that was not going to affect their competitive position ('safety is a matter of governments. What we are interested in is our goods to arrive') (Richards, 1996). As for the mediators in the maritime transport operation, shipbrokers and freight forwarders, not only did they not have any policy input but also the interview process (Pentheroudakis, 1995; Van de Perre, 1996; Sangster, 1996) saw that they were largely uninformed of the actual policy developments. It was only in mid-1996, when the Commission proposed envisaging legislative measures for inflicting pecuniary sanctions on cargo owners who call on ships that do not respect the safety standards (CEU, 1996a), that shippers reacted to the common policy. Notably, whilst unpopular, this concept has not been totally rejected. This shows that 'by exchanging views attitudes have changed' (Richards, 1996). Shippers, who could not be liable for the use of unsafe ships unless they know about it, identified the potential to have full and immediate access to all ship information before signing contracts. What had been difficult to promote at the national level, as individual governments fear the responsibility for providing incorrect information, may be achieved through the EU. As the Commission exploits opportunities and leads the expansion of the agenda, stakeholders adjusted their attitudes aiming to make the most of this expansion rather than rejecting it and attacking it from the outset. The osmosis with policy makers' preferences created a consensual attitude accompanied by the willingness to utilise the new policy framework in a favourable way.

Conclusions

Constructing a view on how the common policy on safe seas has progressed must begin with the features of the economic environment. The common policy developed against the deteriorating safety performance of an increasingly structurally deficient industry, which was accompanied by the incapability of the pre-existing international policy making mechanisms to provide the essential regulatory realignments. The qualitative features and quantitative extent of capital de-localisation undermined the role of self-regulation and international rule making, generated the need for policy reforms, but also confirmed the improbability of national policy responses. This environment fed the perceptions and behaviour of the actionable factors. The presence of 'escape routes' imposed constraints on the preferences of EU policy makers and militated strongly against radical schemes of higher EU safety standards. It also informed the choices of national administrations in the domestic arenas, which in turn are dominated by regulatory concessions to the capital intensive and highly mobile shipping industry, and at EU level, as well as the demands of the interest groups involved in the process. Yet, these factors alone do not explain the development of an EU policy. Antithetically, they had provided a justification for its absence in the past.

The explanation contains additional variables located in the dynamism generated by the institutional framework. Each pole of the institutional triangle Commission-EP-Council, as well as the exchanges of these poles in the light of the economic context, were causally consequential to the policy developments. The opportunism and leadership of the Commission were vital. A selective exercise of its agenda-setting powers, as regards both timing and content of its initiatives, an organisational capacity to activate this selection, and a preference to work as a 'consensus-builder' through a 'problem solving', rather than a 'principle driven' confrontational approach helped the common policy to progress. This policy entrepreneurship was combined with other influential institutional features, notably the obligations and commitments deriving from the Treaties; the fact that the EU law supersedes national legislation; the geographical span of the expanding EU membership; and the identification by the concerned public of the EU as the framework associated with European policy cooperation. However, the Commission could not impose its views, hence, some of its actions were unsuccessful. It was constrained, by the economic context and by the level of support that was offered by other policy actors, member states and contending interest groups. Finally, the policy preferences of this political institution did not remain fixed. As the other actors' preferences or specific constraints became apparent, the policy preferences and strategies of the Commission altered as well.

The EP had a distinctive influence, systematically in line with the pro-integration considerations of the institution. The EP employed its powers to iron out notified disagreements between the Commission and the Council, or between any of these institutions and the involved interest groups. The development of a close EP-Commission relationship helped policy initiatives to progress, not least because it provided a means to absorb domestic national pressures and facilitate a positive member states reaction. That said, when such EP-Commission partnership was not present the ability of the EP to develop legislative developments was minimal.

Member states hold the power to agree collectively on the policy measures they prefer. Still, certain of their activities contributed to the evolution of unintended policy developments. National governments remained preoccupied with short-term targets and the symbolism of EU rules that had their own dynamic or consequences not advocated by all maritime states. Despite their collective powers to determine the rate and direction of integration, the ability of each member state to impose its own preferences without gaining a critical level of support by the other participating policy actors is limited, irrespective of whether they are in favour of more or less integration. This has affected their willingness to maintain isolated stances throughout the process. The culture within the process is such that disagreement does not imply the automatic dismissal of a proposal but a search for an alternative. As consensus may be built within the process member states sharing the same values insist on the search for policy integration.

Furthermore, the Council is not just 'the total of its membership' but a mechanism within which disagreeing member states become committed to a common policy. Whilst its non-binding decisions and political statements legitimised EU actions, its sectoral formation helped the common policy format, but also induced a certain (in this case 'industry', rather than 'environmental', sensitive) direction. Within the Council meetings those national representations holding isolated views decided to corporate before the voting procedures, whilst a non-active non-maritime Council majority systematically favoured the proposal submitted for adoption. In this context, the aim of the presidency to successfully fulfil its bureaucratic role was accompanied even by attempts of state executives to promote policies they would have otherwise opposed. Finally, the policy making process institutionalised a more integrated policy-making framework in which the Commission shares some responsibility in the making, implementing or amending of agreed EU rules, irrespective of the fact that member states forcefully refused a transfer of substantial powers to the EU.

Private actors had their own distinctive input in the examined policy developments. However, this input has been a variable critically interrelated not only to the economic context, but also the institutional framework. The interest groups which represent these actors have been 'locked' in a meaningful policy making process. Therein their pleas and market powers informed and constrained the views of national administrations and EU policy makers. On the other hand, the institutional framework within which the policy making occurred critically shaped the very preferences of the private actors regarding the extent and potential content of the EU policy, as well as the structure of the advocacy of these preferences.

Due to their strong contribution to the market reality, the preferences of shipowners and the need to discourage their flagging-out inclinations influenced the decisions of EU institutions and national administrations to take action, as well as influencing the form that this action has taken. However, the juxtaposition of the shipowners interest to retain the benefits of traditional flag shipping, with the policy makers' decision to set in motion a common policy, resulted in the replacement of the previously maintained non-integration stance by the search for 'workable' EU rules. Moreover, the industrial heterogeneity, and the Europeanised format of interests representation, have been two additional factors systematically contributing towards a more 'Europe minded' standpoint.

Maritime industries had the major input, while in the case of conflicting interests, lobbying resources, the form of interests' representation, and the familiarity with the policy-making process, affected their comparative input. Substantial lobbying resources and expertise enabled shipowners to develop close relationships with the policy makers since the early stages of the process, and increase their input. Yet, the policy agenda and outcomes were ultimately determined by the preferences of policy makers. On the other hand, the momentum of the policy-makers' choices, and organisational incapacity to advocate interests in the early stages of the process, were factors that limited, as much as the diverse industrial characteristics of the port industry did, the abilities of the port industry to achieve a full accommodation to their preconceptions.

Organised labour has been even less influential. To a great extent, the EU reproduced the notified policy making pattern, both nationally and internationally, where seagoing labour has not prevented deregulation. The expansion of employment internationalisation had already weakened the negotiating positions (and declined the membership) of seafarers' unions throughout the last decades. However, the input of organised labour was minimal even when favourable measures were in discussion. Despite their support for a common policy on maritime safety, the strategy of organised labour remained (perhaps logically given the pressures on its membership) focused on the need for tackling FoC shipping. But without re-approaching their agenda, trade unions underplayed their contribution to the meaningful policy making process. Insisting on a reactive interest representation, was an additional parameter that did not help labour to promote its point of view over the specific policy initiatives.

7 The New Economic Environment of European Shortsea Shipping

This chapter concentrates on the major elements of the new economic environment of European shortsea shipping. The complex maritime transport system naturally divides into segments of distinctive features, problems, and policy demands. The types of service, the types of trade, and the relationship of the latter to a country's jurisdiction, are the most used criteria for classifying them. However, the distinctive characteristics of short distance operations, and the development of geographical regions characterised by a substantial interchange of traffic flows, have led to an additional differentiation between deep and short sea shipping. Since there is a lack of a universal definition,[1] European shortsea shipping is understood to cover both purely national transport and cross-border maritime transport services between member states (cabotage and intra-EU trade respectively). It also covers maritime transportation between the EU and adjacent European regions.

The economic environment of the market in question has changed dramatically over the last decade. Some of the changes are the products of intrinsic market developments; they derive mainly from changing behaviours of the market actors either on the supply or the demand side. Others are attributable to external factors, largely beyond the control of shortsea market forces. In conjunction, they have created a new economic environment within which European shortsea shipping operates.

Quantitative and Qualitative Market Changes

Two of the most appreciable market developments are the remarkable expansion and the structural modification of European seaborne trade. During the second half of the 1980s Western Europe experienced one of its longest post-war booms.[2] The economic expansion of the twelve EU member states in the 1990s was accompanied by a 3% increase of goods transport demand. The latter reached 2770 tkm in 1998, growth of over

100% since 1970. The same year passenger transport demand in the EU reached 4.830 billion pkm, an over 120% growth since 1970. Importantly for this analysis, trade between member states grew remarkably faster than economic output, or extra-EU trade. Proportionally, intra-EU(12) trade represented 53%, of the total EU trade at the end of the 1970s, reached 55% in 1985, and topped 60% in 1990. In 1998, it accounted for 63% of the total, and for 13% of the EU GDP.[3] Apparently, this augmentation accelerated, both in absolute and proportional terms, since the re-launch of European integration. The interest in the completion of the SEM was followed by a progressive elimination of non-tariff barriers advancing the unrestricted circulation of goods inside the EU. Notable examples are the lessening of border controls and the mutual recognition of technical regulations and standards. The exact magnitude of the static and dynamic integration effects is impossible to determine, since the rapid growth of intra-EU trade is bound to be influenced by many factors. Nonetheless, the stimulation of cross-frontier flows previously discouraged by non-tariff barriers and a national market ethos drove to a sharp intra-EU trade expansion.

Subsequently, the already substantial intra-EU maritime market began to grow. Eurostat indicates that intra-EU maritime flows are now running at 270 million tonnes per annum but real volumes are higher.[4] Most member states have a close interest in the efficient realisation of shortsea operations, though geographical contiguity and maritime traditions clearly affect the level of this interest. Maritime flows account for almost the entire intra-EU trade of states like Greece, or the British Isles. In the latter case, also in those of France and the Netherlands, intra-EU trade is also substantial in volume terms.

Overall, 61,4% of the total intra-EU(12) maritime flows are recorded in the North part of the Union. A further 23,4% is trade between North and South, leaving 15,2% as intra-Mediterranean movements. The most recent EU enlargement, as well as the level and direction of Nordic and East Baltic countries seaborne trade, suggest a growing impetus in the northern part of the EU. Then, seaborne trade between EU and European non-EU countries has topped 300 million tonnes (52,2% of the total) since 1994, with the northern industrialised states having the major involvement. On the contrary, the 223,7 million tonnes EU cabotage traffic, which is mainly taking place in the Mediterranean countries and the UK (55% and 30,8% of the total respectively), saw negligible growth over the last decade.

To complete the picture, traffic between all non-EU countries should be added but full-scale information does not exist. The most inclusive available figures have documented that, following an average annual increase of 4,7% throughout the 1980s, international shortsea trade between the nineteen European OECD countries exceeded for the first time the 400 million tonnes in 1988.[5]

This uninterrupted traffic growth has been accompanied by an impressive increase of general cargo and containerised commodities. Figure 7.1 illustrates the changing division of maritime trade. Unitised intra-European traffic in 1996 was twice as much as in 1982. Throughout the same period container trade from outside Europe increased by 77%, a substantial part of which (39%) arrived at a European port and then was transhipped to another port. As deep-sea lines move steadily to larger vessels, calls are reduced to one port in each trading area, hence, a stronger intra-European feeder trade to and from the outports develops.[6] The tripling of the feeder activity between 1982 and 1996 contributed to a remarkable 123% growth of containers handled in European ports. With this, and ro/ro traffic being the most expanded market niches, the split of the shortsea shipping market according to loading categories is general cargo 52%, liquid bulk 38% and dry bulk 10% (Zachcial, 1996).

Structural changes are furthered by reforms in goods production and distribution. The increasing application of logistics is an element affecting the profile of the demand for shortsea shipping but also transforming the organisation of the maritime transport process *per se*. Production practices move steadily from the conventional Fordist industrial archetype of mass production and economies of scale towards post-Fordism. The latter is a process dominated by economies of scope, focused manufacturing of specific parts with earlier steps being conducted by outside suppliers, and the integration of production and distribution through information technologies (for a reader: Amin, 1994). New organisational concepts, i.e. lean production, manufacturing island, are driving factors for changes in industrial enterprises' operations. They imply a just-in-time manufacturing and procurement strategy, which is the supply of the exactly required items at exactly the required quality, in exactly the required quantities at exactly the right time (Rothery, 1993). Those involved in this chain, from early suppliers to final customers, favour the synchronisation of the whole transport operation to serve an unbroken management of physical flows.[7]

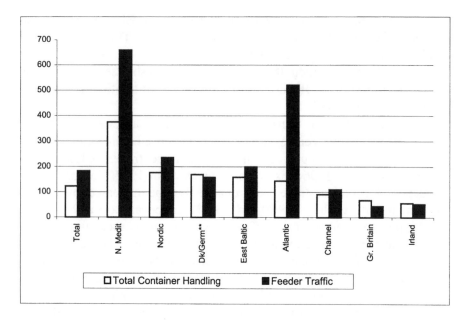

[a] Area Traffic (AT) refers to the number of containers handled in an area (AT = Exports + Imports + Cabotage)

Channel: Channel France, Benelux.   *N. Mediterranean*: South Spain to Black Sea.
Nordic: Norway, Sweden, Finland.   *Atlantic*: Rest of Spain and France, Portugal.
Ireland: Irish Republic and N. Ireland.
East Baltic: Estonia, Russia, Latvia, Poland, Lithuania.
[b] Whilst in 1996 data the former East Germany is part of the Denmark/Germany area, in 1986 it is part of East Baltic.

Sources: MDS Transmodal (1983, 1998).

Figure 7.1 Growth of European Shortsea Container Traffic 1982-1996

By introducing a new trading context, where transportation is an integral part of production and marketing strategies and efficient industrial functioning is endangered whenever bottlenecks and delays are caused by the transport system, logistics alter the industry-transport relationship (McKinnon, 1989; Cooper *et al*, 1991). Least cost is no longer the only criterion for selecting a transport mode. Modern capacity, more frequent consignments, reliable predefined schedules, and services integrated to the other parts of the transport network represent additional factors that concern cargo owners. When logistics determine between 10 to 30% of all costs in industrial enterprises and more than a quarter of these costs is generated by transport activities with the shorter the distance the higher the proportion (Everard, 1995), shippers are also interested in quality and reliability. This is an added dimension with critical repercussions on ship design, cargo handling, communication technologies, the role of ports, and the importance of integrating transport modes. The impact may not be the same in all the segments of the market (i.e. they do not affect tanker operators and oil distribution) but neither individual market actors, nor single industries, can remain competitive if the whole system does not demonstrate an ability to revitalise the new types of demand. To accomplish this objective two types of innovative moves are essential (Winjnolst *et al*, 1995; Peeters and Wergeland, 1997): a product innovation, which is the technological adaptation of the provided services, and a process innovation, implicating the comprehensive reorganisation of maritime operations.

The intensification of competition between transport modes for the same consignments is another feature that strengthens the importance of the required fundamental adjustments. The expanding general cargo figures, particularly their most profitable unitised part, represent commodities exposed to sharp modal competition. Road and air are two modes already involved in business logistics. Rail also competes strongly for intra-European traffic, including traditional international seaborne trade (i.e. English Channel). Excluding the cases which geographical characteristics impose shortsea as the unique viable choice, the competition has sharpened by developments to other transport modes (ECMT, 1993). The construction and operation of high-speed distribution networks within and between areas once mainly served by sea shipping, introduce prospects of growth in highly flexible low-cost inland transport modes. Moreover, road, rail, and waterway, junctions are designed or implemented to join together infrastructural networks, creating continuous land routings and reducing transit times over long journeys (i.e. the planned transalpine tunnels). Together with the plans for connecting high-speed railways, originally designed merely on a domestic basis, to combined international transport traffic, they provide the impetus for further development of modal techniques that exclude the maritime mode. The distinct feeder market provides an illustrative example. Feeder lines are more flexible than other modes insofar as they react quickly with unscheduled movements to meet changes imposed by a customer and absorb large traffic volumes. However, on certain routes road operators now compete effectively, an example being the service between Benelux and Spain where the main feeder traffic is developed without using sea feeders (MDS Transmodal, 1994).

All these changes take place when additional external, beyond the control of the shortsea markets, variables contribute to the generation of a new setting. Foremost, there is a rise of concerns regarding the distortion of the environment by growing demand for transport services. Traditionally, the significance of a mode was related to the geography of an area, the distribution of production sides, and its contribution to the production process. In recent years, environmental problems associated with transport have intensified at all geographical scales. With externalities increasing in parallel to demand, transport qualifies as an economic activity with negative environmental effects. In economic terms, transport traffic results in air pollution that is estimated to cost 0.4% of the EU GDP, noise pollution and congestion are estimated to cost 0.2% and approximately 2% respectively. In total an annual cost of approximately ECU 510 per person is the product of transport activities.

The World Commission on Environment and Development (1987) set the pace for a global commitment for sustainable development which 'meets the present needs without compromising the ability of the future generations to satisfy their own needs'. Environmental considerations lead to mounting pressures from the green lobby to constrain road traffic growth and stimulate the expansion of those modes that combine the lowest energy demands and the less possible negative effects to the environment. Europe has entered a period where these considerations have gained in political importance (cf. Hart, 1994).

Different transport modes result in different environmental impacts. For instance, 25% of all energy consumption in Europe is transport related but its modal variation is impressive. Road transport consumes 78% of the total, yet accounts for only 16% of the total freight transport activity (tonne-miles). The respective percentages of the aviation industry are 11.5% and 0.3%, while those of the rail industry are 3.9% and 17%. Seagoing vessels consume 6.5% of the energy to cover the 66.7% of the transport activity. The external costs associated solely with road transport in the six largest countries of the EU excluding congestion equivalent to around 2% of their GDP (Group Transport 2000, 1990) and EU congestion causes ECU 100 billion in wasted funds per year. Because of the imbalanced external costs that various means of transportation produce, the accommodation of the increasing demand implies fundamental decisions concerning priorities and distributional issues about gains and loses in the transport modal pie. A 'business as usual scenario' estimates a road traffic growth in the EU of around 40-50% between 1990 and 2010 (CEU, 1992a) and forecasts congestion to get worse. Considering that lorry traffic forecasts in 1985 for the year 2000 were reached by 1990, the ability of road transport industries to accommodate such expansion is questionable. The decentralisation and the reorganisation of the economic activities continue to be among the essential conditions but are not enough by themselves.

The geopolitical changes produced by the collapse of the economic efficiency and political institutions in Central and Eastern Europe comprise a second major external variable. For most of the 20th century the division of Europe into East and West and the major differences in the economic systems restricted economic activities, limited policy cooperation, and played a negative role on thinking about transport issues or designing transport policies in pan-European terms. A totally different situation has been evolving since 1989. In economic terms, the liberalisation of the East-West relationships generates demand for transport services, as well as the opportunity to provide them, on a pan-European basis. The East-West rapprochement means that Europe as a whole regained its deeper and more continental dimension, thus, stressing the need for intermodal cooperation and genuine transport chains that can serve this area with the required transport fluidity. As it has been asserted, 'it is difficult not to think of water when fluidity is mentioned' (De Whale, 1993, p. 291). In policy terms, some East European countries wish to be part of the integrative experiment. This fact has already had a significant effect: to accomplish this target they increasingly gravitate their policies around EU initiatives and policy philosophies.

Adjustment Pressures

In this context, market forces have to strive for innovation in order to compete. A major adjustment relates to the type of vessel providing shortsea services around Europe. Along with larger ships to accommodate the expanded demand, the greater use of vessels that employ sophisticated technologies and work as functional machines for the purposes of carrying cargoes on the sea leg of an intermodal movement, is essential. Innovation diffusion may double speed, lessen delivery time, lower logistical costs, increase frequency potential with the same number of ships and, not least, act as a psychological catalyst, similar to the one the introduction of fast trains has been to the use of railroads (Winjnolst *et al*, 1993b). In part, the know-how for ships loaded and discharged under the control of computerised systems is available (i.e. ro/ro units, cellular containerships), in part innovative vessel designs have to be further developed (i.e. catamarans, other high-speed shipping).

The need to modernise vessels upgrades the importance of quality manning. Automation at sea decreases the size of crews but also redefines their role. More qualified and experienced, less 'pure' shipping men represent a presupposition for the enhancement of superior services. The shore-based part of the operation also presumes certain levels of technical knowledge. The premise that all tomorrow's seafarers would be supplied from low-paid unqualified labour forces is challenged by a pattern where qualified labour produces operational savings that compensate for its increased price to the employer. The tendency to employ untrained seafarers holds, yet the reliance of innovation on skilful employees indicates that the commercial future and competitiveness of the sector increasingly rests on the assumption that qualified seafarers exist and operate sophisticated ships.

Furthermore, by demanding a process orientated view of goods and information, logistics and the new types of cargo inaugurate a major change regarding the role of ports (Chlomoudis and Pallis, 1996). The traditional conception of a 'gate' simply providing the facility of transferring cargoes between ship and quayside is no longer adequate (Pesquera and De la Hoz, 1992). Along with conventional operations, ports need to work as load centres providing a range of complementary storage and distribution services. The cargo generating capacity remains a powerful element but other qualitative factors (i.e. inland connections, or provision of electronic data information) come into play. In their absence, ports cannot meet the demand for commodities to be delivered (or transhipped) quickly and predictably, and the user considers the employment of the mode as a disadvantage of the production function. Eventually, shipowners and the port industry become more interdependent than ever. To ports, the means to win traffic and secure the continuity of costly adjustments is to be the shipping lines partners. Such modernisation is of equal importance to shipowners. It influences the variation of the costs associated with the port interface[8] and improves the speed of shortsea shipping. Due to the latter, the range of the potential freights expands and operators who invest in modern and larger shortsea vessels can increase their competitiveness and profitability.

Finally, a growing interdependence also marks the relationship between shippers and shipowners. As chain transportation implies a series of operations frequently supplied by different modes, the accent is not just on the operation of each link but the coordination between the various stages as well. Several shipowners attempt to keep in pace through their transformation to multimodal operators. To compete successfully they have their own road haulage, establish schedule cooperation with rail networks, or operate port terminals. The objective is to control the complete chain and offer profitable, integrated to the inland network, services. To establish this control they need sufficient knowledge that the risks associated with product innovation are sufficiently minimised through the readiness of shippers to employ it (Peters, 1993). On the other hand, relatively higher value goods are travelling via shorter sea distances. The satisfaction of cargo owners' needs for reliable, flexible, and cost-effective transport arrangements is eventually dependent on the options and the quality of the services supplied.

Tracing the Level of Adjustment to the New Economic Environment

In summary, a new economic dynamic has been developing, creating adjustment pressures on the shortsea shipping sector. The considerable quantitative and qualitative changes come with the acquisition or loss of market shares, the break-up of previous market balances, and fresh inter-industry relations. On the one hand, they trigger intra-modal competition. On the other hand, they are forces transforming the commercial relationships between the market players by creating, for a variety of reasons, a growing interdependence of the market actors. None of the players can stimulate its competitive position if the others do not show the same level of adaptability. It is the entire shortsea sector that needs to improve its internal structure to remain competitive within the new reality.

Still, the essential adjustments have been only partially in place. Shortsea shipping is well established in various European corridors but a large part of its market share results from compelling geographical circumstances, or mechanical economic reasons (i.e. low value bulk commodities which benefit from scale economies). The mode has yet to compete effectively in all intra-European markets. For instance, no-bulk trade between countries with major container ports such as France and Germany, is seldom carried in containers by sea.

An overall judgement of the level of the sector's adjustment to the new economic dynamic can be reached by comparing the conclusions of two ECMT round-tables regarding European shortsea shipping that were held in 1982 and 1993 respectively. The optimism of the early 1980s was replaced by more sceptical views in the early 1990s. Whilst the former advocated that 'the industry has in the past shown both adaptability and entrepreneurship' (ECMT, 1983, p. 182), the later stated that 'some experts considered that there has been little innovation in shortsea shipping and that this sector has remained archaic' (ECMT, 1993, p. 106). Unsurprisingly, this has adversely affected the general perception of the mode. Shippers believe that shortsea is a slow, not competitive in terms of price, mode which involves double handling and risks delays and disruption during the loading, or reloading developments (Baasch, 1996).

The size of the vessels has increased[9] but kept up with technological achievements only in limited routes. Obsolete ships are still in operation and several market sections lack the services of available technologies. The structure of the, primarily EU-flagged, EU owned shortsea fleet (Table 7.2) reveals that shortsea operators continue to use multipurpose general cargo or all-round ro/ro vessels (60% and 16% of the total respectively) but cellular containerships, characterised by a high flexibility in their operational possibilities, represent only a minor part (3% comparing to 8% in the case of larger deep-sea vessels). The significant higher average age of shortsea vessels than that of the deep-sea fleet (20 and 17.8 years respectively) confirms a slow replacement cycle. Notably, the nationality breakdown of the fleet ownership is highly concentrated, with owners from seven EU member states controlling 92.8% of the EU and 50% of the total European owned ships, with less than 30% of these vessels conveying trade under non-EU flags.

Although ports specialisation implies substantial investments in infrastructure, the level of these investments in Europe has followed a negative trend, whether it is expressed as a share of the total of the investments in transport infrastructure, or as a percentage of the GDP. The aggregate European OECD investments in transport infrastructure declined from 1.5% of the GDP in 1975 to the relatively low 1% throughout the 1980s with the share of ports decreasing from 5% to 3.5% of the total, a trend that continued in the 1990s (ECMT, 1999). True, the absence of conventional capacity infrastructure is not a generalised problem and, largely due to the vigorous competition that takes place even between ports within the same member state, most of the EU ports have covered such needs. But at the end of the 1980s even the most successful EU ports needed further modernisation to integrate into the logistical systems (Seidenfus, 1987). Moreover, in some EU regions ports had not kept pace, but they needed to do so to overcome their less efficient and less specialised facilities (EP, 1993).

Table 7.1 European Shortsea Fleet by Ownership

| | %-of EU fleet | %-of European fleet | %-flag | | | | Type | |
			EU	RE	RW	Liquid	General cargo	Other cargo
Greece	22.0	11.9	63	15	22	23	45	32
Germany	19.8	10.7	63	14	23	10	71	19
Italy	12.8	6.9	na	na	na	32	29	39
UK	12.6	6.8	68	10	22	26	49	25
Denmark	10.0	5.4	75	7	18	17	60	23
Netherlands	8.9	4.8	67	10	23	10	70	20
Spain	6.7	3.6	84	2	14	10	53	37
EU(12)	100	54.0	71	10	19	19	61	20

RE: Rest of Europe; RW: Rest of World; ships of 500 grt and above; as of 1/1/92.

Source: Grilley and Dean (1992).

The adjustment process has not been facilitated by the national policy frameworks that have either neglected or been ineffective at building up the external environmental parameters that would improve the competitiveness of the shortsea shipping sector. In some cases (i.e. the UK) there is lack of policy harmonisation towards rail and road modes, and combined transport principles do not apply for shortsea shipping. In others, like Greece where all ports are public entities, the national administration has followed a 'road-addicted' investment policy in transport infrastructure failing to modernise port facilities (Chlomoudis and Pallis, 1997). There is also an issue of adequate monitoring effects of policies, and assessment of external costs in markets, implicating even the maintenance of information regarding the current modal accommodation of demand. Recent reviews of all EU national transport policies concluded that comprehensive statutory requirements for environmental assessment exist only in Finland and the Netherlands (Lee and Hughes, 1995) and practical experience is limited (Chadwick and Gleave, 1996). Furthermore, recent UK inland origin/destination data are only available because a private company (Eurotunnel) commissioned it.

It appears then, that shortsea shipping has received little or no recognition as a potential joint contributor to the solution of the environmental problems. According to several interests groups (i.e. BCS, ESC, CLECAT), the tendency for governments to restrict road transport by increasing its costs and prohibiting traffic during the weekends comprises the most positive national initiative. As a recent study of several corridors in Europe concludes, whilst the attitudes of stakeholders towards various transport modes are, in principle, neutral, the tendency of national transport policies to display a comparatively more positive regulatory behaviour towards alternative modes is among the critical socio-political factors that reflect an unfavourable environment for shortsea shipping (Table 7.3; also: Tinsley, 1991). When external, not-controllable by the market, variables contribute to a context that allocates a greater social importance to the future of the sector, and market changes demand radical improvements of its internal characteristics to better its competitive position, national policies have not been channelled in a way that would induce positive changes in the environmental framework characteristics faced by shortsea shipping.

It must be noted, however, that due to the trends in manufacturing, supply, and distribution, processes the dimension of the shortsea operations is experiencing increasing internationalisation. The continuous integration of domestic cabotage services into a wider network where they are often relegated to the minor and subordinate role of a mere link in the chain, as well as the stagnated size of cabotage (which remain at the same level since 1984, whilst the level of intra-EU trade increased by almost 20%) highlight this change. National authorities cannot easily administer expansive international trade and growing multimodal operations of a wide geographical scale. It was in the second half of the 1980s and within this context that the various EU policy initiatives were introduced.

Table 7.2 National Governments and Shortsea Shipping*

	UK-NI/Ger/Dk	Ir-NI/B	Ir-UK	UK-Gr	UK-It	Nl-Gr	Nl-Fin
Government regulation toward alternative modes[a]	+	E	E	+	+	+	+
Relationships of shortsea operators with regulators	–	E	E	E	E	E	–
Attitudes of stakeholders towards various modes[b]	E	E	E	E	E	E	E

[a] A 5-point scale is used: (++) extremely attractive (+) attractive (E) neutral (-) unattractive (--) extremely unattractive.

[b] A high score for alternative modes reflects an unfavourable environment for shortsea shipping

Source: Peeters *et al*, 1995.

Notes

1   In 1970, shortsea shipping was conceived as 'the part of maritime traffic which is operated among countries without ocean connections' and excluded seaborne trade conducted within national borders (Rochdale Report, 1970). More recently, La Saponara (1993, p. 10) anticipates that a workable definition 'must cover the whole of the trading and shipping operations traditionally, termed international and cabotage shipping, carried on in a comprehensive geographic area characterised by a substantial interchange of traffic flows and by similar production techniques in the field'. ISL (1992, p. 1) provides a practical definition of European shortsea shipping including 'all the maritime traffic in the area stretching from Iceland in the North to the Mediterranean Sea in the South ad from the Atlantic coast in the West of the Baltic and the Black Sea in the East'.

2   From 1985 to 1990 the economies of the twelve EU member states grew annually by a rate of 3.1 comparing to averages of 2.5 and 1.4 for the periods 1974-79 and 1980-84 respectively (average annual percentage change of real GDP at constant prices; based on 1985 price levels and exchange rates). Source: OECD, Basic Indicators.

3   Sources: Eurostat, Basic indicators; Transport in Figures.
4   Eurostat database is compiled through import/export data, thus registers as maritime flows only the trade, which travels by sea at the point that it leaves a member state. For instance, cargo transported (un)accompanied on trucks by ro/ro ships is excluded, hence, only 74.1% of the total of Ireland's trade is recorded as 'seaborne'. Although needing to be treated with some caution, Eurostat figures remain the most valid shortsea shipping statistics available (cf. Winjnolst *et al*, 1993a).
5   European OECD countries: EU(15) plus Iceland, Norway, Turkey and ex-Yugoslavia; the preceded limits of Eurostat database are applicable; Source: ECMT, Statistical Trends in Transport.
6   For instance, many lines already call in Europe only at either Hamburg or Bremen (alternatively, either Rotterdam or Antwerp) and shortsea operators undertake transportation to other ports. The feeder market carries cargoes to the requirement of their customers, and the carriage of empty containers for deep-sea lines where the latter's trade is imbalanced and container repositioning in Europe is necessary.
7   US-based companies, in particular, have been among the first to take this view with many of them selecting a single European port of entry, to serve a wider geographical markets through a just-in-time process. According to a World Bank (1995) survey, by 1990 some 28% of all shipments in the US and EC were carried on a just-in-time basis and the portion projected for 1995 was over one-third.
8   Which according to shipowners, currently stand on average above the 50% of the total shortsea transport costs (Everard, 1995).
9   The 1988 average size of over 3000 dwt per vessel was more than twice the size of ten years before (Struchtey and Zachcial, 1989). That said, there is not a clear cut of vessels operating in the shortsea market. Searching for an accurate criterion, Grilley and Dean (1992) prefer the 5000 grt upper limit, and this book has benefited for their detailed analysis of this fleet. Peeters (1995) favours the 6000 grt. Yet, when these ships do not operate exclusively in shortsea routes, some bigger vessels operate in the shortsea market.

8 Towards a Common Policy on Shortsea Shipping

An EU policy addressing the integral European shortsea market became a component of the EU agenda in 1991. Before this, shortsea shipping was not recognised as a genuine economic sector with its own significance and attributes. The considerably different geopolitical structure of the continent was a variable that constrained the scope of thinking of all trade flows in the continent within a unified pan-European dimension. Maritime exchanges between the EU and the East European nations were subject to the total of the relationships between the two blocs, so the need for a policy differentiating between short- and deep-sea maritime operations with state trading countries around the world was limited. The development that reflects the troublesome maritime relationships before 1989 was the willingness of some member states, but also exporters and operators, to seek retaliatory responses to East Bloc countries practices.

Neither was there any EU activity regarding the policy framework governing the considerable maritime flows between EU member states before the middle of the 1980s. From 1957 to 1974 this absence can be ascribed to the exclusion of the maritime mode from the CTP. Maritime traffic between or within the six founding members of the EU was relatively unimportant (only 5% of the total intra-EU(6) trade) contributing to the non-appearance of any supranational policy making interest. Yet, for reasons discussed in Chapter 3, there was no change after the first EU enlargement (1973) and the legal confirmation of the Commission's maritime transport policy-making authority (1974). The importance of the internal maritime transport market increased but its regulatory framework remained subject to national policies and/or bilateral agreements. Nevertheless, the Brussels package (1979) had a certain impact on the operation of the internal maritime market: it provided that liner trade between member states would not be covered by the UNCTAD Code cargo sharing formula but would be redistributed among them on the basis of commercial criteria. Apart from its market consequences, the provision was substantial in policy terms. In essence, it recognised that maritime relations within the internal market could be developed under a distinctive EU regulatory framework rather than the international.

Establishing the Freedom to Provide Services

The turning point was the 1984 ECJ judgement that the Council had failed, *inter alia*, to ensure the freedom to provide services in the sphere of international transport and to lay down the conditions under which non-resident carriers may operate transport services in a member state (Chapter 3). By ruling that the Commission was obliged to elaborate relevant proposals the ECJ led to the first EU initiatives intrinsically related to the European shortsea market. In 1985, the Commission proposed the application of the freedom to provide shipping services in both intra-EU and cabotage maritime trade (CEU, 1985a). The same year, the Commission argued that this was one of the seventeen specified transport related barriers that prevented the realisation of an 'area without internal frontiers' in which the freedom of movement of goods, persons, services, and capital can be realised. In its report on the necessary conditions for the establishment of the SEM it called for a change in this 'crucial but largely unrealised component of the single market', and called for freedom to provide transport between member states be established by the end of 1986 at the latest, though with the possibility of a limited restriction period of phasing out certain types of restrictions (CEU 1985b, p. 20).

The proposals focused on the need to converge the heterogeneous national policy frameworks in line with the transport title of the Rome Treaty. Following national traditions that preceded the inception of the EU, intra-EU maritime flows were subject to several cargo reservations.[1] Maritime cabotage trade was liberalised in the North states (B, Dk, Ir, Ger, Nl, UK)[2] but all five Mediterranean states (Fr, Gr, It, Pr, Sp) allowed the provision of services only to their national flags. To the Commission, opening competition and creating a wider market would be a much-needed assistance for the expansion and efficiency of the mode. However, none of the proposals was easy to progress. Whilst an agreement regarding intra-EU trade finally became part of the 1986 regulatory measures, the removal of cabotage restrictions was more controversial, and following further discussions positively concluded in 1992.

Interest Groups Mobilisation

The Commission's proposals mobilised stakeholders to articulate their interests via two routes. Within the national arena, interest groups tried to influence the positions of the national administrations. As regards the Mediterranean states, shipowners enjoying the advantage of protected national markets, even subject to manning requirements and price controls, supported the continuation of the *status quo*. Precisely because cabotage restrictions were accompanied by strict manning requirements and crews composed only by nationals, trade unions opposed liberalisation as a means of securing jobs and called for the co-operation of national administrations and MEPs to protect national employment (Tselentis, 1996). The less, or not at all, organised shippers operating at local or national level (a not so rare phenomenon in the Mediterranean regions) were not mobilised against regulated prices and frequent services. These views empowered national administrations to retain their objections, and informed counterproposals, i.e. France, and induced two-track approaches. Because of their extensive involvement in cross-trade, Greek shipowners lobbied for an immediate liberalisation of any non-cabotage trades but for the maintenance of cabotage restrictions (Peppa, 1996). Being economic elite that has a strong influence in the country's maritime policy, irrespective of the political party in power, their position was clearly mirrored by the stance of the Greek administration throughout the negotiations.

Similar mobilisation was observed within the domestic arenas of the northern states.[3] Shipowners were supportive of unconditional trade liberalisation, as it would open the scope for new or interlinking voyages increasing the utilisation of their vessels (Southorn, 1996). Notwithstanding that, with a substantial part of Mediterranean cabotage being unprofitable and subject to seasonal fluctuations, the potential benefits from building up regular business in these national markets was expected to be limited, and to be obtained only on some routes and some types of services (Tinsley, 1991). For many owners cabotage was a measure that would strengthen the direction of the EU policy in line with shipping liberalism. Shippers' councils also offered their support to both proposals. To them 'any trade restriction represents a constraint to the qualitativeness and modernisation of shipping services; and moreover, these measures would be a means to press for a widespread liberalisation that would include inland transport services as well, (Baasch, 1996). Trade unions remained focused to the international changes of manning conditions irrespective of flag or ownership. Nonetheless, having nothing to lose by the opening of the Mediterranean trade they supported the Commission's proposals (Aspinwall, 1995a).

Despite the aforementioned divergent national priorities shipowners, shippers, and trade unions expressed their views collectively at an EU level.[4] Trade unions did so through ITF, the other two through their Euro-federations. Shipowners faced the greatest problems in reaching a common position. ECSA finally supported the early enactment of the Commission proposals. It acknowledged, however, that transitional periods might be necessary for the harmonisation of other policies affecting the costs of EU shipowners, as well as for social and political sensitivities of the sectors involved to be fully dealt with within the context of the cabotage rule. Shippers did not face similar internal disputes as all major national shippers councils (British, French, German) agreed on the same line. Reflecting their views, ESC lobbied for an immediate total liberalisation in that it would widen the choice of services available to shippers. Given the variance of national unions positions, the achievement of a collective trade unions stance could also be problematic. However, ITF did not specifically point to the internal market or any other proposals and this eroded internal disputes. Backed by all European trade unions, the ITF rejected the whole Commission policy and put forward a different philosophy targeting the competitive position of European shipping *vis-à-vis* low cost FoC shipping.

Policy Makers Reactions

The diversity of national policies produced analogously different positions of national governments. The difficulties could be (and have been: Bredima-Savopoulou, 1990) portrayed as a division between the North and South part of the EU, however reality was far more complex. The protected cabotage was clustered in the Mediterranean states and all these states were in favour of retaining these restrictions as a mean to fulfil public service obligations to islands and remote regions. However, the additional reasoning, and subsequent positioning, advanced by some of these governments differed from others. Italy, Spain, and Portugal subordinated liberalisation to harmonisation of social costs and employment conditions, in order to preserve their national fleets and seafarers' jobs. France initially rejected the whole idea of liberalisation but during the discussions this attitude changed. In November 1985 her administration proposed, similarly to French and other trade unions, the creation of an EU maritime space where national restrictions would be abolished in favour of an EU flag (Aspinwall, 1995a). Then, France, Portugal, and Spain demanded a long phase out period before the abolition of their intra-EU cargo reservations (Bredima-Savopoulou, 1990).

The fifth Mediterranean state, Greece, argued for the immediate liberalisation of intra-EU trade but opposed the cabotage proposal outright on the grounds of strategic location and national security derived from the long-term troublesome relationships with Turkey. On the other hand, all north member states insisted on the immediate lifting of any restrictions regarding trade between member states and cabotage. Nonetheless, it was the neo-liberal UK government that, having the most significant liberalised cabotage trade of all member states and substantial shipowning interests championed the movement for liberalisation.

The EP Transport Committee produced its own report in controversy. Therein, it suggested the gradual market liberalisation on the basis of reciprocity but considered important that certain exemptions regarding cabotage could be made, and member states should be able on national security grounds to restrict their coastal trade. A minority opinion remained on record, arguing that liberalisation without harmonisation is a logically flawed policy that pursues the free market approach in imperfectly competitive markets.[5] It needs to stress however that the positioning of the EU policy against FoC shipping, rather than the questions over the internal maritime market policy, produced the major controversies during the EP discussions. Then, the Ecosoc appointed two Rapporteurs representing shipowners and trade unions respectively.[6] Its consultative opinion offered a unanimous support to the opening of the internal market to the EU registered ships but not to European shipowners that would prefer to exploit the cost advantages of operating under FoC (Ecosoc, 1985).

The controversies expressed during the consultation process appeared in the Council as well. Member states disagreements on several issues led discussions to a temporary standstill. Cabotage was one of the major impediments. On the other hand, none of the member states was advocating a fundamentally different policy regarding intra-EU maritime trade, objections referred only to the implementation timetable. When the British government, which was keen to see all the Commission proposals agreed, assumed the presidency in the second half of 1986, it recommended the disassociation of the most controversial issues from the rest of the proposals under discussion (Bredima-Savopoulou, 1990). This practice concluded in the agreement on four Regulations one of them embracing a decision regarding intra-EU traffic. The latter provided a three-stage elimination of unilateral restrictions, lasting until January 1993.[7] Four member states, Germany, Greece, the Netherlands and the UK itself, found the specific outcome unsatisfactory. Yet, despite that each of them alone or collectively could veto the decision, they restricted themselves to the expression of their discontent in the minutes of the Council.[8]

Resolving Cabotage: The Second Successful Attempt

Although the 1986 Council failed to unanimously agree on cabotage its decision stated that further considerations on the issue were necessary, and instructed the Commission to do so. The latter had tabled a proposal in line with the *raison d'être* of the Community. The EP and the Ecosoc had supported the concept but questioned its terms. A number of national administrations had expressed a favourable stance, and several private actors had supported the proposal at national and EU level. Therefore, the output failure did not produce the withdrawal of the proposal. Notably, the British administration, which acting at the capacity of the Council presidency had provoked the specific compromise solution, was the first to react by threatening to proceed to the ECJ against the decision on cabotage. Moreover, it passed the 1988 Merchant Shipping Act that allowed for retaliation against EU states that would not voluntarily give up their restrictions. This provision was never implemented but, in intergovernmentalist terms, for the British government liberalising cabotage trade turn, probably on political dogma and not economical grounds, to an issue of high politics, or perhaps high symbolism, with the British Prime Minister M. Thatcher making a reference to the issue in her famous 1989 Bruges speech.

The Council's guidance provided a stimulus for the Commission to return to the issue, and to search for an agreement that 'would unprecedented reorganise the national markets' (Jones, 1996). Following further contacts with both stakeholders and national administrations, the Commission submitted in 1989 an amended proposal that incorporated some of the sceptical considerations (CEU, 1989a). Recognising the severe objections for the initial project of an immediate and, most critical, unconditional abolition of national restrictions, the Commission adopted the view that policy integration progress should be achieved through derogations with regard to timing, vessel size threshold, and conditional liberalisation of specific routes. Member states would be allowed considerable time to implement the rule, while special provisions regarding the sensitive trade to and from islands were esteemed as necessary. The reviewed proposal also associated liberalisation with converging conditions of operation, through the instrument of the parallel EU register, which was already part of the EU agenda.

Interest Groups Mobilisation

This initiative received a mixed perception. All the stakeholders repeated earlier stances, suggesting that their views were not altered. However, the accommodation of some initial objections, as well as the progress of the SEM project, transformed the intent of those that had opposed the initial proposal. In particular, the position of the ITF and of the, newly formatted, CTWUEC offered a conditional support holding that 'cabotage and all intra-EU traffic should be reserved to EU shipping carrying the Euros flag' (De Villele, 1996). The priority was the establishment of a European area served by Euros-flagged vessels manned with European seafarers. This view did not satisfy the Mediterranean unions, which maintained a hard-line and organised several strikes against the visible EU agreement in 1992. Nevertheless, when the most active Greek trade union 'went alone' to lobby the EP, it did not do so objecting the entire idea. On the contrary, it promoted five 'constructive' amendments to be incorporated in the final proposal to the Council and three of them were finally embodied in the EP report (Tselentis, 1996). As Euros was becoming increasingly controversial, one of their main concerns was to secure that the vessels operating in cabotage would be manned according to the rules of their host-state and, therefore, would provide a more favourable crew composition to its nationals.

The change was apparent in the case of the sceptical shipowners. Greek shipowners acknowledged that, as integration progresses, the principle to provide free services had to be implemented in the case of maritime transport as in all other sectors of the economy. According to an interviewee, irrespective of the position that Greek shipowners would hold, a decision for the abolition of cabotage restrictions was something that would happen (Mavrommati, 1996). Although formally retaining a negative position (UGS, 1991), their informal contacts focused more on the possibilities of a long term adjustment process, and other aspects of the operating conditions that would govern a liberalised market, in particular the substantial information and transparency on subsidies that shortsea shipowners receive in other states and inhibit free competition and the achievement of a level playing field. Based on their competitive record, they started thinking of potential market opportunities rather than devoting efforts to objecting to the opening of national trade. More recently, in a further attempt to come to terms with the agreed regulation, Greek, French, and Italian shipowners engaged in informal discussions to the formation of a common adjustment policy, discussions that have been continuing. In Spain and Italy, shipowners left the national trade unions to be the main voice against the Commission proposal (Aspinwall, 1995a), Besides, the domestic traffic routes are dominated by a state owned carrier in competition with smaller private operators having less commercial interests at stake.[9]

Those shipowners that had been frustrated by the absence of a decision reluctantly agreed under the circumstances to the proposed derogated liberalisation; it 'offered a better option than the maintenance of the status quo', and the expectation was that the discrepancies would be ironed out in an early review (BSC, 1992). To understand this positioning one should not disregard that, insofar as many niches of the market are concerned, the effects of the rule were expected to be modest. The first report on the implementation of the cabotage regulation provides a valuable, though *ex post*, insight (CEU, 1995e). Liberalised bulk cargoes, which are transported between mainland ports in the south of Europe are of little interest to foreign shipowners, either because freight rates are too low, or there is no return cargo available. Foreign flags operate when there is a lack of sufficient national flag tonnage, carry only 6% of the liberalised trade and, moreover, these foreign flagged ships are often under the control of nationals. Shippers and freight forwarders tend to stay with their traditional national carriers at least as long as foreigners do not offer regular services. The consumers of the services acknowledge its limited impact: (according to Sangster (1996) 'it helps to a certain degree but we cannot get too excited'), though they suggest that this is because liberalisation happens very slowly and remains subject to severe distractions. In fact, when the revised proposal was published cargo owners remained firmly in favour of an unconditional full liberalisation of transport services in Europe (Baasch, 1996).

Still, some conditions of the revised proposal were totally unsatisfactory to north shipowners, foremost the reciprocal rather than unconditional character of market opening, whilst the link of the proposal with Euros was unacceptable to the whole industry. Notably, with the position of the UK administration driven by political ideology, strong government/industry joint statements for unilateral action against the absence of any EU decision accompanied British shipowners conditional acceptance of the reviewed proposal. These statements incorporated proposals for retaliation and/or taking a test case to the ECJ either by the government or mounted by the industry with the support of the government (DoT, 1990).

Policy Makers Reactions

The Ecosoc delivered an opinion that welcomed the new Commission proposal on the condition that harmonisation of other legislation affecting cabotage would provide the essential material and legal background for an effective EU regime (Ecosoc, 1989). Similarly, the EP was keen on promoting further integration but retained its wider concerns that harmonisation should parallel liberalisation. The report of its Transport Committee suggested amendments on that direction.[10] Specifically, it emphasised the distinctiveness of island cabotage demanding a special operating regime, an argument that had been strongly promoted in the Rapporteur's national constituency, and incorporated provisions for a longer phase out period. These EP amendments were endorsed by the Commission, which incorporated them in its final proposal (CEU, 1991b). Thus, the Commission was able, to build an institutional coalition as the EP reading supported the Commission proposal and *vice versa*, which had not been evident during the 1986 discussions. Simultaneously, by endorsing the EP amendments the Commission accommodated further conditions that sceptical stakeholders, or national administrations, had called for.

The problem that eventually perplexed the reviewed proposal was the association of cabotage with Euros. The latter was not in the minds of states either favouring or opposing the abolition of cabotage, and was disapproved, for a variety of reasons, by both shipowners and trade unions, thus this association destabilised the compromise potential. Otherwise, with the exception of the Greek administration that maintained its anti-abolitionist view, the main disagreement was in the matter of the implementation timetable. Reportedly (Tinsley, 1991), all states but Greece proceeded to the December 1990 Council meeting declaring their desire for all coasts being open to all EU operators but with a range of opinions regarding the time-scale. The UK sought for implementation at the beginning of 1993, while France and Italy argued for 1995. The Greek Minister of Mercantile Marine called the Italian presidency to defer any discussions before the presentation of a full report on the status of domestic shipping in all states.[11] The latter is a hint that, with changing positions in the domestic arena and a 'mild' proposal on the table, even this administration had started to think of a 'liberalisation after harmonisation'.

Yet, the Council presidency decided to work on the Commission's proposal insofar as it satisfied her long maintained position that some form of public service regime would be necessary when flag-preferential cabotage traffic would be eliminated. The Italian administration followed a similar presidency strategy to the one followed by the UK in 1986: a focus on what could be agreed (progressive cabotage liberalisation) disassociated from its controversial elements (the Euros initiative). A decision on the establishment of Euros as well as its would be relationship with the cabotage rule were left for future discussions, although the Italian administration was interested to see a common position on issues of registration. Transport Ministers, with the Greek official being the exception, reached an informal agreement that certain parts of the market should be opened by the end of 1993 at the latest. There was still a decision to be reached regarding the possible exemptions and the timetable of the second stage of the programme. A subsequent legal opinion issued by the Commission, suggested that while the second phase of liberalisation could be delayed, implementation of the agreed first phase after the entry into force of the SEM (beginning of 1993) could breach the Treaty and should be justified on exceptional socio-economic grounds.[12]

Satisfied by the outcome, those states that had been the most energetic advocates of liberalisation (Dk, UK, Nl) acknowledged the great concern with which the matter was viewed in other countries and on that basis alone indicated that they were prepared to make concessions, though they retained their initial hard line as a starting negotiating position.[13] This helped the Dutch presidency of the second half of 1991 to work on the unsettled issues (meanwhile the landlocked Luxembourg presidency had shown little interest to promote an accord). A political agreement was in principle reached at that point of time, though the regulation was detailed and formally adopted in 1992. The outcome was not close to optimal for several states. Yet, Denmark, the Netherlands, and the UK, did not form a blocking minority that would prevent the adoption of the Regulation. Nor did Greece, which had grounded her opposition to cabotage on vital national interests and has been among the members that sit tight in isolated national positions in the Council, decide to veto the decision by using the paragraph that the same member state had insisted to accompany the SEA amendment of Article 84(2) and provides for a unanimous voting on maritime issues of vital national interest.

The Regulation, that came into force in January 1993, satisfied the 'freedom to provide services' principle, as it stated that any vessel flying the flag of a member state is able to provide cabotage services within the EU.[14] Still it offered concessions to opposing administrations and stakeholders. National administrations retain the ability to maintain public service contracts on specific routes, under which they may regulate capacity, quality, and rate, obligations though on a non-discriminatory basis in respect of all EU-flagged vessels. A special implementation regime spans over a period of 12 years allowing considerable time to adjust to the incoming conditions, a provision that satisfied sceptical shipowning views. Antithetically to its 'national security' argument, the Greek objections on market peculiarities were taken into account so this is the last member state to implement the Regulation in 2004. Besides, the regulation provided that ships operating in island cabotage should apply the manning rules of the state in which the vessel is performing a maritime transport service, rather than the rules of its flag-state. This satisfied trade unions which maintain a privileged position *vis-à-vis* non-EU nationals in the liberalised cabotage trades. Given all these exemptions, the more protective southern national administrations would face fewer reactions in the domestic arenas.

Furthermore, the agreement increased the Commission's competence over the implementation process. The right of adopting safeguard measures in the event of 'a serious disturbance of the internal transport market due to cabotage liberalisation' is reserved for the Commission, and in limited circumstances to member states which in such events should request the Commission to adopt measures on its own initiative after consultation. The ongoing evaluation of the implementation also rests with the Commission, which monitors the functioning of the internal market and suggests further adaptations in the light of experience, when member states should submit proposals to the Commission.

In this context, the Danish and Portuguese administrations demanded the opening of cabotage to vessels operating under the international registries that they have established (DIS and MAR flags respectively). However, the Commission's first evaluation report did not propose the amendment of the initial regulation (CEU, 1995e). The lower manning costs of these flags, due to less nationality requirements, offer a competitive advantage to vessels registered under these flags so their full access to EU cabotage would be opposed by other shipowners. Dutch and Greek shipowning associations have already expressed their opposition (Peppa, 1996). Moreover, as the minimum manning requirements allow the employment of non-nationals these flags are strongly opposed by all trade unions (Tselentis, 1996). Then, several national administrations had based their support or final agreement to the cabotage regulation with a view to creating more satisfactory condition for their national flags. While the establishment of international flags has not been followed by several states whenever this is the case (Dk, Fr, Nl, Pr, Sp, UK) operating conditions differ considerably.

This was a proposal, therefore, with limited support either by governments other than those already offering access to these vessels (British and German domestic trades are fully liberalised), or private actors who were preparing for the implementation of the existing agreement. The main problem would not be the small MAR, especially as these ships operate within their national cabotage. However, allowing DIS vessels in EU cabotage trade could have twofold significance. First, it would allow the operation of vessels enjoying a considerable regulatory advantage. Second, DIS vessels do not operate in the Danish cabotage, although waivers may be granted. Providing them a permanent access to the cabotage of other states would open the potential for market liberalisation to other third flags. The feeling has been that the reopening of the discussion could create the potential of moving towards a different direction (Goulielmos, 1996).

Indeed, the Commission adopted the view that the 'delicate political compromise between the positions of Northern and Southern member states' (CEU, 1995e) should not be amended to include the specific provision and, at least to date, rejects the request. To the extent, however, that the proposal serves the idea of market liberalism, the Commission argues that modification of the national legislation might be one way to give DIS and MAR vessels permanent access to the cabotage trade of the other member state. The Council of December 1995 had a debate on the timeliness of extending certain derogations granted in 1992 and on the EU's position concerning the possible extension but agreed to return to the issues in the future on the basis of a new Commission report.[15]

In 1998 the Commission put forward a proposal for an amendment of the initial Regulation (CEU, 1998). The proposal alters the allocation of responsibilities between the flag-state and the host-state for matters relating to the crew. Specifically, it distinguishes between (a) ships providing regular passenger transport and ferry services, for which the rules of the host-state (i.e. the country in which the ship provides its services) apply in respect of the proportion of EU nationals in the crew and the rules of the flag-state apply to any other matter relating to the crew; and (b) other ships engaged in cabotage, for which the rules of the flag-state apply to all matters relating to the crew. The EP has approved the proposal subject to certain amendments, and the proposal is before the Council for a common position, following the rules governing the co-decision procedure.

The latest report regarding the implementation of the EU Regulation reviews that during the period 1997-98, two cabotage segments were liberalised in the southern member states: services involving the transport of strategic goods (oil, oil products, drinking water) and services by ships smaller than 650 grt. As a consequence, the foreign flag share in the total cabotage trade of the southern member states rose from 8.35 million tonnes in 1995 to 9.05 million tonnes in 1997. The participation of non-national EU carriers in the liberalised sector of the southern European cabotage on the basis of the Regulation decreased in relative terms from 9.4% of the liberalised cargoes in 1995 to 8.1% in 1997, but increased in terms of volume carried from 3 to 5.75 million tonnes (CEU, 2000d).

Shortsea Shipping as Part of the Horizontal Approach

Meanwhile, in September 1991, a Commission communication to the other EU institutions put on the agenda the need to develop an EU policy framework dealing explicitly with the integral European shortsea shipping sector. Although it did not include regulatory proposals, the document advocated a new strategy to prepare the EU maritime transport system for the advent of the SEM. Grounding on the already high trade and transport demand in Europe, and expecting their further increase due to the completion of the internal market and the transition process in central and eastern Europe, the Commission documented its aim as to promote the competitiveness and encourage the greater use of transport along Europe's geographic coastline plus the Mediterranean, the Baltic Sea, and Black sea coasts (CEU, 1991a, p. 5). In 1992, the White Paper on the CTP strategy expressed a similar aim (CEU, 1992a). Analysis derived from three strong trends: the growing demand for transport services; the increasing imbalance between the different modes; and the stagnation of the investments in maritime transport infrastructure. This intention was re-addressed in the 1992 Green Paper wherein shortsea shipping was identified as a priority field in accordance with the need to reconcile transport demand with the requirements of the environment (CEU, 1992b). Motivated by the environmental and energy efficiency advantages of the mode, the Commission indicated that the potential shift of cargo from land modes to the maritime mode should be fully developed.

The novel 'shortsea concept' was introduced as a joint idea of two Commission departments, DG-VII (transport) and DG-III (industry) respectively. However, it is an idea associated with the latter. As an interviewee recalls, the programme was adopted soon after a change of the Transport Commissioner and when such changes take place a new Commissioner needs time to be informed about his portfolio before promoting issues (Economou, 1996). But when DG-III approached maritime transport as a derived market that had to be linked with industrial policy, DG-VII enthusiastically promoted the initiative, aiming to undo deficiencies of previous policies: Is view was that there was an imbalance not only in the work of the Commission but also at a member states level: there had been a lot of work to promote the use of rail as an alternative to road but not shortsea shipping (Ferreira, 1996). Then, by addressing shortsea shipping through an horizontal approach, the Commission decided an 'essential and by nature horizontal change of direction ensued by the recognition that maritime transport had to become much more a part of the transport policy than it had been before' (ibid.). According to its then director, the maritime division of DG-VII endorsed the view that it should generate more efforts than in the past on developing the shortsea shipping sector as an alternative to land transport (Blonk, 1994).

These developments were followed by some practical measures. The development of multimodal trans-European transport network (TENs) had started as a project to complete the inland networks, and expand them to inland waterways and air transport in order to accommodate the expected demand growth. Road and rail links to ports were included only for the lagging regions of the EU. It was only when the Community institutions started thinking about shortsea shipping, that ports became a component of this concept (Morales, 1996). In deploying a policy for shortsea shipping improvements of ports, as well as their connection and interoperability with the other modal networks, were regarded as essential. In this vein, the EU legislation on combined transport was amended extending the traditional combination of inland modes to include sea journeys as well.

Such decisions gave access to financial resources, distributed by the EU institutions, for the economic development of maritime transport as part of the European combined network (i.e. the Pilot Action for Combined Transport framework). Then, shortsea shipping projects were included in R&D programmes. The normal DG-VII budget provides funds for actions with a view of promoting shortsea shipping, and the 4th R&D Framework had for the first time a line for the development of maritime transport technologies. Although these are a recent development, which implies unfamiliarity with the provided frameworks, several market actors have started working on these opportunities. Even the Greek shipowners, who remained unconvinced of the usefulness of an EU shortsea shipping policy, acknowledge that available funds are of strategic importance and the 4th Research Framework has been a unique opportunity for the modernisation of the maritime transport services and the promotion of shortsea shipping at a European and Balkan level (Mavrommati, 1996).

Interest Groups Mobilisation

Shipowners welcomed the 'new product of the Commission's work' as a sign of a more constructive EU policy development than the policy approaches and ideas that the Commission tried in the 1980s (Southorn, 1996). Compared to the failure of the 1989 measures, it was conceived as a positive move that could have to a certain extent some impact. When it became apparent that external factors assisted the European institutions to think of it more seriously, their Euro-federation adjusted its lobbying practice:

Realising that the advancement of the environmental friendly transport modes is among the main targets of the EU transport policy, ECSA decided to campaign for a greater institutional focus on the potential of the shortsea shipping sector. Therefore 'it put some views to the European institutions regarding possible EU initiatives' because 'the potential of a greater shortsea shipping share of the, increasing in size, modal pie'. Expecting further progress of a policy that could enhance their competitive position, ECSA formed a special committee on shortsea shipping to detail shipowners' views. To them, the real test was whether the initiative would go beyond a very initial phase; so, they accompanied their reaction with demands for a more detailed programme. The emphasis was on promoting port infrastructure and offshore facilities, as developments that could benefit the position of the sector. Given the Commission decisions that followed, they assess that 'this was proved to be the right moment to demand a greater emphasis on the sector's potential' (Economou, 1996).

When the Commission introduced its initiative, it expected shipowners to react more positively than other industries, as by nature shipowners have much more to gain by boosting shortsea shipping than ports or shippers (Vanroye, 1996). Indeed, shippers perceived it as a policy serving purposes other than those of their immediate interests. According to the European Shippers' Council secretariat, this was just a policy related to European shipping industry, employment, offshore industries, and questions like the environment, and what is politically right or not. From a general perspective all of them are very important issues. But they are not the immediate concern of shippers. Shippers want to use good shipping services and only secondly are concerned whether European shipping provides these services, or not.

Shippers were surprised by the emphasis that was given to 'the outcome of a coalition between the Commission and certain industries, pushed forward by the Commissioner responsible for the industry, who was concerned about employment with a particularly clear European view'. Notably, at that point of time their Euro-federation was not yet located in Brussels. A year later, they assessed this as a characteristic contributing to the lack of an essential information exchange with the EU institutions. Still, as they were not being particular interested in a modal shift, shippers remained unimpressed by the decision of the European institutions to promote a policy that 'is probably exaggerated simply because most of the cargoes that are on the roads cannot be shifted anywhere else' (Baasch, 1996).

However, they have developed a more positive attitude towards the new policy agenda. This is not the product of mere environmental consciousness, which is anyway subject to cost effectiveness.[16] Shippers identified possible benefits, particularly the potential of leading to a more competitive maritime process that would widen their modal options. Dissatisfactions from national policies strengthened a greater attention to EU initiatives, giving rise to expectations of a more constructive policy framework. For instance, British shippers 'welcome what has occurred and would like to see more' (Richards, 1996). This is not least because actions of the national government had been assessed as detracting UK based shippers from the use of shortsea shipping. The prospect of EU developments to alter the unfavourable direction of the national policy became evident when, following the EU initiative, the British DoT decided to begin consultations on the possibility of permitting, similarly to the rest of Europe, specific technical concessions for intermodal operators. Previously excluded from consultation, British shippers came to see the EU agenda as a means of achieving things in the domestic arena.

By addressing port issues as an integral part of this agenda, the Commission initiative greatly affected the views of the port industry, as well as the organisation of the representation of these views. In the absence of any general directive, or policy statement, concerning an EU ports policy having been drafted, port authorities had preferred to remain informally associated, primarily for coordinating their activities within a working group organised by DG-VII for almost two decades. But the new EU strategy produced the view that a more coherent interest representation was essential if the demands of shipowners and the willingness of the Commission were not to develop a common policy with a negative influence on their activities. Specifically, the port industry estimated that the Commission could drive for structural intervention that would interfere with the commercial flexibility of ports and distort their commercial position and success, when the bulk of shortsea shipping works extremely well. To port authorities, there was no necessity to intervene either on issues of competition or infrastructure, because the industry was undergoing changes automatically by basic economic necessity. Appreciating, however, that in several cases shortsea shipping is not integrated to logistics and multimodal transport operations, those responsible for European ports decided to get better organised in order to ensure that the agenda is directed towards the question how to expand maritime trade where it is possible (Jeffery, 1996). They formed their own European association in 1993 but according to ESPO secretariat it was already late. As they had not been organised at all when the policy was introduced they found the whole policy designed in a 'biased and inefficient direction' (Suykens and Le Garrec, 1996).

In a similar line, private port operators responded to the developments arguing for the necessity to refrain from any structural intervention in the port industry, or the development of an all-embracing port policy, and decided to articulate it collectively through direct contacts with EU institutions. On the other hand, owing to the development of the industry to resent national deregulatory and privatisation policies, they recognised a useful initiative that could advance further deregulatory moves in European ports (Verhoeven, 1996). It is the absence of rapid progress of the EU policy towards that direction is conceived as a negative development ascribed to the fact that 'the Commission tries hard to develop a maritime strategy but specifically for port issues it has not managed to find how ports can be developed as a part of a coherent strategy' (Laino, 1996).

A major problem for the port industry derived from the fact that the EU move to promote shortsea shipping was followed by a greater attention to infrastructure issues and the inclusion of ports within the TENs project. Ports differ from other parts of the transport network insofar as they are more in competition with each other than other modes; when funds are allocated to a port and advance its development they do so largely at the expense of nearby ports, and therefore introduce questions of distorting competition. Initially, the industry complained about its exclusion from the first TENs plans and demanded funds for optimal road and rail links to any EU port. But when the focus turned to port infrastructure per se complaints escalated with port authorities firmly opposing a plan of 'ports of community interest' as a discriminatory practice. To them, ports like any other commercial enterprise should be responsible for the finance of their infrastructure. Funding of port projects was acceptable only in the case of the cohesion fund countries. Still, given the heterogeneous characteristics of European ports (cf. Pallis, 1997), objections were mainly coming from those ports located in the northern part of the EU and compete strongly with each other. Many ports in the southern member states, which could nevertheless continue to be financed by the regional and cohesion funds, are public entities and intra-state competition is less significant to their authorities and operators (Hatsakos, 1996).

Another industry that demonstrated a growing interest in the new EU agenda was freight forwarding. As changes accompanying the progress towards a SEM had eliminated customs' documentation in intra-EU trade, forwarders looked for further deregulation of the transportation process. Expecting the support for the maritime mode to change the operative framework and increase modal choices, their Euro-federation predominantly demanded EU measures to advance the transparency of port tariffs. This was grounded on the port users need to known precisely the costs of alternatives options and not be charged any hidden tarrifs (Van de Perre, 1996). They also advocated the inclusion of ports in TENs as a means to provide more opportunities for those operating close to the ports that would be funded. The intensity of the articulation of these interests was disadvantaged by the minimal interest of several CLECAT members in maritime transport, and by internal disputes. While the British association has withdrawn from CLECAT due to 'the ineffectiveness of the organisation', large companies discussed the possibilities of a breakthrough and the formation of another organisation (Sangster, 1996). These moves limited the resources and subsequently the activities of the specific interest group.

On the other hand, labour representatives did not denote any significant interest in the shortsea project. National trade unions, and their European committee, remained focused to social and employment issues and more 'traditional' industrial problems affecting working opportunities of seafarers, like FoC shipping. As the new concept was not directly addressing such problems, labour demonstrated little interest in providing an input into the debate. Notwithstanding that, CTWUEC emphasised the contradiction between the initiative to promote shortsea shipping and the parallel decision to liberalise cabotage within a policy framework that rejects the creation of a EU maritime space (De Villele, 1996). Moreover, they criticised the short-term nature of the initiative suggesting that more long-term movements are essential for a project that goes beyond the EU and demands cooperation between EU and non-EU countries (Steinvorth, 1996).

Maritime Industries Forum

The increasing interest of the preceding actors to develop a stance *vis-à-vis* the 'new' EU agenda, and to devote resources to its articulation through EU-level interest groups, is inextricably linked to another Commission initiative, that is the evolution of the Maritime Industries Forum (MIF). A critical proposal of the Commission strategy was for the institutionalisation of the cooperation between policy makers and stakeholders. Specifically, the Commission proposed the creation of a forum for an efficient and a permanent dialogue between representatives from all the industries concerned, trade unions, research institutes, MEPs, the Ecosoc, representatives of national administrations, and the Commission itself (CEU, 1991a).

This was a multi-target idea aiming to satisfy both Commission necessities and industries' demands. According to a Commission official, the industries wanted a forum to discuss their own problems, but the MIF was also in the interest of the Commission: instead of having all these associations lobbying on the wrong side it was better to create a type of organisation in which they could be together and produce common thoughts and recommendations (Ferreira, 1996). Through closer vertical and horizontal links the Commission would secure the consistency of business-governments cooperation and provide the structure for the different industries to meet regularly and develop formal and informal networking. National administrations would also be involved more consistently in the development of the EU policy, at least by coordinating the activities of this forum at national or regional level. Furthermore, it would engage the European institutions to a contribution to the development of policy proposals to a greater extent than what is assumed by the EU decision-making rules. This initiative would be the medium for the active contribution of all actors on the identification of common aims, EU level projects and market-lead strategies, as well as on the definition and detailed preparation of common policy initiatives.

The MIF commenced its work in January 1992. Policy makers and interest groups decided to set up three panels that parallel the agenda of the Commission, thus one panel was devoted to shortsea shipping.[17] In June 1993, the MIF agreed to a detailed report that focused on the work of this panel. Being critical of the inefficiencies in various EU ports, it called for more and improved port services, more competition in services, and increased charging fees openness. This report also referred to the liability system for goods carried on shortsea routes as 'an impediment to the transfer of goods from land modes to sea'. Finally, it demanded R&D programmes to help the sector adjust to the new types of demand.[18] These suggestions, including a call to the associations representing shippers and shipowners for discussing, together with the Commission, potential changes in the liability system, informed the Commission's conclusion on 'the first tangible results of the horizontal strategy' (CEU, 1993d). Therein, the preparation of further proposals for concrete action was also declared.

The first meetings of the shortsea panel were organised only by the Commission. An official participating in these meetings recalls that in the beginning the feeling was that the industry was trying to reinvent the wheel and there would not be anything new (Vanroye, 1996). However, the situation has changed: the meetings are organised by the representatives of the industry, who have gained experience through the discussions and the participating Commission provides a supportive role. This process represents an effective medium for the Commission, as 'it is able to bring the problems to them and a lot of things to discuss' (Ferreira, 1996), so, the panel of shortsea shipping is by far the one that has more meetings and has produced the more constructive results. The input of the Commission can be detected in the MIF decision to be organised through a network of national and regional working groups. This plan was initially drawn up by the Commission, which wanted to formalise consultation. The Commission also preferred to see actions that fulfil the EU objectives taken at the lowest possible level, in order to promote the idea of subsidiarity and give in practice more practical sense to the power of its initiatives.

To the Commission, the shortsea panel has also been helpful in channelling the industry away from 'unrealistic' policy demands. During the first MIF meetings there were calls for the Commission to support through the Community funding, the shipowner to buy new ships for starting a new life in specific ports or that the Commission should support the operating costs, for instance port dues, crew costs, or fuel. Because to finance the mobile assets to assist the setting of specific services would result in complaints from other companies, the Commission was of the view that these were not realistic demands, although this would be a way to compete with the other transport modes. Through the MIF, 'fortunately, the industry realised that this would be a very sensitive development and they did not mention it in their documents, although some people mention it to the Commission' (Ferreira, 1996).

As a result, the MIF enjoys a privileged status in the making of the CMTP. According to an interviewee, even though the MIF does not have any legislative powers and does not play any role within the scheme of the EU, it is a Commission generated body. So, what is discussed and raised at the MIF is important and is going to be taken by DG VII, and be formulated to European initiatives (Verhoeven, 1996). Indeed, while there are other industrial initiatives that attempt to have an input on the policy making process, the Commission's *modus operandi* is selective. On the one hand, 'in policy terms the Commission does not have to co-ordinate and consult all the industrial initiatives, or define its policy on their inputs', on the other hand, 'the very constructive MIF reports are examined very carefully and many of their recommendations have been taken onboard by the Commission' (Vanroye, 1996). This practice is not, however, unconstrained. The dimension of the MIF recommendations is critical. There are issues that the member states have the last say on and the DGs cannot do anything to change the existing legislation, even if they desire so, or problems involving more that one department of the Commission so there is a lengthy process of discussion and cooperation between the DGs.

Interest Groups and the MIF Shortsea Panel

Most shipowners welcomed the MIF as a means of clarifying what business demand from the European policy and what they actually receive Still, when the Commission published its proposal, the industry was surprised, not well prepared and, hence, sceptical on its potential direction (Economou, 1996). Five years later it was recognising that the MIF has been able to look at practical difficulties of shortsea shipping, and 'the fact that it is looking for the way forward gives an added weight to what has been achieved' (Southorn, 1996).

Estimating that the MIF would be 'more than another forum' ECSA welcomed the idea to chair its shortsea panel. To a Brussels based executive of the association, shipowners proved right in practice: The major product has been the generation of a habit to discuss and act at European level. Many of the European level groups that were involved in the MIF had just been formatted and did not have the experience of what it means to have a voice at EU level. The MIF gave them the opportunity to realise how ECSA and ECS were operated, as both of them had already a coherent view regarding European policy developments. So, 'looking at some smaller organisations it can be realised that before the MIF they did not have an equal treatment by the European institutions' (Economou, 1996). This process has significant benefits for the shipowners themselves as through the MIF they had the opportunity to communicate with these small organisations and realise that there are common interests where they could work together instead of going separately and publishing individual positions.

Since the beginning of the project, however, Greek shipowners remained remarkably critical. Specifically, they objected to the MIF as another bureaucratic secretariat that in practice challenges the fundamental global character of shipping (Peppa, 1996). To the then vice-president of the Greek union, the MIF provided 'an example of the Commission's attempt to breakdown international solutions to shipping'.[19] The dominance of deep-sea operators, and the minimal interest by shortsea operators which enjoyed the closed domestic market, may ground that position. An additional justification to this stance is that Greek shipowners feel happy with the nature of their relationships with the Greek Ministry of Mercantile Marine and are able to represent their views at the European level through the very active representation of Greece in the COREPER. So, they believe that they have little to gain from the MIF. According to them the latter is a mechanism introduced by the Commission and those interests that do not have the potential to influence COREPER but wanted to be represented more effectively. The fact that the state executives dealing with the actions of the MIF in Greece are those of the Ministry of Industry rather than that of Mercantile Marine added to the dissatisfaction of Greek shipowners (Goulielmos, 1996). Notwithstanding that, Greek shipowners decided to provide an input to the shortsea panel expressing a high interest on infrastructure matters and the debate on the role of the ports.

The shippers' reaction to the establishment of the MIF reflects the scepticism regarding the whole shortsea initiative. They are less enthusiastic about what has been achieved (Baasch, 1996) and challenge its usefulness. Concentrating on a different agenda, European shippers have conceived the MIF as a mechanism contributing to the redirection of the CMTP. Besides, it perplexed the policy-making arena by bringing in more market players and respective interest groups that, because of organisational structures, market conditions, or the themes of the previous EU policy agenda, had little input in the process. Nevertheless, whilst arguing that a permanent industries forum is not a panacea as the Commission thinks sometimes, they see the shortsea panel as a process that may direct minds and find solutions in the long-term but is difficult to achieve something in the short-term (Southorn, 1996).

The newcomers have a more positive approach to the activities of the forum. The Euro-federations representing the port industry offered their support because there was the need for maritime industries to have a unified voice (Suykens and Le Garrec, 1996). Port authorities have focused on the necessity for MIF to move on areas where the whole maritime sector can work together. Private port operators share this stance; hence, the two interest groups have closely coordinated their actions aiming to promote it more effectively. Yet, as the MIF shortsea panel has not redirected the Commission agenda, ESPO and FEPORT appear to be the most disappointed interest groups. They are unhappy with the critical analysis of ports in the MIF reports, especially as so many of these critical arguments about ports have been reproduced in the shortsea shipping document by the Commission. The nature of the problem according to the FEPORT secretariat is the product of the fact that the MIF is 'a forum where shipowners, which is a strong lobby, tend to dominate when the position of ports could and should be stronger' (Verhoeven, 1996).

Freight forwarders remain more supportive of the MIF shortsea panel feeling that 'the panel has done a great job, and has been the main factor behind the developments' (Van de Perre, 1996). With a great part of the ongoing debate concentrated on port infrastructure and tariffs transparency, CLECAT conceives the main advantage to be the fact that this mechanism gave the industry the opportunity to promote useful proposals. Notably, the British forwarders association (BIFA) that has withdrawn from CLECAT since 1992 and follows EU policy developments through the British Business Bureau does not have any contacts with the MIF. In fact, BIFA was not aware at all of the MIF presence.

Whilst initially regarding the MIF as a positive step, trade unions became progressively more sceptical. There was no reason to reject the specific form of the debate and, importantly for organised labour, it was a sign that the Commission acknowledged that the maritime industry is not only shipowners but a whole range of knowledge behind several European industries which needs to be maintained (Orrell, 1996). Yet, trade unions believe that in practice MIF has not produced a great deal of positive results but some good reports during its first plenary sessions (De Villele, 1996). This is not irrelevant to the fact that labour tried to redirect the agenda that the Commission had put forward but they failed to do so. Although they pressed for the establishment of a panel on human resources, such panel was not established. Instead there is only a working group on the subject, resulting in growing scepticism. According to the CTWUEC secretariat, it remains doubtful whether the MIF discussions have contributed to the current EU policy approach at all.

Policy Makers Reactions

The Commission was of the view that part of its responsibilities was to act when governments need to be co-ordinated at a bigger scale, so it had the competence to promote initiatives like shortsea shipping and the MIF (Vanroye, 1996). Yet, these innovative moves did not match the priorities and policies of some national administrations, a critical parameter that influenced the reactions of the latter. The debate had started with the Delors concept to harmonise the different national environments but was rather problematic as the member states faced different interests (Goulielmos, 1996). Moreover, the Commission's initiative challenged well-established administrative hierarchies in the national domestic arenas. Being a common DG-VII and DG-III initiative, and involving other Commission Departments, like DG-XII (environment), it introduced a departmentalisation of responsibilities not necessary being followed at national level. This unconventional administration of the project was a reason (reinforced by the aforementioned, and inextricably linked, negative Greek shipowners' reactions, as well as the minor interests of specialised trade unions) that impeded the willingness of the Greek Ministry of Mercantile Marine to open a policy debate at national level. When it was realised that 'shortsea represents a case that has become bigger than the idea and everybody talks about it, although this concept itself talks only about a part of maritime transport' the initiative became reluctantly at play in the domestic arena as well (Bantias, 1996).

The reactions of the British administration have been more critical. To the UK Department of Transport the new concept represented another unnecessary involvement of the Commission in an otherwise liberalised, thus competitive, maritime market (Mann, 1996). When the EU began to focus on shortsea shipping, the British government anticipated that there was limited scope to do so. It endorsed a series of initiatives to encourage a shift of traffic away from road but within the traditional concept of combined transport that excluded the sea journeys.[20] At the moment that the Commission decided to move forward, the DoT produced its own draft, which was not dependent at all on the Commission's work, and concluded that this concept would have much more influence on the continent than the

UK. Therefore, there was no justification for developing in detail national level policies or implementing non-obligatory EU frameworks. The MIF was useful for different parts of the industry but not to governments, hence, the DoT expressed little interest in its development.

However, such critical views did not restrict the Council from reaching a political agreement only a month after the Commission's initiative (November 1991) arguing for the need to develop an EU policy addressing European shortsea shipping, and to put in place the MIF. Some member states agreed and decided to work in the direction fostered by the Commission and the EP wanting or believing that moving cargoes from road onto rail and sea can solve a number of environmental problems. These states are identifiable by Europe's geography: shortsea must be a possible combination, and this is the case in the North Sea and Portugal, but only in certain areas of the rest of the Mediterranean sea (Baasch, 1996).

Before the first results of the MIF had been published, the Ecosoc demanded further and speedier progress of the shortsea policy (Ecosoc, 1993a). Specifically, it recommended priority policy measures aiming to optimise shortsea shipping, a coherent intermodal strategy for long distance intra-EU transport, and specialised port installations to be built at strategic points to handle this traffic, all of them to be taken in parallel with the lifting of the cabotage restrictions. Following the submission of opinions by its Committees on the Environment, Transport, and Economic and Monetary affairs and Industrial Policy respectively, the EP received a resolution responding to the horizontal approach including the progress of the EU policy on shortsea shipping. When the first of the preceding EP Committees focused on the necessary inclusion of maritime safety issues, the two others gave favourable opinions on the Commission initiative emphasising the need for follow-up action. The latter referred to the development of the external dimension of the EU policy to open competition on a reciprocal basis, and concrete action after having the agreement of the industries involved. Moreover, the EP focused on the disadvantages produced by the Commission's departmentalisation. In this vein, it emphasised that the Commission should ensure that its own internal organisation and the many different DGs involved respond effectively and show the proper leadership for the development of the common policy.[21]

Still, some MEPs were not entirely satisfied with the development of the MIF. Several regional authorities had advocated that the presence of an industrial forum would create a powerful lobby and centralise the EU policy-making, thus minimising their input in the policy-making process (Seidel, 1996). MEPs who embraced these views decided to sponsor politically the creation of a non-profit organisation targeting a stronger regional impact than that provided by the MIF.[22] The idea was to provide a permanent secretariat that would build more on social issues, training, employment, environmental issues, protection of coastlines, as well as a stronger regional approach. In 1993 this movement was backed by the EP and supported by the Commission as long as it did not result in unnecessary duplication with the activities of the MIF, and transformed to AMRIE, with the principal aim of bringing together different organisations and lobbying for policy developments in a proactive way.

So, the EP has provided to regional interests the infrastructure to develop the necessary networking to put 'justifiable' cases to the Commission, and the political relevance to act at the European level, which is not available when regional organisations articulate their interests alone (Seidel, 1996). The feeling that the Commission initiatives continued to favour the central areas of the EU also led peripheral regions to join forces and articulate their interests collectively.[23] This infrastructure has been used by several local organisations, and effectively promoted human resources stabilisation and more impetus to research. Notably, apart from capitalising on an alternative road to an insight into the EU initiatives, its membership has also used it to establish links with member states governments through the MEPs (AMRIE, 1995)

The 'Shortsea Shipping' Document

This phase of the common policy led to the publication, in summer 1995, of a Commission document outlining specific policy actions to be undertaken at EU level, and where appropriate by the national, regional, and local authorities, even the industries themselves, in order to improve the quality and efficiency of the shortsea shipping (CEU, 1995a). The first axis of this programme was directed to the port element, and especially infrastructure involving European institutions in devoting funds, and member states contributing through the submission of projects and the distribution of the available regional funds. Therein, the Commission declared that, because of the difficulties in designating ports of European interest, it would not list a defined strategic or priority network that should be constructed within a set time. Furthermore, the Commission announced its decision to study the transparency of port accounts and publish guidelines on state aids to ports. The second axis referred to further R&D actions. In line with the EP demands, the third axis referred to external relations and focused on the Commission actions to get stakeholders and policy makers together with their counterparts from non-EU states. The final axis documented further financial and technical assistance to setting up working groups to specify further actions and translate them into EU policies. Today, these groups exist in several member states (i.e. Ger, B, Nl, Pr, Sp). Yet, their formation remains subject to national governments' interpretation. The way that the UK translated this particular initiative was to devise the lobbying system as an informal national roundtable (Richards, 1996).

The preparation of this document had been announced at the end of 1993 following the welcome of the shortsea concept by the European institutions and stakeholders. However, the Commission found difficulties to detail the document as by going to the MIF meetings it realised that the concept to promote the use of shortsea shipping without creating artificial advantages over the other transport modes is very much related to industrial actions (Ferreira, 1996). The problems amounted to practical difficulties. To give an example, the MIF demanded measures to ease unfavourable documentation procedures, arguing that the current situation results in a modal discrimination. The support by DG-VII was not enough as the responsible DG-XXI emphasised the potential of the simplification to allow owners to act fraudulently. Hence, the issue became subject to a study rather than regulatory developments.

In fact, any legal instrument did not accompany the document. Nevertheless, the Commission decided to produce a policy document that would support the MIF work and detail 'non-legislative but important' policy initiatives. Its authors acknowledge that, in the absence of regulatory implications, it seemed more a Green paper for setting policy options but pointed out that there is still a comprehensive action programme to be implemented which without our document would never be part of the debate (Morales, 1996). The progress of the R&D programme is conceived as an indication that through the Commission's political action the commercial side of shortsea shipping has been promoted, and the shipowners use elements of the European policy to be more competitive.

An additional major effect of this document advocated the raising of a political interest and debate for the usefulness of the EU policy at regional, national and European level. In other words, the Commission activities created a critical momentum. The 1991 paper (introduction of the horizontal approach) and the MIF have resulted in several actions and studies on shortsea shipping. The periodical Commission reports revise all the actions that have been made affecting the sector and promotes further policy actions. The short shipping document has created 'a very good political basis from which policy makers and the industry can start translating the philosophy into action' (Ferreira, 1996).

Interest Groups Mobilisation

As this document closely followed the conclusions of the MIF panel, incorporating limited 'new' proposals, it was conceived as the confirmation of policy directions that have already been agreed. However, all the private actors acknowledge to its presence a noticeable importance. Whilst none of the Commission's political documents seems to have substantial practical effects there is a major effect, which is political awareness (Verhoeven, 1996). Although the document did not result in a comprehensive European policy, the, supportive of its content, shipowners emphasised the confidence that it has given on the effectiveness of the consultation process. Despite the fact that from a first view the shortsea document seemed insignificant, as it was all very interlinked to the MIF, they emphasise that it is different to have an official document taking some MIF thoughts and publishing them. This is because 'if the industry's views get corporate like that and then reappear in a Commission's documents it means that the message is getting across' (Richards, 1996). In this vein, they welcomed its presence, though more than the recommendations of the MIF were included into the publication in order to accommodate wider EU issues.

Those actors that had been critical of the outcome of the MIF discussion underlined the 'negative' implications of the process. The unconvinced port industry representatives stressed that the Commission's document and the EP support raise the profile of shortsea shipping at the commercial level as a viable mode. But port representatives did not consider this as necessarily right because 'it implicates tremendous amounts of risk and money, when businesses do not know how they are going to compete' (Jeffery, 1996). In the position documents that they submitted to a hearing organised by the EP Transport Committee, ESPO and FEPORT reacted strongly to the 'very wrong idea that the Commission has about shortsea shipping' (Suykens and Le Garrec, 1996). Arguing that the document simplistically overemphasises port deficiencies, they objected the study and development of guidelines on port tariffs, on the grounds of 'difficulties in defining what is state aid', or 'where a port starts or ends?' (i.e. which part of the hinterland should be accounted as part of the port – also: Verhoeven, 1996). These calls were without any effect though and the investigation announced by the Commission is underway. Finally, to trade unions the determination of the Commission to put forward a clear framework could prove useful if it would overcome omissions on the social side (Orrell, 1996). So, since its publication the CTWUEC focused on the weakness of the social aspects, and lobbied the Ecosoc and the Transport Committee of the EP of the need for a better expression of the employment aspects for the European seafarers that had been overlooked completely in the Commission document.

Policy Makers Reactions

Following a report by its Transport Committee, the EP adopted a resolution, which welcomed the Commission's document as a means to speed up a comprehensive policy, but objected to two of its dimensions. Firstly, the fact that through its actions to improve efficiency in ports the Commission 'almost as an aside and in an annex', drew up a general seaport policy. Second, the EP considered the absence of any social aspect as a serious omission from both the social and the economic point of view. Therefore, it called for concrete action to increase the number of qualified personnel that is a vital part of the quality and reliability of the sector. These priorities should be developed in a close liaison with the MIF shortsea panel in order to establish further policy priorities but also monitoring of the relevant actions and achievements.[24]

The respective Ecosoc opinion, which was drafted by a consultant of Greek shipowners, was more critical (Ecosoc, 1996). The Ecosoc pointed out that the EU approach needed a detailed analysis of the different market segments, rather than addressing the whole sector in an integral way. Moreover, it focused on the social dimension albeit in a different direction than the EP. The emphasis was on the essential 'flexibility' of labour, i.e. in working conditions in ports. The Committee of the Regions also had an input in the process, publishing its first ever report on CMTP issues. Proceeding to more generalised comments, the CoR stressed the need for harmonising national regulatory and social systems, as they could have only positive repercussions on the efficiency of the sector. Happy to see local authorities participate in the implementation of several measures, it demanded a further role for them in the policy making as well as the support of the work they had already carried out (CoR, 1996). Off the record, this has been assessed as a 'not well drafted' document, even though its critics stress that this could be understood by the inexperience of the Committee.

The publication of the Commission's document found Spain holding the Council presidency. Being one of the first states to support the EU-level activities, its national administration submitted a paper for discussion on further actions including measures to improve the qualifications and flexibility of the personnel. In line with the ongoing reform of its national ports policy,[25] Spain also prioritised the need for harmonised and uniform accountancy systems for European ports. So, it used its presidency capacity to promote the idea of a system of common criteria aiming to reach an acceptable level of transparency in the field, the latter being already part of the Commission proposals. The December 1995 Council debated the Commission's initiative and agreed on the text of a favourable resolution that would formally be approved without discussion during the forthcoming Council session.[26] Though it incorporated the additional measures that the Spanish administration had brought forward, the resolution text made no reference to the considerations of the EP and the Ecosoc regarding the social dimension of the common policy. On the other hand, the Council recognised the need to achieve a balanced growth and a positive integration of shortsea shipping into the intermodal transport chain. To this end, it 'invited' the Commission as well as the member states to endorse active and comprehensive policy-action.

This decision concluded a process that succeeded in establishing the promotion of shortsea as a priority EU goal and in 'tying' the policy makers on further actions. Despite the power of this vision, however, it is still unclear whether this will finally result in a comprehensive policy framework. Nevertheless, and most importantly to this analysis, within the new situation the outcome depends heavily on the, as yet uncertain, success of the EU policy makers to develop a long-term strategy. The view that has prevailed is that, 'the Commission, the EP and the Council try to find a programme at a European level and when they manage to do that shortsea shipping will become more a national issue' (Laino, 1996).

Indeed, the Commission produced a progress report in 1997 and the Council responded to the progress report by inviting the Commission to submit progress reports at two-yearly intervals, which should include an evaluation of the results of the actions undertaken in order to promote short sea shipping.[27] In 1999 the Commission produced its second two-yearly progress report (CEU, 1999), wherein and it also addressed some broader issues and recommended further actions to be undertaken by four distinguished actors: national and sub-national level authorities, maritime industries, the port industry alone, and the Commission itself. All these actions are considered as part of the application of the Community law and the establishment of the internal European market.

Summary

This chapter contained the analysis of the progress towards a common policy on shortsea shipping and the transformation of such policy to a subject figuring dominantly in the EU agenda. Following the establishment of the freedom to provide services between member states in 1986, the EU finally adopted a regulation for applying the freedom to provide services within the member states domestic maritime markets. Moreover, in recent years the Commission and the other EU institutions have increasingly concerned themselves with a policy promoting the use of shortsea shipping in Europe. Despite the difficulties in establishing a comprehensive legislative framework, or the doubts as to the feasibility of the operation, it is clear that the EU has created a policy context and commitment to further action administered at the EU-level, though implemented at national, local, regional, or even pan-European level.

Notes

1   France, Spain, and Portugal, reserved 'government' cargoes to national flag ships. France reserved 66% of her crude oil imports and 40% of her coal imports to French cargoes. Spain reserved oil cereals and tobacco to Spanish fleets (Davies, 1992)
2   Denmark was the only one of these member states having some but of inconsiderable total cabotage restrictions (regarding small so-called 'paragraph ships' under 500 grt

and trade to Faeroes islands) and agreed to abolish them.

3   See the debate of the Select committee of the UK House of Lords: House of Lords, 1986.

4   This paragraph is based on the views presented by the respective interests groups to a Hearing organised by the EP on 26.2.1986 (for a detailed presentation: Bredima-Savopoulou, 1990).

5   EP Doc A 2-95/86, Rapporteur: K. Anastasopoulos, PPE, Gr.

6   A consultant of the Greek shipowners (Dr. Bredima-Savopoulou) and a representative of the Danish seafarers' association (Mr. Sørensen) respectively. As analysis suggests, these interest groups were advocating diametrically different positions regarding cabotage liberalisation.

7   Council Regulation 4055/86, of 22.12.86.

8   Council of Ministers, Statement for the Council Minutes 11584/86, of 19.12.1986.

9   Finnmare, a state owned company, carries around two-thirds of Italian cabotage traffic.

10   EP Doc A3-199/90. Rapporteur: P. Sarlis, PPE, Gr.

11   *Lloyd's List*, Greek Minister calls EU to delay cabotage discussions, 17.11.1990.

12   *Lloyd's List*, Cabotage plans face a rethinking, 29.2.1991.

13   *Lloyd's List*, Argument throws cabotage scheme into confusion, 20.3.1991.

14   Council Regulation 3577/92, of 7.12.1992.

15   *Agence Europe*, 9.12.1995.

16   According to an interviewee, 'if a shipper can do a good deal and send the goods by a coastal vessel rather than put them on a road vehicle he would be happy to do that, and he will be happy that there is an environmental benefit. If the price is an increased cost then he will not prefer maritime transport. What counts above all is cost effectiveness' (Richards, 1996).

17   The other two MIF panels deal with issues covering maritime resources and ship financing respectively.

18   MIF (1993), Results of the Plenary Session of the MIF, 27th/28th June 1993, Athens Greece.

19   Lyras, J. (1992). Shipping Today: The Threat of Regulatory Chaos. In: Hellenic Chamber of Shipping, *Shipping Report*, No 125, July-September 1992, pp. 5-8.

20   The then UK Secretary of State for Transport (M. Rifkind) announced in May 1991 four initiatives promoting intermodalism, focusing in his press release to the 'major new opportunities for combined transport using road haulage at either end of a journey with rail taking the main burden', without any reference to the use of the maritime mode (DoT Press Release, No 147, 28.5.1991).

21   EP Doc. A3 -111/93. Rapporteur: A. Donelly, PPE, UK.

22   The three MEPs that developed this idea were: A. Donnelly, UK; B. Langenhagen, Ger; and R. Speciale, It.

23   *Lloyd's List*, Fighting back against the Blue banana: The Atlantic Arc Commission, 3.12.1994.

24   EP Doc. A4-167/96. Rapporteur: N. Sindal, PES, Dk.

25   Including the transformation of state owned ports to autonomous authorities (cf. *Seatrade Review*, Seatrade Report: Spain. June 1994).

26   Council Resolution of 11.03.1996.

27   Council Conclusions of 18.06.1997.

9 Shortsea Shipping: Policy Actors, Process, Outcome

Policy developments concerning the framework of maritime transport within the EU, or between the EU and adjacent European countries, encompass two regulations establishing the freedom to provide international maritime transport and cabotage services within the EU respectively. They also embrace the evolution of 'soft law' activities, which are political agreements and statements, non-legislative policy measures, and the commitment to further EU action aiming to promote the competitiveness of shortsea shipping services in Europe. These 'soft law' rules are not legally enforceable but nonetheless guide the acts of the EU institutions, the member states, and those undertaking economic activities, (Wellens and Borchardt, 1989). This chapter discusses, and draws conclusion, on the findings from studying the transformation of shortsea shipping activities to a subject figuring predominantly on the CMTP agenda.

Economic Environment

The two regulatory measures establishing the freedom to provide services within the EU are quintessentially associated with the new economic reality produced by the SEM project. Maritime transport services within this market could not continue to be governed by national regulatory frameworks that were inconsistent with the basic principles of free capital, goods, persons, and services circulation. However, this condition alone was not enough to see the two rules progress. The consistency of the transport sector to these principles had been a policy target since 1957 and maritime transport part of the CTP since 1974, but the conception was that the presence of different national policies regarding a uniquely international business did not contradict or pose a serious hindrance to the common market. The slow and controversial progress of the cabotage rule consolidates that agreeing general policy targets in the Treaty context may direct common policies, yet, it does not imply an automatic policy integration in the related sectors of the economy, thus the continued absence of a genuinely single market in many sectors of industry compared to the '1992' target (Butt Philip and Porter, 1995). These targets remain subject to interpretations by the actors involved in the policy making process. Without an immediate change in the desirability for an EU policy there was no initiative before the mid-1980s.

Aspects of the profoundly new economic environment also act as critical parameters to the innovative EU policy addressing European shortsea shipping in an integral way. The policy activities examined developed as the absence of market and policy adjustments jeopardised the competitiveness of the maritime transport system in Europe. The expansion and structural modification of transport demand, coupled with the transformation of transport services to an integral part of post-fordist 'internationalised, flexible (but also regionalised) production systems' (Jessop, 1993), have necessitated fundamental adjustments, including the technological adaptation and the comprehensive reorganisation of the provided services. However, the essential market responses, whether product or process innovations, are only partially present. Then, the simultaneous increase of intra-modal and inter-modal market interdependence has critical implications. First, market actors, either firms or industries, cannot stimulate their competitive position unless the others demonstrate the same degree of adaptability. Each of them has self-interest to see the others moving decisively towards modernisation.

Secondly, market interdependence upgrades the role of the framework conditions within which the mode operates. However, national transport and infrastructure policies have negatively affected these conditions, creating a considerable disadvantage to the sector's ability to serve the new type of demand, and remain competitive vis-à-vis the other transport modes. Moreover, as trade and, consequently, transport operations experience increasing internationalisation, the probability of effective responses by the pre-existing non-EU policy frameworks diminishes. The economic and geopolitical changes in both Western and Eastern Europe (the progress of the SEM project, and the collapse of the economic and political regimes, respectively) increase international exchanges. Most importantly, a core characteristic of the new trends in manufacturing, supply and distribution processes is the integration of local production in transnational trade chains. National authorities are decisively weakened to administer, or proceed with the alteration of, this internationalised framework unilaterally. These facts along with the notified tendency of the national policy making frameworks to favour other transport modes and the slow adjustment progress of the market itself had adversely affected the competitive position of the mode. In addition, the unprecedented high levels of transport demand have generated the saturation and congestion of the inland transport system, and public concerns regarding environmental implications. Though taken alone these features of the contemporary economic environment and the 'policy-gaps' that they created may not suffice to fully explain the process, they provided causal variables for policy Europeanisation.

The Regulatory Policy Developments

Having stressed from the outset that the economic background contains some critical explanatory variables, what are the other factors that influenced the progress of the two regulatory measures? The ECJ, specifically its 1983 ruling against the Council's inaction, has been pivotal in shaping policy integration. It had the effect of altering the behaviour of another institution, the Commission, which had preferred to treat the maritime mode differently from the rest of the transport sector. It was because of this Court judgement that some member states and private actors turned to the EU framework for a policy reform. By standing alongside the Commission, they assisted the latter in assuming policy authority. The Commission captured the opportunity to issue proposals dealing with the internal maritime transport market along with the Treaty provisions, albeit confronting preferences of several national administrations and stakeholders.

This was the second time that the ECJ acted as a CMTP agenda-setter. The first had been in 1974 when another ruling incorporated the maritime mode in the CTP strategy. Still, the ECJ ability depends, according to the Rome Treaty, on other actors to force issues onto the agenda and condone its interpretations. Importantly, both the preceding rulings had been provoked by other EU political institutions, the Commission in the 1970s and the first elected EP in the 1980s that were trying to establish their own role, but also test how far they could push member states to progress common policy legislation against the noticeable absence of any interest or strategy towards such progress. It is also interesting that these moves took place in periods associated with 'critical junctures' of European integration, i.e. the first enlargement and the early discussions of the SEM project by a more maritime orientation of the EU respectively. More recently, the Commission took advantage of the climate created by the TEU discussions to introduce a common policy addressing the entire shortsea mode. In several cases, the EU institutions have managed to benefit from the dynamic of the 'historic' moments of European integration to further the developments of the CMTP.

Domestic politics and intrastate coalitions led to an inter-governmental bargaining that played a critical role in the process of establishing the freedom to provide services within the EU. National policy traditions, some dating back centuries, embedded the preferences of national administrations and stakeholders. A reciprocal interest to defend such traditions led to intrastate coalitions, empowered by the fact that on a national basis all stakeholders lined behind the same positions. These coalitions decided the initial member states' positioning *vis-à-vis* the potential of a common policy, induced two-track approaches regarding intra-EU and cabotage trade, and disproportionate to the potential economic consequences support/opposition to the Commission's proposals. The ideological stances of state executives were also deterministic to the standpoints of the national administrations *vis-à-vis* the proposals of the Commission (i.e. the neo-liberal and the populist 'national-security' rhetoric that dominated the British and Greek positions respectively). The consequent split between north-south member states appeared to prevail, creating a no-decision situation, and limiting integration. It was only the Commission's proposals referring to intra-EU trade, to which there were not major objections but time derogation demands for the abolition of the contradictory practices, which became part of the 1986 regulatory package.

Yet, inaction on cabotage proved to be temporary. As the Council did not resolve the issue, those member states favouring integration relied on the Commission for leadership. This gave the Commission allies for continuing its search for a common rule. On the other hand, the commitment to the SEM constrained member states from a permanent opposition to a reciprocal opening of their cabotage trade. As scholars who examined other EU policy developments of that period observe (cf. Mazey and Richardson, 1993b), member states became reluctant to be perceived as blocking legislation related to the internal market and become the target of the criticism. Knowing the setting, and exploiting the spillover effect of the SEM project, the Commission had the opportunity to work on the particular issue for three years, notably alone rather than in parallel with the Council mechanisms as it happens during the formal policy-making process. It finally redrafted the proposal in a way that crafted consensus among most of the member states without abandoning the principles of a great liberalised maritime transport market advocated by the first proposals.

The development of a partnership between the Commission and the EP helped the building of consensus, as allowed for further refinements. This time the EP proved to be more influential than when the cabotage rule had first been discussed. This was not least because the EP focused on the implications of the specific rule, rather than on a debate about a CMTP grand design, as it had done (and in many respects had been obliged by the nature of the then-current regulatory proposals to do) in mid-1980s. Via the selective accommodation of societal demands, notably in line with the views developed in the national constituency of the MEP that drafted the report of the EP Committee, the EP became part of an influential interaction. When endorsed by the Commission, as the cooperation procedure allowed, the EP amendments impelled a final agreement.

This institutional exchange had multiple effects to the positioning of the other, public and private, actors involved in the process. Firstly, it lessened the force of disapproval in the domestic arenas of Mediterranean states, facilitating the compromise by state executives. Second, by re-balancing the front with the 'status-quo oriented' parties, it softened the ideas of those who had not wanted to compromise on derogated cabotage liberalisation. The national administrations, as well as private actors, who had supported the Commission in the 1980s, did so again, otherwise they faced the prospect that the whole negotiation might break down indefinitely. The refinement of the rule diluted the repetition of the bloc positioning developed during the earlier discussions. Besides, neither the inter-state north front coalition, nor the south one, was cohesive as regards the details of the rule. To several states cabotage was an issue of minor importance, thus they abandoned their initial position converging in support for the new 'mild liberalisation' proposal, facilitating in that sense a policy agreement. Bearing in mind that Euros as well as other issues were already part of the agenda makes it plausible that to some member states cabotage was already downgraded to a secondary theme of the CMTP discussions and disagreements were worthy of being reserved for other more important battles (i.e. Euros). Others continued to make known their different approaches, threatening but not carrying out retaliatory practices (the UK) or vetoing any cabotage regulation (Greece). Still, the only significant effect of their stances was to give the impression of hard fighting for their scope.

Moreover, EU membership directed national administrations to specific behaviours. The voting procedures configured in the Treaty were underplayed as member states restricted themselves from utilising them to block decisions according to their own preferences. Perhaps in 1986 member states restrained their objections to the minutes of the Council, rather than making a unanimous decision impossible, due to the unwillingness to destabilise a balance between different rules. Nonetheless, the member states that were dissatisfied with the refined cabotage proposal neither formed a blocking minority, nor opted for vetoing. Characteristically, the Greek government had argued against the rule on national security grounds. This would normally invoke the veto, especially as it had been on the request of the same state (and Portugal's) that a paragraph in the SEA provides for unanimity in vital CMTP decisions. However, when this administration found itself isolated, it retracted its veto and demanded further negotiations. Looking into the details of the final decision, market peculiarities and socio-economic reasons, rather than the veto probability on 'national security' grounds, led to special provisions for certain (island) cabotage routes. As member states came to accept an EU decision, threatening to veto the refined proposal gained, if anything, a lengthier implementation timetable.

Notably, when holding the Council presidency national administrations had an active role in promoting policy integration even against their own preferences. Member states used the presidency capacity as a device to promote compromises rather than continue to delay policy developments until they matched their standpoint. The British administration did not hesitate to promote an indefinite inaction on cabotage, despite that it had proclaimed full market liberalisation as a matter of principle. The Italian presidency decided to put cabotage in its agenda, although it had to contribute to the dissociation of the cabotage rule from Euros, against its preference for an agreement on issues of registration. It could have exploited the opportunity offered by Greece though allowing for further negotiations and seeking a better outcome than the one that was in the agenda, especially as the inaction experienced over the same regulation (cabotage) had secured amendments precisely towards the direction that Italy had advocated during the policy making process. However, the interest for, or perhaps the long-term benefits from, avoiding a fight against the majority of its European partners and the European institutions, or the facilitation of agreements on other issues which at the specific point of time seemed increasingly improbable, were perceived as more significant than a focus on what was thought to be the optimum outcome. As in other EU sectoral policies, the search of the presidencies for 'qualified home runs' (Héretier, 1996) contributed to 'second choice for all participants', rather than the 'winner takes all', policy outcomes (see: Peterson and Bomberg, 1999).

To sum up, although member states preferences and the consequent divisions, empowered by the support in the domestic national arenas, slowed down the progress of integration and affected the details of the final regulations, they did not exercise a deterministic control over policy integration. Whilst the interactions of the institutional framework gave to member states the incentives to act as shapers of a common policy that they had previously either disregarded or objected to, national administrations also found their actions being shaped by this policy-making process and the cultural effects of the TEU membership. As a result the different, to some member states 'vital', interests and preferences were not by themselves factors enough to lead to the absence of certain policy developments.

What then was the role of shipowners, shippers, and trade unions that contended to influence these regulatory developments? Clearly, the fact that the EU proposals did not gain the acquiescence of more than half the shipping industry and organised labour made the rules difficult to progress, especially as the social partners converged in defence of their national policy *status quo* and formed coalitions with national administrations, the importance of which has already been analysed. With private policy actors divided on national lines, domestic lobbying of national administrations paralleled, and when successful prevailed, interest representation in Brussels through Euro-groups. On the other hand, policy makers need the support of the vested interests to forward a policy agreement. Notwithstanding that, it was only when the actions of the EU institutions (i.e. ECJ ruling, Commission proposals) created incentives that shippers, North-European shipowners and, to a less extent, North-European trade unions, mobilised in support of policy integration. Before that, there had been no indication of a desirability to see the EU amending the regulatory framework of the internal maritime transport market.

The institutional variables of the sort outlined above, had an effect on the stakeholders that went beyond the initial sphere of their actions. As the Commission led to a new proposal on cabotage, the preferences (though not the rhetoric) of stakeholders altered. Assessing the commitment of their national governments to the SEM as more powerful than the interest to maintain national coalitions over the specific policy issue, Mediterranean shipowners searched for intra-industry responses rather than fighting the forthcoming rule alone. British shipowners also worked with the rest of the industry on certain details of a compromise, and thus less satisfactory, rule than simply advocating an uncritical liberalisation. That said, the changing attitude of both associations paralleled the continuation of their support to the hard-line stand of their isolated in the process national administrations. This 'double-face' approach was evident in the stance of the organised labour as well. When the EP, and its Greek Rapporteur, offered avenues to influence the process, the sceptical Greek union's industrial actions in the domestic arena coexisted with Euro-lobbying which was not about rejecting but about promoting conditions for the proposed rule.

All these stakeholders accepted, to various extents, the shift of the agenda and the wider contextual changes produced by the macro-objective of establishing a SEM. Preconceptions changed, with stakeholders deciding to work alongside the EU institutions aiming to be more effective in ironing out the policy proposal, or generating the climate for a future favourable refinement of the legislative outcome, rather than attack the established agenda from the outset. Yet, this happened only because institutional variables had been capable of stimulating the search for a common rule in the aftermath of a member states disagreement and in the presence of divided societal preferences. Notably, in the aftermath of a non-decision outcome those private actors who accepted, to various degrees, the compromise possibility managed to secure some favourable details in the final regulation, not least because the Commission and the EP were keen to accommodate some of their stances in order to see the rule agreed. On the other hand, a process that was otherwise open to interest groups excluded those whose stance remained immovable, even though they supported the very aims of the initial Commission proposal. Shippers opposed the refined proposal, not least because they were attempting to press for liberalisation in all transport modes rather than maritime cabotage alone, and were the first complaining of the eventual agreement demanding a major refinement.

The definition and articulation of interests through Euro-groups were not irrelevant to the notified restructuring of tactics and preconceptions that were expressed by the stakeholders. Searching for collective European action was a process that directed national-level trade unions and shipowners associations to the expression of different approaches from those expressed within the domestic arenas. Euro-groups predominantly articulated the stances of their more 'Europe-minded' membership, rather than that, which emphasised inaction on the basis of national differences. All shippers' councils supported the unconditional liberalisation of maritime services, so they did not face such dilemmas. But the Euro-federation representing shipowners advocated the conditional liberalisation of cabotage since the early discussions of the rule. Similarly, when cabotage came back on the agenda, the Brussels committee of the (regulatory prone) trade unions offered its conditional support to an EU rule, rather than adopting the negative position of southern unions. Conclusions cannot, however, be drawn from the earlier stance of labour as its representatives had remained focused to an alternative CMTP than an explicit response to each rule of the agenda. Overall, the policy-making process motivated participation in Euro-groups which resulted not just in collaboration at different levels of organisation, but also a completely new environment of interests representation contributing to a more cooperative attitude towards EU policy activities.

The details of the cabotage regulation and its first evaluation report emphasise the extent and the constraints of the Commission powers respectively, both of them the outcome of the 'mutual dependence' conditions that have been developed among the actionable factors. Foremost, the Commission needs to gain the support of member states and stakeholders otherwise its actions are ineffectual and its views irrelevant to policy outcome. It could by no means run away from the absence of this support and promote cabotage alongside Euros. Derailed by the generalised (though on different grounds) opposition to Euros, the Commission had to accept the unwanted disassociation of the two issues, exactly as it had done in 1986 with the initial cabotage rule which expressed the Commission's, as well as the North European member states, very preferences.

On the other hand, fighting almost a decade for the essence of the rule, none of the involved actors emphasised the fact that long-term implementation, and regulatory evaluation, powers were secured for the Commission. By interpreting the divergent demands of member states and vested interests according to its assessment of the new market conditions, the Commission has already shown that within the new system it has the capacity to deploy such unanticipated powers towards its preferred direction. The unwillingness to reopen the political compromise, notably opposing some member states that had earlier allied with the Commission over the issue (and in general conceived as 'powerful') like the UK and Germany, and the decision to condition the opening of cabotage to non-traditional flag (in practice the restraint of the rule to a reciprocal market opening rather than full liberalisation) are revealing.

The Non-Regulatory Policy Developments

It is difficult to precisely apportion responsibility for policy innovation. However, by addressing the problems of European 'shortsea shipping' as a sector with its own characteristics and undertaking non-legislative activities to promote its competitive position, the Commission acted as a principal source of such innovation. The compartmentalisation of the institution played a key role in these developments. It produced self-interested DGs and contestants in a bureaucratic competition for policy innovation and coalition building, with both member states and private actors that would help them promote it. When one department (DG-III) was interested in promoting the competitiveness of transport industries, a second one (DG-VII) detected an idea lying within its field of competence and actively championed its promotion. Notwithstanding that, the Commission's actions as a policy entrepreneur were made possible because of a favourable climate that had been produced by the juxtaposition of a changing economic context, which, *inter alia*, created a new internationalised dimension to certain sectoral problems, and the increasing public considerations regarding the environmental implications of the expanding transport demand.

It is important however that, when informed by these features and legitimised by the advent of the TEU, which touched upon such environmental questions, the Commission was able to exercise already developed capacities, including powers over budget distribution, a strong basis for strategic research, and its contribution to the TENs project configuration, to stimulate the new policy directions in the agenda, taking into account this reference to, and the utilisation of, a string of other EU policies (i.e. environment, R&D) having their legal base on the SEA, the Commission managed to expand the capacities that have been provided for it, in order to extend and develop its agenda-setter role.

Member states responded with varying degrees of support to an idea, which, as the directions of the pre-existing national policy activities highlight, had not been part of their own priorities, It is hard to judge whether member states influenced the Commission to pursue its new policy strategy or were 'followers' of the Commission's initiatives. Whilst it should not be forgotten that member states, in particular the industrialised north European states where the expansion of shortsea mode is conceived to be more viable, might expect substantial economic and environmental benefits, such 'rationality' had not been demonstrated in the domestic policy choices. Assuming, that the detected Commission's innovation had been informally credited by some of the member states before its formal expression, rather than *post hoc* as a mere documentation analysis would conclude, then emphasis should be given to the fact that it was the conjunction of EU membership and the dimension of the problem, rather than the latter alone, which adduced the readiness of national administrations to share (at least some) responsibilities with the new institutional framework. Nonetheless, in the absence of coherent national policies to defend, the reaction to the Commission's initiative was not an intergovernmental bargaining, but a comparatively greater reliance on the Commission, its ideas, and coalition-building activities to lead developments.

The standpoints of the member states throughout the process have been anything but fixed around a defined preconception of what issues a maritime transport policy should be about. By establishing the MIF, the Commission exploited opportunities offered by wider member states commitments in the context of integration (in this case the subsidiarity principle) to build alliances with private actors at supranational and subnational level, secure the promotion of its policy idea, and the establishment of policy actions administered at an EU level. None of the member states did object to the development of a structured network between policy makers and private actors, though it would be orchestrated by the Commission itself rather than by state executives. It was not long before this move had several consequences, foremost on the attitudes of the member states towards a policy domain that was challenging their policy priorities. Through the MIF function, as well as its pending vertical and horizontal expansion, which in turn questions domestic administrative hierarchies, all (sceptical or not) national administrations have been 'locked in' a consistent debate and eventually committed to the establishment of a comprehensive common policy.

The actions of the Commission modified the role of the other EU institutions over this policy area. By becoming part of the MIF discussions they were allowed to participate in policy formation at an extent unforeseen by the Treaty context. That way the Commission gained the support and legitimisation for further actions but also created the conditions for further unintentional developments. The EP has taken advantage of playing a more dynamic role according to its own preferences. When the Commission and the member states focused on the input of the maritime industries, the EP configured a framework offering to local authorities and organisations in the maritime regions the opportunity to build relationships and become part of this process. Exploiting the opportunity to overcome organisational incapacity subnational actors participate without being directly dependent on national authorities. As they also used their association with 'Brussels', notably the national MEPs and the Commission, as a medium to be informally linked with and influence the national capitals member states had to follow, or be superseded. The British example is noticeable. As regional authorities from the UK maritime regions energetically followed the provided routes of direct participation, the sceptical British government reluctantly followed the 'Brussels' activities and created an informal national forum linking societal interests and policy makers, In that sense, the EP has acted as a pattern in the governance of policy developments.

Still, the EP relies, and therefore consistently pressures, on the Commission's policy initiating activities, which would allow the EP to be involved in an expanded agenda. Foremost, it depends on the Commission's willingness to respond positively to its policy proposals. In the absence of such willingness, the EP calls for a greater emphasis on the social aspects of the common policy lacked the dynamic that would lead to their endorsement by the Council, Similarly ineffectual were the policy proposals of the Ecosoc in response to the 'shortsea' document. A more generalised problem regarding the consultative EU institutions has been revealed. None of the examined policy developments was actually influenced by the Ecosoc opinions. Whilst reaching the same conclusion regarding the CoR may be unjustifiable, as the limited contribution of its first opinion in maritime issues may be attributed to the 'inexperience' of the institution, the examined policy developments raise questions on whether a 'matured but consultative' CoR would have exercised a more influential role or whether its consultative character is deterministically limiting of its contribution.

Returning to the MIF, it has to be stressed that at the time of its establishment the affected industries were not in a general agreement regarding the usefulness of developing a common policy concerning shortsea shipping, or the need for market reorganisation. Nor were all these industries active participators in a consistent exchange of views with the EU institutions. On the other hand, the Commission lacked the information to produce the necessary policy developments, or the capacity to enforce market adjustments. Since the Commission realised the need for a closer cooperation with those industries controlling significant parts of the maritime transport system, it drew a variety of market actors into the policy-making process. The major effect has been the transformation of policy-making to a widely participatory but structured process that secured the advice and acquiescence of maritime industries to the policy that the Commission had introduced. The plans and the specific policy commitments that supranational, national, and subnational, authorities have undertaken since the publication of the shortsea document were in essence decided in the MIF, outside procedures associated with institutional configurations of the Treaties.

This means that the industrial input has been critical to the common policy developments, especially as policy makers realised that the achievement of their specific policy targets largely depends on non-regulatory decisions and the adjustment actions of the market players. However, the fact that this input was provided through channels and arenas of politics which were selected by the Commission and, thus, enjoy a privileged position *vis-à-vis* other industrial initiatives has been pivotal. Positioning in the middle of the institutionalised network was not simply functional. The Commission coordinated the process in the early days of its formation, filtered the agenda, and guided policy demands towards certain directions. In short, it acted as a transmitter of its policy ideas, as well as a selective receiver of industrial demands (in particular those that activated in support of its ideas) hence, the concrete results of the shortsea panel discussions. It was this interaction that generated an active coalition of the Commission and the maritime industries deciding the content of the 'shortsea' document.

Moreover, the MIF structured the representation system of an inevitably, due to the expansion of the agenda themes, increasing number of interest groups. On the one hand, the Commission managed to avoid an overload of 'realistic' and 'unrealistic' demands of organised interests. Simultaneously, it built into this system an institutionalised hierarchical positioning where European associations enjoy the advantage of closer cooperation with the EU institutions, and especially the Commission. This has had a critical effect on the organisation of interests representation. Choosing not to participate in Euro-groups associating the rest of the EU industry, but to rely on the support offered by national administrations became problematic. The case of British forwarders who relied exclusively on the British Bureau of Business as a means to follow policy developments, suggests that it may be akin to 'living in the dark'. Neither decisions nor information flows are anymore entirely under the control of state executives and national governments' mechanisms. On the other hand, those that have reluctantly become part of the game, even if they may do so reflecting intra-industry traditions, rather than remain isolated to the good relationships with national administrations, are better informed and able to extract more from the process (i.e. Greek shipowners).

Nevertheless, this process does not imply a balanced input as far as the involved private actors are concerned. The market powers of an industry and its structural importance for the maritime transport system; its self-interest to support the EU project; the knowledge of, and familiarity with, the Brussels game; as well as the organisational capacity to exploit the lobbying opportunities; have been the parameters that determined the input of the various interest groups. The locus of power to influence policy developments belonged to the shipowners who topped the scale in all these categories. Despite initial surprise about some developments, in particular the creation of the MIF (also: Ronit, 1995) shipowners had the advantage of working with the Commission since the early days of the CMTP, the organisational ability to adjust in a more formal and structured interests representation game, and a very clear interest to see the specific Commission initiative progress. Through the submission of specific proposals for concrete policy measures, and pressures for the shortsea policy to go beyond an initial phase, they developed a close cooperation with the Commission and had a major input to the policy developments.

Ports were equally interested in promoting the shortsea policy, and within the new economic reality became equally important to the competitiveness of the system. They demanded and legitimised policy developments, but found that the main directions of the common policy had been provided by those 'ready and interested' to help the Commission in the early days of the process, in this case shipowners. Being late comers, and comparatively inexperienced, due to the absence of collective industry representation before 1993, port authorities and operators were less influential and unable to reverse any unwelcome policy directions that a Commission-shipowners common stance was promoting. Moreover, the diverse characteristics of European ports handicapped the efforts of those parts of the industry that opposed the increasing attention of the EU policy on infrastructure issues, as several ports offered their support to these moves.

Knowing the rules of the game better, but not particularly interested in becoming engaged in a debate about modal shifts, which is the essence of the EU policy activities, shippers were unhappy to see the agenda reformulated. In particular, as the MIF formally brought into the process more market players, but also Commission departments, eroding shippers' privilege as one of the two industries (the other being shipowners) providing a regular input to the CMTP developments. Yet, the growing interest of shippers who initially looked askance upon the whole project, suggest that when industries began to participate in the institutionalised process it was the whole policy logic of their position that was affected, not only their organisation. Especially whenever the EU was conceived, justifiably or not, as the arena to compensate for dissatisfactions and impose favourable developments in the domestic arenas, a preference was developed for the common policy to expand. The change of strategy was more apparent in the case of freight forwarders, who were offered the opportunity to become part of the game, against a limited participation in previous CMTP developments. However, two parameters limited their actual input: first, the fact that, compared to other market actors, this industry is less important to the maritime transport system; second, the organisational disadvantages generated by the lack of cohesion of freight forwarders' interests. Internal disputes on the capacities of the existing Euro-federation to effectively represent all the forwarding firms, and the different priorities of its membership (including the absence of any interest regarding the maritime mode by some) where factors that restricted the industry to general statements rather than detailed policy proposals.

On the other hand, the policy actors most completely excluded from the process were trade unions. This is not only because labour was more focused on traditional issues, i.e. FoC, and virtually boycotted the early stages of the developments. Later on, organised labour demonstrated a growing interest in the activities of MIF and asked for a greater focus of the shortsea policy on social aspects. Still, there was limited support by policy makers. Neither the increasing importance of seafarers for the modernisation of the system, nor the familiarity of their representatives with the lobbying system and the organisational capacity to advocate specific measures, managed to redirect the agenda. As already discussed, labour has also played little role in the changes in the domestic national arena. In that respect, the Commission initiatives duplicated and reinforced this balance, when it was interested to forge an alliance with the maritime industries to achieve its policy targets. For organised labour, securing the explicit support of the EP in the aftermath of the shortsea document publication was an ineffectual outcome. As confirmed by the Council, the different balance, which developed by the industrialists-Commission coalition, prevailed.

It has to be emphasised, however, that taking onboard organised interests and agreeing with them on certain directions of a common policy was not something that secured the 'mechanical' introduction of a comprehensive EU-level policy. First, the fact that the economic environments and the new internationalised dimension of the problems offered policy-making opportunities, does not mean that the EU can assume policy implementation authority. A number of initiatives have been recognised as needing, due to their economic dimension, to be taken at national, or subnational level. Then, the organisational structures of the Commission have promoted but also hindered the developments; different departments of this 'fragmented multi-organisation' (Cram, 1994) compete to promote different priorities. as much as they compete for policy innovation, a frequently noticeable bureaucratic characteristic. Foremost, the whole process ultimately depends on member states: their agreement was essential to seal the commitment to further initiatives. Thus, in the pending progress of the common policy, national administrations and EU institutions have become integral parts of a two-way relationship which is *shaped by*, but is also *shaping*, the policy demands of the stakeholders.

Conclusions

The development of a new economic environment has been a critical variable to the progress of the examined EU 'hard' and 'soft' law policy activities concerning shortsea shipping. The profound market changes as well as the wider economic and geopolitical changes, including the progress of European economic integration *per se*, have resulted in the increase and structural modification of the transnational regional trade and demands for rapid and fundamental adjustments. The common policy develops in pursuit of filling the 'policy gaps' that followed these contextual changes. These gaps are the divergent national policy traditions of member states that have become part of a SEM, the slow adjustment of market forces to the new economic environment, and the apparent ineffectiveness of the pre-existing national policy frameworks to produce policy realignments. Still, whilst the economic dynamic advanced the progress of the EU level responses, it was not enough to produce policy Europeanisation.

The institutional web of the EU had a vital role in the considerable progress of the developments examined. As regards the two regulatory measures, an ECJ ruling against policy inaction created a favourable climate for the Commission to deploy its agenda-setter capacities and challenge the dominant conception that maritime transport should be treated differently than any other sector. North European national administrations and market forces mobilised in support of policy integration only in the aftermath of this inter-institutional exchange. Thereafter, the Commission exercised key coalition and consensus building functions, which secured the initial aims. Even in a non-decision situation, the Commission lead, in the name of member states commitment to a single liberalised European market, to a refined cabotage proposal that reversed the situation, but also increased its implementation competencies. The final agreement on cabotage gained impetus by a partnership of the Commission and the EP which selectively absorbed further societal demands that followed the refined proposal. The EP had influenced the examined regulatory developments in a more fundamental way, as it was the policy actor that provoked the preceding ECJ ruling.

National administrations retained a major role, empowered by coherent intrastate coalitions with private actors. Inter-governmental bargaining and domestic policies explain several details of the final regulations, but also the temporary indecision regarding cabotage. Notwithstanding that, the initial preferences of national administrations were reformed, partly because of the preceding institutional activities and partially because of the effects of the EU membership. The EP-ECJ-Commission interaction provided the incentives to support a common policy that had been previously disregarded; the Commission's leadership enabled state executives to compromise, as societal pressures lessened; and the SEM project constrained a permanent opposition to open cabotage trade, compared to the former the latter was 'low' politics. Furthermore, the consensual culture of EU membership disinclined vetoing or blocking Council decisions, and the willingness to avoid a conflict with the European partners, facilitating agreements on other issues, and successfully fulfilling bureaucratic responsibilities, led successive Council presidencies to work towards compromises putting aside national preferences.

These inter-institutional exchanges and inter-governmental bargaining were critically informed by the views of the private policy actors. The direction of the common policy was strengthened by the support of North European shipowners, trade unions, and shippers, but restrained by the conflicting views of Mediterranean shipowners and unions. However, the institutional framework stimulated the search for a compromise and affected the conceptions of most private actors. Even though clustering in support of national traditions had led to domestic coalitions, a progressive transformation of shipowners and trade unions preferences created the background for policy progression. Acknowledging the consensual ethos of national administrations and the importance of the SEM project, as well as the opportunities offered to shape the final rules when working alongside the EU institutions, they accepted (to various degrees) a compromise possibility. Moreover, the collective articulation of interests through Euro-groups resulted in a more cooperative attitude, as the stances of these groups was dominated by the more 'Europe-minded' membership. On the other hand, shippers who remained immovable in support of uncritical maritime services liberalisation strengthened the direction of the regulatory measures towards economic liberalism but had less input to the detail of the final regulatory compromise.

As regards the non-regulatory policy activities, the Commission was a principal source of innovation, and a policy entrepreneur that effectively utilised the favourable climate and the internationalised dimension of certain sectoral problems to enter new policy areas. By leading to the establishment of the MIF, it structured a participatory policy-making process, guided the demands of private actors towards certain directions, and actively built the essential alliances with maritime industries for the promotion of policy actions administered at an EU level. Moreover, it provided the means for a greater participation of the other EU institutions in policy formation than member states had anticipated. The EP was capable of further exploiting this opportunity offering to authorities and organisations in maritime regions the paths to counterbalance, in some respect, the major input of the maritime industries. Yet, the EP was unable to promote its preferred policy directions against the generated MIF-Commission coalition. On the other hand, neither the Ecosoc nor the CoR, had a noteworthy influence on the examined policy developments.

Member states' support for the promotion of the Commission's innovative policy ideas, conditioned their progress to concrete policy measures, and the implementation of the latter. However, in the absence of coherent national policies to defend, the reliance on the Commission, its ideas, and lead towards policy developments increased. The development of a structured and permanent forum discussing potential developments eventually 'locked' member states into policy directions agreed primarily between the Commission and the maritime industries. Although some of these actions challenged national policy priorities and administrative hierarchies, several member states became active advocates and promoters of plans and policy commitments that were in essence decided outside the institutional configurations of the Treaties.

Maritime industries provided a critical input the extent of which was determined by four parameters: (a) the market power of each industry; (b) the self-interest of the industry to support the EU project; (c) the knowledge of the Brussels game; and (d) the organisational capacities to exploit the lobbying opportunities. Shipowners topped all these categories, hence, they enjoyed a privileged position. The port industries topped the first two but were unfamiliar with the interest representation system, so were unable to reverse unfavourable policy directions. Whilst shippers were less interested in the development of the policy, the influence of freight forwarders was handicapped by the secondary importance of the industry for the function of the maritime system and the subsequent limited capacities of the respective Euro-federation. The diverse interests expressed by parts of the industry were, precisely as in the case of the port industry, an additional factor that limited the input of freight forwarders.

Overall, the progression of the institutionalised debate altered both the 'logic of influence' and the 'logic of collective action' of interests representation. The sceptical shippers developed a more positive attitude regarding the Commission's idea, conceiving the emerging policy as the means to reverse unfavourable national policies, freight forwarders become active players against a limited previous participation in previous CMTP developments, whilst the introduction of the MIF contributed to the organisation of port industries to Euro-groups, and a growing interest of organised labour regarding the MIF work and the content of the common policy. However, organised labour was the least influential policy actor despite the increasing importance of qualitative manning, the familiarity of trade unions with the Brussels game and the capacity to advocate specific policy proposals. The Commission forged a powerful alliance with those maritime industries sharing its target to augment the use of the maritime mode. As this practice duplicated the policy making pattern already observed in the domestic arenas, the Council endorsed the policy directions it produced, ignoring the objections of the EP and the consultative EU institutions.

10 Policy Europeanisation in Retrospect

The intention of this book was to generate knowledge on the determinants of the progress and courses of the CMTP in the 1990s. Recent studies of European integration suggest an analytical emphasis on economic internationalisation and on the interactions of the public and private policy actors involved in the EU policy-making process as a helpful way to understand the progress and content of the EU policies. Motivated by these suggestions, it was assumed that finding how these policy actors have influenced the policy-making process would be helpful in achieving a better understanding of the factors determining the CMTP developments. Taking into account the attempts to explain earlier phases of the sectoral common policy in question, and equipped with the assumption that the changing economic context and some institutional features of the EU are central factors to the emerging common policy, two main issue-areas of the CMTP were studied: the establishment of a common policy on safe seas and shortsea shipping. Having distilled the main findings of each policy area examined, this final chapter considers the general picture they adduce.

The Common Maritime Transport Policy in the 1990s

Economic Environment

Two major elements of the maritime transport's contemporary economic environment had a distinctive contribution to the examined downward, i.e. from international fora to the EU (first case-study), or upward, i.e. from national to the EU (second case-study) shifts in policy legitimacy. Developed in an also changing wider economic and geopolitical context, these elements are products of what might be abstracted as 'economic internationalisation' but are a complex phenomenon with multidimensional repercussions even to the historically internationalised maritime mode. The first element is the nature of the fundamental modifications in both the supply and demand sides of the market throughout the last two decades, modifications that derived from both changing behaviour of market actors and external factors. The second element, in many respects a consequence of the first, is the ineffective response of the pre-existing policy making frameworks, whether international, national, or self-regulatory, to the new economic reality. The permanent nature of this ineffectiveness might be debatable, yet, the infirm responses of the well established non-EU policy-making frameworks generated apparent 'policy gaps' and a critical background for the expansion of the CMTP themes in the issue-areas examined.

The first case-study revealed the major effects of the unprecedented ownership, registration, and employment internationalisation of the shipping industry on its structural deficiencies and deteriorating safety performance. In other words, it revealed the effects of these forms of internationalisation on the trends that the common policy attempts to reverse. In policy terms, these changes exacerbated the difficulties of international decision-making, implementation, and enforcement. As mobile vessels and mobile labour are exposed *par excellence* to international competition, a strong tradition of international rules has attempted to create a global level-playing field. However, a growing membership sharing conflicting social and economic priorities undermines IMO's ability to be as potent as in the past. The progress of self-regulatory measures has also been hindered: first, by the different business ethics of parts of the shipping industry, in turn the result of changes in ownership structures and registration partners; second, by the increase of shipowners' negotiating powers *vis-à-vis* those of organised labour, in turn the result of the worldwide expansion of registries which demand few manning requirements.

Although referring to more 'regionalised' (European) phenomena, the second case-study emphasised the impact of another kind of economic internationalisation. More than being an industry of economic importance (shipping), maritime transport is a service activity facilitating the production and distribution functions of an economy. Geopolitical changes in East Europe, the progress of the single market project in the West, and the diffusion of post-fordist production systems, expand the transnational European trade and transform the role of transport in the economic process. These noticeable changes, as well as the environmental questions they result in, demand the product modernisation and process reorganisation of the maritime transport system. Here, the 'policy gap' refers to the relative ineffectiveness, to some the *de facto* 'hollow out' (Jessop, 1993), of national level governance. When policy reforms are needed in response to the new conditions, the interconnection of national European economies suggests that transnational policy cooperation can be more effective.

Consistent with the pattern of behaviour noted in other economic sectors (cf. Pickering and Matthews, 1997), policy makers acting within the EU framework adjusted their policy approaches and proposals to the peculiar requirements that arose from the nature of the markets. Maritime member states demonstrated their unease with the failures of the IMO, however, they maintained a preference for international safety policy realignments and, as domestic developments highlight, in the aftermath of a flagging-out crisis they became highly sensitive to unilateral policies that would increase the costs of their registries and might regenerate flagging-out. Then, the progress of the SEM had a causal effect on the advocacy by some member states of the freedom to provide maritime services within this market, whilst the acceleration of transport demand contributed to a positive stance regarding an EU policy promoting shortsea shipping. On the other hand, the pressures of the EU institutions for common policy responses were based precisely on the specifics of these economic developments and the exacerbating policy instability. In Kingdon's (1984) terms, the economic changes fed the 'problem stream' with widely recognised problems, and the 'political stream' with favourable to policy change preconceptions, hence, they created the essential 'policy windows' for EU institutions to put forward common policy proposals.[1] At the same time, the economic context constrained them from the idea of promoting higher EU safety standards, as they would create competitive disadvantages for those shipowners operating EU flags.

The structural economic changes also had fundamental impacts on private actors' policy concerns, the common denominator being the generation of self-interest for policy reforms. Whilst the transformation of FoC shipping to a generalised practice strengthened the objections of shipowners operating EU-flags to any non-international safety rules, the hijacking of the registration dualism by the parts of the industry that do not comply to the international rules has lead to indirect cost increases and severe concerns. Then, the increasingly interdependent maritime industries developed an interest in seeing the whole system adjusting and its framework policy conditions changing, though they do so to various degrees and expressing diverse policy demands. On the other hand, European seagoing labour became increasingly concerned about the internationalisation of employment resources, with its policy agenda, at all levels, and dominated by calls for regulatory arrangements that would compensate for the undermined employment opportunities.

In many respects, these conclusions echo claims that the 'pendulum' swings towards policy integration as the contextual internationalisation has significant implications for a European region which shares transnational economic interconnections and a long attachment to similar socio-economic values (Wallace and Wallace, 2000; also: Keohane and Hoffman, 1991b; studying the CMTP: Cafruny, 1987). We must not, however, disregard that, as the CMTP examination in a historical perspective reveals (Chapter 3), it was precisely the ever present 'globalisation' of the shipping industry which grounded a long disapproval of EU resolutions to the remarkable but 'highly internationalised' maritime safety problems, limiting EU activities to policy recommendations. The same factor induced the long absence of EU intervention in the *status quo* of the internal maritime market. Moreover, the absence of policy support to the shortsea mode in a national context emphasises the very different choices that member states had endorsed in responding to a specific set of economic and geopolitical changes rather than those that they ultimately committed to within the EU. In short, the changing economic situation and the 'policy gaps' cast up problems to be resolved and created the context of policy actors' choices, but did not dictate decisions, or the development of common EU strategies.

In that sense, claims developed within the economic interdependence paradigm contain certain explanatory powers for the CMTP developments but only insofar as they are conceived as background situations which become subject to a competition regarding policy choices on how, and not least 'at what level', to respond to them (as some scholars have already argued: cf. Wallace and Wallace, 2000; Risse Kappen, 1996). If left alone, conceived as systemic reasons which determine policy integration, they would not explain why a common policy did not develop simply when several of the current economic characteristics became apparent, in other words, the inertia of the past against the current choice of the EU as the 'venue for policy-making' (Richardson, 1996). In turn, this justifies the analytical focus on the understanding of the role of policy actors involved in the making of the CMTP. As Caporaso (1998) argues, to understand EU policy developments, one needs to look, apart from the 'external forces', the 'internal logic' of integration as well.

A *first conclusion* can be detailed: the CMTP progressed as the vastly changing internationalisation of the sector's economic environment, in turn the outcome of both intrinsic market changes and external factors, created the need for regulatory and policy realignments. As the pre-existing non-EU policy making levels, whether national, international, or industrial self-regulation, did not produce effective policy responses, apparent 'policy gaps' were generated. This context informed the preconceptions of all the policy actors involved in the meaningful EU policy making process, and provided the stimulus for discussing EU policy developments, though did not dictate the choice of the EU-level as the venue for policy making.

Institutional Dynamism

European Institutions The reference to the presence of an institutional dynamism should start from the pivotal role of the Commission. Consistent with what scholars have already suggested (cf. Peters, 1994), much of its influence stemmed from its policy initiating powers provided in the Treaties. Notwithstanding that, it was the emergence of a proactive, as recently suggested 'maturing' (Christiansen, 1996) Commission, which delicately exercised its agenda-setting capacities, in terms of content and timing, and had a strong contribution to the change of pace in both issue areas examined.

The capacity that those Directorates Generals of the Commission involved in the development of CMTP initiatives has shown to promote common policy initiatives when policy opportunities offered focuses our attention on its leadership and opportunism. Controlling 'when' to introduce 'which' initiative, the Commission took advantage of the public attitudes (safe seas document; ro/ro safety), the discontent from non-EU rules (minimum training directive), and the euphoria created by the advent of critical junctures of European integration (SEM-freedom to provide services; TEU-shortsea framework), to challenge long-term preconceptions against EU-level activities. Then, detailing the draft proposals DG-VII (and to a certain extend DG-III) was able to put forward consensual approaches that increased the feasibility of policy agreements (safe seas), and advance phenomenally symbolic rules which generated the momentum and legitimacy to instigate in more controversial areas (ro/ro safety). Demonstrating a longer horizon than states' executives, the Commission's officials engaged in the parallel preparation of future proposals, free from member states that remained focused on the then-current agenda alone.

That objections to these proposals were expressed only after their initiation (ro/ro safety) works in favour of the argument that the capacities provided for the Commission at a point of time T_0 allowed this institution to act with a greater autonomy in a future point T_1 (Marks *et al*, 1996; Pierson, 1996). As does the fact that the accumulation of competencies in other issue-areas, or policy fields, as well as standard EU practices, i.e. mutual recognition (minimum training), became the tools to stabilise novel initiatives in the non-legislative policy arena (shortsea), to expeditiously detail policy proposals when 'policy gaps' become apparent (ro/ro), and the status to intervene when the lax implementation of international rule by member states became apparent (STWC).

The presence of quasi-autonomous capacities advanced as the Commission DGs also led with ideas and a degree of innovation. The second case-study saw that, as its initial interest in resolving issues that hindered the SEM project soon became claims for more ambitious policy projects (a progressive expansion of institutional interests noted in other policy areas as well: cf. Butt Philip, 1994), the Commission entered arenas where it directed developments without worrying about, or being restrained by, different national policy traditions. Precisely as Wincott (1995) has argued, supporting initiatives before member states consider the issues, the precondition for intergovernmental bargains eclipsed and the Commission enjoyed a higher autonomy. On the other hand, while the intra-bureaucratic competition advanced policy innovation, the involved DGs were also engaged in divergent perspectives and priorities. Importantly, the departmentalised (rather than coherent and unitary) apparatus of the Commission implied 'intra-institutional norms' (Bulmer, 1994a) which both impelled and hindered CMTP developments, making it also plausible that one DG might have referred to the role of the other to become more autonomous from other policy actors' demands.

Emphasis also needs to be given to the substantive role of the Commission's multi-directed, as addressed towards both national administrations and vested interests, consensus-building function over a period which extended the final decision making stage. Remarkably, in the aftermath of a non-decision on cabotage this function contributed decisively to the reversal of the situation via a rule that also increased the Commission competencies over policy implementation. As divergent demands from member states and vested interests followed the new market conditions, the Commission has already deployed such powers to interpret these conditions according to its own assessment. In line with Marks and his collaborators (Marks *et al*, 1996; Hooghe and Marks, 1997), the divisions of member states over policy proposals allowed the Commission to enter more energetically into the process. Notably, this happened even when such divisions were expressed in other than the EU international fora, i.e. IMO (ro/ro safety). Several national administrations conceived the Commission as a useful ally to achieve their aims within the EU, eventually supporting the rhythm and specifics of policy integration that the Commission defined. In this vein, the latter, but also the Commissioner himself, have not been simple 'go-betweens' but active promoters of coalitions with other actors. As regards the Commissioner, a COREPER member observes that 'his role is more important in things where the member states disagree'. Then, 'it is up to the Commissioner to bring his personal influence to progress certain issues' (Jones, 1996). Concession making is however a two-way process. To generate the support, which conditioned the progress of, its proposals to adopted rules the Commission did not hesitate to substantially modify its draft proposals as long as they fitted into a wider target framework.

Towards this end, an inter-institutional Commission-EP relationship consistent with Westlake's (1994, p. 225) assertion that whilst 'theoretically rivals the two are de facto partners' has raised. The case-studies findings suggest that the two institutions were engaged in a partnership of substantial importance: first, the Commission endorsed fundamental EP amendments, even when the EP was trying to secure competencies at the expense of those the Commission advocated for itself (minimum training); second, when searching for the critical mass of support, the Commission had the political capital to enhance the EP participation (via MIF) to policy formation at an extent unforeseen by the Treaty context. This partnership increased the dynamic of policy frameworks and defined significant details of regulatory measures (SBT; cabotage). Yet, it was neither a consistent nor a balanced partnership as the advantage remained with the Commission: when the latter was more interested in accepting a Council position (i.e. ro/ro safety), or policy directions agreed with maritime industries (shortsea), the EP was unable to draw a different line.

In turn, this partnership was a means for the EP to establish a certain degree of influence. But it was also one that affected its actions: facilitation of this partnership, rather than party politics, prevailed and shaped its stance *vis-à-vis* private actors demands. That said, the EP developed activities which successfully challenged the dominant (insofar as being preferred by the Commission, member states, and maritime industries) conceptions in at least two policy episodes: first, when it provoked the ECJ ruling that triggered CMTP developments; second, when it took the involvement of subnational authorities and organisations in policy-making one stage further. The Commission and member states, either individual (shortsea) or collective (internal market), following up activities suggest that despite the formal inter-institutional balance, the changing status of the EP to an elected institution with expanded formal decision-making powers has increased its political resources allowing it to play a more effectual role in progressing, and detailing sectoral policies like the CMTP.

As the history of the CMTP relates, exercising the ability to bring cases to the ECJ gave the EP and the Commission the opportunity to push the CMTP according to the general obligations prescribed in the Treaties but which member states were deliberately neglecting. The ECJ rulings had a major effect on the EU capacities to act, as it challenged the attitudes of member states and private actors which had been hesitant to see the CMTP dealing with any other issues than the reverse of flagging-out crises. Furthermore, several measures regarding maritime safety were based on the relationship between the EU and the national law, more precisely the fact that the former supersedes the latter. These findings come close to what Weiler (1982) has aptly described as a 'judicial normative dynamic', with an emphasis on treaty provisions and ultimately judicial review by the Court, which accompanies the 'political decisional dynamic' of integration. Clearly, by actively exercising their formal powers, the decision-making EU institutions and primarily the Commission shaped the CMTP developments examined.

On the other hand, none of the consultative EU institutions has been effective in doing so. Though further observations regarding the CoR are required (as it is judged on the basis of its first ever opinion on maritime issues alone) the consultative non-binding status of the Ecosoc was deterministic, not least because those who are supposed to be represented by this institution were offered other, more direct, channels and arenas to build a privileged relationship with decision makers. The recent institutionalisation of these arenas (MIF) justifies wider questions on the long term future of the Ecosoc (cf. Greenwood, 1994) and on whether the CoR can exercise a more influential role, or the factors that marginalised the Ecosoc will inevitably minimise its actual capacities as well.

In other words, there has been an institutional dynamism of functional orientation, which derived from the capability of the EU decision-making institutions to expediently deploy their formal powers in order to strengthen the perspective of common responses to apparent industrial problems. Yet, neither the Commission, nor any other EU institution, has responded to the neofunctionalist assumption of a 'clear independent political authority' (Coombes, 1970). These institutions also failed to secure some of their original targets, whether details of the examined rules or breakthroughs regarding their competencies (minimum training; freedom to provide services). Employing Pollack's (1997) argument, the EU institutions 'push through' legislative proposals and policy frameworks, but could not 'run amok' in an unconstrained pursuit of their own policy preferences. At the same time, policy-making was a learning process: searching for the critical mass of support the Commission has reshaped its strategy and vision regarding CMTP. With a great part of scepticism about common safety rules based on the heterogeneous intra-EU industrial structures, the Commission's recent proposals explicitly differentiate between kinds of maritime operations whilst in the past such differentiation was conceived as 'derogations' to the common policy.

Conversely, one could still argue that even these activities were epiphenomena of a process defined by the preferences of member states, or vested interest. What challenges this argument is the second type of institutional dynamism that has been described, this is the development of noticeable 'autonomy gaps' (Pierson, 1996) in the relationship between the EU institutions and their creators. What corrupts the claim that the EU institutions simply functionally facilitated the CMTP developments via an 'operational optimum', as the functional transaction costs approach would suggest, or that these institutions were in practice controlled by vested interests, as the neofunctionalist approach would maintain, is the third type of institutional dynamism revealed by the two case-studies. This is, the mediation of the extant institutional framework in the preferences of the other policy actors, whether member states or organised interests, and eventually on CMTP developments. Turning our attention to the other two clusters of actionable factors makes the presence of this type of institutional dynamism apparent.

At this point, however, a *second conclusion* can be outlined: the EU decision-making institutions, primarily the Commission, played a decisive role in the CMTP developments examined. This is because of (a) a functional dynamism deriving from the capability of the EU institutions to expediently deploy their formal powers in order to strengthen the perspective of common responses to apparent industrial problems; and (b) the fact that leadership, policy innovation (ideas), the accumulation of competencies, inter-institutional partnerships and exchanges, a judicial normative dynamic, and not least member states divisions, allowed the Commission, the EP, and the ECJ, to act with more autonomy in their relationship with national administrations.

Member States Establishing the pivotal role of the EU institutions does not imply an adverse trend for the powers of the member states. As already discussed, reversing the deteriorating maritime safety performance, facilitating the establishment of competitive maritime services within a SEM governed by the principles of economic liberalism, and tackling the environmental implications of the expanding transport demand, were all aims that member states were disinclined to or were incapable of tackling nationally and, hence, became interested to respond at a supranational level. Such developments affected the CMTP progression, precisely as did three more factors, namely national policy traditions, ideological standings of national administrations, interest of national administrations to develop common policies through consensus in the domestic arenas, and the intergovernmental bargaining that resulted. Besides this, both case studies provided evidence that member states' power to decide according to their collective preferences was more than a formality. When confronted collectively the agenda of the Commission, the EP, or both of them, member states had the power to prevail (minimum training directive), when the Council was divided integration halted (cabotage).

Interestingly, however, the case of the minimum training directive also records that when the Council drew a different line than that advocated by the Commission the latter preserved its position further than would be the outcome of mere members states exchanges. Moreover, the resolve of the cabotage issue suggests that the absence of a common denominator, or the objections grounded on 'vital' national interests, did not halt policy integration but temporarily. Apparently, policy-making has been more than a process exclusively controlled by national administrations that proceeded to intergovernmental negotiations holding pre-fixed preferences about what a common policy should be about. A critical point was that whilst the pressures from the economic context and domestic politics contributed to member states' preconceptions regarding the CMTP, the constellation of their preferences and their positioning in the policy-making process were eventually affected by the activities of the EU institutions, and the cultural impacts of the EU membership. In accord with scholars who suggest that 'membership matters' (cf. Sandholtz, 1996; Sbragia, 1996), these states acted, either individually or collectively, in different ways as members of EU than that they would have done without it.

Primarily, all the member states bar Greece, and to a certain extent the UK, treated the CMTP as an issue of 'low' politics. Thus, they accepted compromises in order to bring the CMTP in line with policy targets to which they have subscribed in the EU context and conceived as more important, e.g. the SEM, or environmental targets, or in line with public attitudes, e.g. ro/ro safety. Then, in a context of economic pressures and policy uncertainty the majority of maritime member states was ready to make concessions in order to establish effective alternatives. This was easier within the EU than in other international fora for two reasons: first, because EU membership has more in common than the membership of international organisations like IMO; and second because the bargaining position of member states *vis-à-vis* the private actors was strengthened by the commitments resulting from the participation in the EU (the 'paradox of weakness': Grande, 1996), as well as by the preceding consensus-building activities of the Commission. Given the spatial dimension of maritime activities, the expanding geographical span of the EU membership was a feature that facilitated the adoption of this approach (PSC directive), though it should not be forgotten that the same factors provided rigid difficulties for an agreement on ro/ro 'stability'.

The 'sense' of community was also important in the case of those member states that were less keen to compromise: isolation was perceived as a real danger. Despite hard bargaining, they become willing to accept losses rather than face the criticism and frustration of their partners, e.g. as the other Mediterranean states renounced their ambitions to retain cabotage restrictions Greece had to follow (similar events are notified in the air sector: Mény *et al*, 1996). The fact that a group of member states does not maintain a core, or any, interest in the sector under discussion had another critical implication. This is the presence of a non-active majority of member states that, in the absence of national policy targets to defend, consistently supported and empowered the Commission's initiatives. As the obligations and commitments deriving from the Treaties created a degree of spillover, and the CMTP decisions created pressures for further initiatives, this non-active majority enhanced the political momentum that the EU initiatives contained. This practice contributed to a process that member states did not (even collectively) fully control.

In the structures and functions of the supposedly intergovernmental Council this study identified additional intra-institutional norms and rules that critically affected the decisions that national administrations were ready to make. First, the problem solving decisional style of the Council (also: Westlake, 1995) means that fundamental disagreements did not imply the demise of the proposal in discussion but further negotiations in search for accommodation and a common denominator (freedom to provide services). Second, in the presence of a non-active majority, the 'edge effect'[2] minimised the ability of states opposing integration, or the already suggested terms of the latter, to extract high prices (safe seas). Third, the consensual culture disinclined those states retaining objections until the voting stage from vetoing, or forming blocking minorities: insofar as the CMTP is concerned the progress of the cabotage rule, gives some credence to Teasdale's (1993) pronouncement of the national veto as 'dead'. Fourth, the sectoral formation of the Council means the isolation, when it came to detailed decisions, of transport ministers in an 'industry sensitive' apparatus facilitating agreements (safe seas). Fifth, successive Council presidencies put aside national preferences in order to successfully fulfil their bureaucratic responsibilities, facilitate agreements on other CMTP issues, or use the presidency as a device to ensure that 'inevitable' EU policy outcomes would be closer to its national priorities.

Although not explicitly referred to in the CMTP developments examined, a critical parameter must be added at this point of analysis. This is the vital role that the Commission, and not least the Commissioner himself, exercises, within the Council mechanisms, whether these are working groups, or the meeting of Transport Ministers per se. An insider can undoubtedly state it more forcefully than any researcher: 'The Commission is really the engine of the Community. The Council can only work on the basis of a Commission proposal. If there is nothing coming from the Commission then the Council cannot do anything. Then, once the Commission has made a proposal it is up to the Commission officials to ask for discussions on these proposals. We have seen proposals falling asleep and nobody taking them up. The Commission has to ask for meetings, and once the negotiations start they have to animate the debate. They have to explain and defend their file. If there is a group meeting, or a sub-committee at a group level, half of the time the microphone is held by the Commission official. It is a kind of dialogue between the Commission and the rest of the room. If you have a bad official then you have a file that turns to nowhere. If you have a bad Commissioner you have a bad Council' (Vermote, 1996).

Inaugurating this comment in the context of the case studies, it is not surprising that the Council has systematically agreed to share policy administration and implementation competencies with the Commission. True, it used the 'comitology' as a means of control. But, as the empirical discussion of 'comitology' by Docksey and Williams (1994) suggests, these procedures also strengthen the Commission's control of the agenda: its draft must be voted upon and a decision must be taken within the deadlines laid down.

To fully understand the repercussions of an institutional framework involving multiple locus of decision making powers to its creators, one should also consider the new dimensions in the relationships of organised interests and national administration. The preceding 'paradox of weakness' coexists with its very opposite phenomena: an emerging, in a very neofunctional manner, 'weakness' of member states because of the direct exchanges between EU institutions and organised interests. This study revealed (for similar arguments: van Schendelen, 1993; Mazey and Richardson, 1994) that member states became less successful in coordinating national private interests regarding the CMTP agenda (cabotage), or found themselves reacting to an agenda, or terms of regulations, which had effectively been set elsewhere (shortsea; SBT). Following the vertical expansion of the MIF, and to a lesser extent the EP attempts to form a direct communication between subnational authorities and EU institutions, national administrations found themselves in something of a 'subcentral government situation' (Allum, 1995). They adjusted domestic policy administration hierarchies, structured their relationships with organised interests and regional authorities, and ultimately committed to common policies, according to the terms agreed within the MIF procedures. In other words, the exchanges of the Commission and interest groups (see below) restricted the actual role of member states to a loosely supervisory one. 'Low politics' it might be, but this does not challenge the fact that details of the CMTP frameworks and specific rules were in essence determined even before member states began bargaining.

In retrospect, a *third conclusion* can be detailed: whilst member states retained a prominent role in the CMTP developments, EU membership *per se* and the norms of the institutionalised national administrations interaction (Council), shaped their preferences and policy actions. Beyond this, the research findings discussed in the last two sections suggest that member states *de facto* superiority in policy formulation has been absent because of three reasons: (a) the dynamism of the formal powers member states have ceded to the EU decision-making institutions; (b) the feedback that a non-active majority of member states, and the behaviour of the rest as 'member' rather than 'nation' states, provided to this dynamism; and (c) the reform of the relationships between policy actors and private interests.

Contending Interest Groups The evidence of the case-studies as regards the role of private actors also fits in very well with a picture of prominent actors interacting within rules and norms that affect their policy preferences and actions. On the one hand, the within-case analyses suggest that organised interests provided a distinctive input into the policy developments; in some cases they stand among the driving forces of the CMTP. Maritime industries developed multi-level lobbying activities that advanced and constrained the CMTP developments examined. The ability of each industry to do so depended on factors that can be summarised in two broad categories: (a) the market powers and structural importance of the industry for the maritime transport system; and (b) the organisational capacities of the industry to exploit the lobbying opportunities offered.

The shipping industry enjoyed a privileged position and its input was systematically greater than that of the maritime industries. Being the core of the system resulted in apparent advantages, i.e. shipowners' consensus was *de facto* critical to securing the promotion of the shortsea policy from an idea to a policy framework, hence their major impact to the agreed policy. Moreover, the first case study highlights that these advantages were furthered by shipowners' capability to avoid undesirable regulatory frameworks through the re-registration of their mobile assets. In line with

Aspinwall's (1995a) thesis, the fluidity of shipping capital in a context of internationalisation induced a 'shipowners' bias' that decisively helped their cause against higher European safety standards. Besides, in some of the member states the preceding factors had already contributed to a tradition of close relationships between the industry and national administrations and the disinclination of the latter to openly confront them.

Three organisational features of shipowners' interests representation generated a particularly effective readiness to lobby and offer 'technical expertise' at every stage of the process: (a) the remarkable tradition of collective associability, which helped agreements on a common stance even in dividing themes (cabotage; but not 'stability' where the geographical features made the achievement of a collective stand impossible); (b) the familiarity with the complex and unstructured Brussels game; and (c) the devotion of substantial resources to interest representation.

By contrast, none of the other maritime industries that mobilised to influence the process shared such characteristics; hence, they have all been less effective. In brief, port industries, whether authorities or operators, are remarkably embedded to specific locations, a factor that facilitates rules imposition, and transnational collective interests representation was only recently developed, a factor that limited the exploration of lobbying channels and exaggerated the difficulties which the intra-industry heterogeneity produces to achieve and advocate collective stances. Shippers were less affected by the safe seas policies, less interested in the development of a shortsea policy, and in comparison to shipowners they devoted less resources to a daily exchange with 'Brussels'. Freight forwarders were handicapped by the secondary importance of the industry, the limited lobbying resources, and the internal disputes of a Euro-federation whose membership is not necessarily involved in maritime transportation. Finally, shipbrokers remained uninformed of the actual developments as they decided not to be involved in lobbying on the details of a policy that did not affect their competitive position directly.

On the other hand, it would be a mistake to understand the role of organised interests as a one-way causal arrow determining the pace of the CMTP developments. Rather than that, attempting to influence the plurality of decision-makers, the contending interests were 'locked' into a complex policy-making process within which three interrelated sets of parameters affected their policy demands, the structure of their advocacy and, foremost, their actual influence.

The first set of parameters lies in the fact that organised interests found themselves lobbying decision makers that have gained relative autonomy to act. Not only were private actors less powerful against national administrations 'tied' to the EU project, but they also did so against a Commission invoking its formal policy-making obligations and authority to act. The persistent incapability to control the CMTP agenda offers noticeable evidences that this factor has undermined the actual input of organised interests. The institutional exchanges, and the spillover of the SEM, produced the intrusion of the CMTP in issues dealing with the internal market; in other words, neither shipowners, nor trade unions, nor even the latent support of their views by national administrations managed to limit the CMTP to external issues, nor had shippers achieved putting maritime services liberalisation into discussions earlier. Then, as in the light of public concerns policy makers converged over a policy framework, shipowners' forceful objections did not restrain the CMTP expansion in the issue-area of safety.

The second set of parameters lies with the 'channels of access' that the DGs of the Commission and the EP have offered to interests groups. Given the aforementioned capacities of the 'interested to be lobbied' EU institutions (as they needed information and acquiescence in order to detail policy initiatives, legitimise EU-level developments, improve their position in the inter-institutional triangle Council-Commission-EP, and secure rules implementation), organised interests have striven to exploit these channels trying to enhance their participation in policy making. Whilst many details were decided within the interactions developed between EU institutions and maritime industries, implicit to these interactions was a 'bias', which strengthened and extended the progress of Europeanisation.

Four findings lead to this conclusion. First, the potential of these exchanges, and not least the 'political momentum' of the Commission initiatives, provoked a generalised tendency to work alongside this institution in a cooperative fashion rather than attack its initiatives from the outset. As the Commission led the expansion of the agenda, or attempted to reverse a non-decision situation, even those having a record of long-standing opposition to specific EU rules eventually adopted this strategy. Second, the tendency of the EU institutions to balance the input of private interests transformed the reluctant acceptance of 'second best' policies to active support for them, in order to counterbalance the possible gains of competing interests (shipping industry/SBT). Third, the observed EP-interest groups interplay indicates that when the latter opted to work within the pro-integration considerations of the EP, even if at the same time they were vigorously lobbying the Council members against the progress of the Commission proposals, this helped to amend critical details of policy initiatives (cabotage/trade unions; SBT/port industries); but when they attempted to halt integration or challenge the logic of the Commission, i.e. by exploiting the presence of a helpful Rapporteur, this path to influence the actual developments was systematically restricted by the plenary EP session, and that was irrespective of their relative powers (shipowners/minimum training Directive; seafarers/1986 rules).

The most striking example is the establishment and privileged position of the MIF. As it attempted to form policy coalitions through a deliberate strategy of institutionalising interests' participation, the Commission affected both the forms of collective action and the actual influence of interest groups. Not only did it encourage the emergence of EU level interest groups by pursuing a policy of preferential treatment (consistent with what scholars have observed: cf. Butt Philip, 1985; Greenwood *et al*, 1992) but also interest groups were driven and shaped by this initiative. Some of them, even among those that had not expressed any interest, now consciously see themselves as not only responding but also creating policy or correcting national policies (i.e. shippers). Within this process, however, DG-VII and DG-III have been more than *primus inter pares*: it had the political capital required to transmit its ideas, filter the agenda, 'rationalise' demands in line with its preferences, and privilege those interest groups which supported its ideas. Although when isolated some of these findings can be possibly interpreted as tactical calculations, when put in perspective a consistent pro-integrative filtering of the stances organised interests advocated becomes apparent.

The third set of parameters are the endogenous characteristics of the industries mobilised to influence the CMTP developments through a Euro-federation format of interest representation, in turn a response to the explicit EU institutions preference to deal with one group representing the whole industry throughout the EU. Whilst those associated collectively at EU-level share many common social and commercial interests, they are also separated by heterogenous commercial practices and traditions, distinct domestic policies and political backgrounds, even the divergent geographical morphologies within which they develop their economic activities. Thus, there is frequently a noticeable variation of intra-industry preferences. The examination of interest groups mobilisation suggests that with the Euro-groups predominantly articulating the stances of their more 'Europe-minded' membership, those interests positioned negatively *vis-à-vis* policy Europeanisation were *de facto* weakened. In short, the structure and preferences of the EU institutions resulted in a 'new' environment of interests' representation, which provided incentives for collective action (see also: Greenwood and Aspinwall, 1998) and contributed to a more cooperative attitude towards EU policy activities.

Reflecting on the preceding discussion, a *fourth conclusion* can be drawn: interest groups representing maritime industries have been prominent actors with variable powers and provided a distinctive input to the policy making process, however, the institutional framework in which policy making took place influenced their input. The influence of these actors was related to the economic position of the industry, and to a certain extent the resources devoted to interests representation. But the logic of the decision making process, that is the channels of access and the new forms of actors' relationships it implied, influenced interest groups strategies, induced a Europeanised format of interests advocacy, which in turn induced a 'pro-integration' bias to policy demands. Beyond these, it limited the actual input of private actors. The two case-studies suggest that although both national administrations and the EU decision-making institutions developed their actions having in mind what they were pressured to do by the most powerful of these interests, or what they could do given the economic environment, they have gained an autonomy that has an adverse effect to the direct interest groups input.

In the light of these findings, it is worth saying something more about the powers that the shipping industry extracted from 'capital mobility' (Aspinwall, 1995a). The advantages that shipowners gained by their capital exit powers was comparative but not absolute: it was enough to secure an advantage when their interests confronted other private actors' interests, i.e. port authorities (SBT) or organised labour (minimum training), but could neither secure that issues like safety or the internal market would remain 'no-go' areas for the EU, nor allow shipowners to define EU rules according to their preferences. Besides, shipowners' 'loyalty' to traditional flags is also economically driven, which means that capital exit is not unlimited and, moreover, there is a self-interest in being part of the process that defines the regulatory framework of these flags. Furthermore, as the

CMTP agenda expands not all the policies in question involve the issue of 'capital exit'.

The latter also suggests that whilst employment and registration internationalisation had an adverse effect on the negotiating powers of organised labour, these market changes are not variables that can explain the consistency of this weakness. The deficiencies of trade unions interest representation strategy including an insistence on their own agenda, which is an indirect effect of the pressures that 'capital exit' exercises on its membership, stand as additional causes. Still, these factors cannot parsimoniously explain why labour did not have a greater input in the developments examined in the second case study: aspects of economic internationalisation increase the importance of quality seafaring for the achievement of the common policy targets and trade unions adjusted to the EU agenda, however their policy demands were neglected. Juxtaposing the facts that the Commission preferred to agree policy directions through an alliance with maritime industries and that the weakness of trade unions is a frequent phenomenon in EU policy developments (McLaughlin and Greenwood, 1995) one can bring into the analysis suggestions that the conjunction of a liberal democratic polity and a capitalist economy confers an unusual degree of systemic power on capital (in the sense that irrespective of whether they take concrete action to actualise it or not industrialists are better placed to influence policy developments than labour: Hall, 1986, p. 262-3; also: Lindblom, 1977), and conclude that the EU, as an entity based on these principles, duplicates and reinforces the balance observed in the domestic arenas of its member states.

The Common Maritime Transport Policy in Retrospect

It should be clear by now that the previous studies concerning the CMTP cannot explain precisely the factors that have influenced the CMTP developments examined. In particular, the intergovernmental approach of the first CMTP studies (Cafruny, 1987; Bredima-Savopoulou, 1990) explains too little. True, member states have shifted to the EU due to their incapability to solve sectoral problems at the national level, or the difficulties of the international policy-making regimes. It is also true that national governments exercise a prominent role throughout the policy-making process. But these phenomena should be disconnected from the particular intergovernmentalist argument. First, policy-making has not been a mere collection of national governments bargaining with each other, nor have member states been in an exclusive control of the policy agenda and outcomes. As the detailed conclusions suggest, an explanatory model that omits the role of both the EU institutions and interest groups, as well as the influence of the institutional dynamism on the actions of member states, ignores some of the factors that influenced decisively the CMTP developments.[3]

On the other hand, by focusing on the importance of the interactions between private interests, national governments, and supranational actors, Aspinwall's (1995a) analysis explains much more. Foremost, the preceding analysis confirms that interest groups, involved in multi-level lobbying game with variable powers, played an eminent role. In many respects, this research also confirms that 'capital exit' was relevant for the determination of these interest groups' powers to influence the policy making process. Moreover, this research identified similar economic factors to motivate policy actions. To review them employing Aspinwall's (1995a) terms, domestic priorities, global regimes, collective competitiveness of the maritime industries, and a functional spillover, have put apparent pressures on both policy makers and private actors; nonetheless, all these bar the latter confirm the conclusions of the earlier CMTP studies. What is missing however from the pluralist domestic politics paradigm that emerges as the most important point of Aspinwall's studies is the presence of an institutional dynamic, which goes beyond a functional dimension. Policy developments were not always a direct product of group conflict, nor the importance of capital exit was as deterministic as Aspinwall suggests. As detailed earlier in this chapter, understanding which economic interests have gained economic strength and political power due to economic internationalisation does not mean that we could predict the CMTP agenda, or how specific rules would be likely to change. In the light of the preceding actors-analysis and the conclusions that have been drawn it would be argued that whilst Aspinwall's analysis doesn't represent an intellectual failure it is dominated by the role of pressure groups power and undermines the actual role of the institutional framework.

The examination of the common policy on safe seas and shortsea shipping suggests that an 'explanatory' model of the factors that determined the progress and courses of the CMTP should also focus on the distinctive institutional dynamics of the EU. First, it needs to put centre stage the capacities of the EU decision-making institutions. The making of the CMTP policy has been a process within which the Commission had a decisive role in shaping policy developments through: its leadership; policy innovation; exploitation of formal powers; consensus-building function; the relative autonomy it gained from its creators when it built coalitions with maritime industries, or when member states seek an alliance with it to promote their targets; and its ability to have a prime role within the 'channels of access' it has opened to private actors. As also did, to a lesser extent, the EP, primarily through an inter-institutional EP-Commission partnership, and secondarily through the political resources that it has developed, and the ECJ. Second, such a model needs also to focus on the impacts (detailed in the preceding conclusions) that the rules and norms governing the EU policy-making process exercised on the activities of all the involved policy actors. When contextual economic changes provoked policy instability, these factors had a major impact on the noticeable policy Europeanisation in both of the issue-areas examined.

At the same time, however, this model should not be reductionist insofar as the input of the other policy actors is concerned. To express it in the form of a *fifth conclusion*, rather than positioning these actors in an hierarchical order (where some of them would be dismissed as being, or becoming, irrelevant) we should understand member states, organised interests, and EU institutions, as 'autonomous but interdependent' actors involved in a triangular relationship. Each one strengthened its bargaining position against the other by referring to its relationships to the third. The prospects of a balance that would advance favourable policy responses to the changing economic environment, intensified these exchanges and the search for 'winning' coalitions at the expense of each actor 'autonomy'. The dynamic of this process eventually affected the relationships between them, but also favoured policy actions and outcomes that advanced integration: one of the poles of the triangle (i.e. EU institutions) advances by definition this aim. When integrated, the detailed research results provide the explanatory model delineated in Figure 9.1.

Whilst the results work in favour of the central proposition of this study, they also draw our attention to some critical facts. First, that the institutional dynamism should not be taken to mean that the actions of the EU institutions were in fundamental respects autonomous from member states, or organised interests; policy arenas, the logic of participation, and policy preferences were shaped, but the accord of other actors was also important. Second, that we should not homogenise clusters of actors but be conscious that within each cluster there are actors sharing variable powers and interests for the policy developments that are taking place. Among others, this means that it is not enough to say that institutions 'mattered', but we also need to specify which of them, and how, did they matter. Third, that rather than a stable process with a predefined outcome, the common policy changes are the result of a dynamic process within which policy actors need consensus in order to develop policy ideas to policy rules. A final point needs also to be clarified: this model helps us understand better the dynamic of policy making process and define the factors that influence it, it does not imply, however, that the solutions produced are by definition better, or worse.

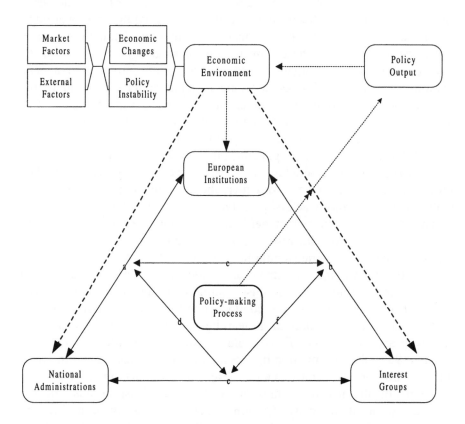

Figure 10.1 Economic Environment, Policy Actors and the CMTP

The Prospects of the Common Maritime Transport Policy

Given the highly complex political and economic parameters that are at play assessing the CMTP prospects is not a simple task. Implicit to the described dynamic of the policy-making process is an inherent uncertainty and, in addition, the 'policy gaps' of the future are unpredictable.

With the characteristics of the economic environment suggesting a continuing transition of maritime transport member states will undoubtedly remain in search for effective policy alternatives at the most international level possible. As the international scene is becoming more fraught and complex, 'membership' of a Union sharing common principles will stimulate the debate for EU initiatives, especially as the commitments that this membership implies can help overcome some of the domestic pressures, i.e. demands for further incentives to operate their national flags, or calls against the deregulation of manning conditions. On the other hand, given the 'openness' of the EU institutions, particularly the pursuit of the Commission for allies, organised interests will shift further their agenda towards the EU. Besides, as domestic national policies respond to the changes of the economic environment in different ways, the stakeholders are interested in seeing a level-playing field established and the maritime mode to integrate in multimodal transport operations.

All these do not however guarantee that common policy initiatives will develop and rules will be adopted. A critical factor for the further CMTP progress will be the extent to which the dynamic opportunism of the Commission and those actors perceiving the need for EU level action (whether private actors, member states, or the EP) will manage to encapsulate the various interests in policy realignments into a set of policy initiatives that will generate a minimum consensus. The results of this study indicate that the Commission stands as a policy entrepreneur and a political ally that create options and mobilise coalitions in favour of collective EU action. The 1996 review of the common maritime strategy (CEU, 1996a; 1996b) suggests that through a learning process which implied both successes and failures (i.e., Euros), and an extensive consultation (i.e. Core Group, 1996), the Commission has been particularly effective in providing a framework for discussions on a policy agenda encompassing all the major problems of the maritime transport system, not least because of the presence of a 'high status' Commissioner who has given a different dimension to the transport portfolio.[4] Still, these discussions are inevitably conditioned by the economics of the sector, i.e. the means to address collectively questions of EU flagged shipping competitiveness and European seafarers employment within an internationalised economic context remain questionable.

The developments in the latter area provide an illuminating example of the powers and limits of the institutional dynamism, as well as the prospects of the CMTP. Notwithstanding claims that a common policy can be successful without necessarily establishing a European flag (Roe, 1996), the failure of the Euros proposal could be conceived as a challenge to the aforementioned conclusions. At the peak of the flagging-out crisis the Commission put forward an ambitious proposal implying a revolutionary effect to the regulatory regime of the industry. Whilst in conditions of crisis this initiative generated enthusiasm and discussions, it was soon realised that there was no desire to proceed with this particular idea. At the end, several member states and both social partners insist that it was 'their stance' that led to the withdrawal of the proposal.[5]

Yet, having formally withdrawn Euros, the Commission put forward a different set of proposals that will draw up minimum standards for the EU registries (CEU, 1996a). As happened in the case of cabotage, the EU institutions might lead to a reform of a non-decision situation, this time via indirect means. The fourfold strategy (i.e. safety standards, open markets, measures for securing competitiveness, and harmonisation of national level state aids) under development comprises an incremental alternative of regulating EU-registration to the breakthrough and symbolism of the tried but failed Single European Flag approach.

In this vein, maritime safety policy has already progressed beyond the 'safe seas' framework. The authority and experience that the Commission has gained, the EP pressures, and not least the fact that the EU works as a force for pressure on IMO developments, have provided a critical background. However, the expanding agenda needs to acknowledge the different operating conditions that exist throughout the EU. The outcome of the ongoing discussion regarding ro/ro stability provides an interesting test for the capacities of the Commission to find a path towards common rules against the heterogeneity of the expanding EU membership and the divergent demands that this induces.

A second test for the prospects of the CMPT is its implementation record. Effective implementation reinforces the Commission's legitimacy, and eventually increases the pressures of the EU institutions and some member states (i.e. the non-active majority and states having relatively modern fleet) for EU safety legislation that will go beyond agreed IMO standards. The vital question will then be how can regional rules be consistent with shipping safety as an international global concept. On the other hand, the loose implementation and the consequent ineffectiveness of the EU rules raise a different question: whether the EU policy-making authority is irreversible. The preceded conclusions suggest that in such case the EU will continue to develop initiatives that duplicate the IMO standards, and in moments when maritime incidents will weaken the position of powerful interests, i.e. shipowners, or the scepticism of maritime states, the Commission and the EP will attempt to generate consensus for further policy initiatives. The recent policy proposals following the *Erica* incident (CEU, 2000c) confirm this suggestion.

As regards shortsea shipping, it can be anticipated that the current Commission-maritime industries exchanges, foremost with the shipping industry, will provide further sets of proposals aiming to enhance the share of the maritime mode in the modal pie. Still, much depends on the application of the subsidiarity principle in practice, as the progress of non-regulatory measures depends on national and subnational level policy actions. On the other hand, assisted by the formal competence it has gained, the Commission will continue to exercise a key role in the monitoring and progressive implementation of the cabotage rule, especially as the ensuing fundamental changes to the maritime markets will result in demands for amending the existing political compromise.

European Integration: Reflections on the Theoretical Debate

The findings of this analysis on policy Europeanisation add to recent studies that have inserted a neoinstitutional perspective when conceptualising EU policy developments. This perspective has been most useful to draw our attention to features of the CMTP developments that had been neglected, or at least underestimated, notably the key role of the Commission, the EP, and the ECJ in shaping the policy developments that have taken place, as well as the several ways that the rules and norms of the EU policy-making game have affected the ways in which national governments and private actors perceived and pursued their interests. The neoinstitutionalist perspective has provided a major help in understanding the CMTP developments precisely because it has suggested (contrasting the 'other' institutionalist accounts: Hall and Taylor, 1996; Dowding, 2000) that, rather than attempting to read everything done by the institutions alone, we should focus on the matrix of the interactions that take place between them and the rest of the actors that are involved in the governance of a polity (Thelen and Sletmo, 1992). This study certainly indicates that an explanation of CMTP focused solely on the EU institutions, solely the member states, or that focused too much on the role of private actors would give only a partial view. At a general level, neoinstitutionalism provides a useful theoretical focus on the dynamics of the EU policy-making and has much to commend it.

The underpinning factor for the usefulness of such a 'comparative politics' framework is that an internal EU policy arena with its own characteristics (the most obvious being the pluralization of policy actors and a 'multi-level' decision making process) and complexity has grown considerably. Member states and organised interests think and act as parts of 'a new system of governance' (W. Wallace, 1983) rather than as part of a 'two-levels diplomacy game' (Putnam, 1988): they all take into account the choices of their EU partners prioritising collective EU-level actions and interests representation, rather than emphasising their national differences, whilst the EU institutions share policy setting and shaping capacities. In that sense, the emerging approach of the EU as a 'polity like' entity does appear to be an appropriate analytical device to use, at the very least for sectoral EU policy analysis and, just as Aspinwall (1995a) claims, the CMTP analysis in particular. At a more general level Hix (1994; 1999) argues, therefore, the analytical tools of *comparative politics* rather than those of *international relations* should increasingly be used for the study of EU policy making.

Nonetheless, such argument needs some qualification. Clearly, in order to understand sectoral policy developments one needs to move beyond questions of sovereignty, or the nature of the EU and, as for instance Caporaso (1996) suggests, employ a post-ontological focus on the internal dynamics of the EU. Intergovernmentalist refinements have focused on the instrumentality of the EU institutions for reasons that the transaction-costs approaches illuminate (cf. Moravcsik, 1993) or the 'symbiosis' of the Commission and member states (Taylor, 1996), but there is still a lack of exploration of the dynamics of the system to produce and implement binding decisions that member states have created, the EU institutions as actors with their own capacities, or the substantive role of private actors and the 'new' interstate interests representation system that develops, all distinctive features of this research findings. On the other hand, whilst some of the findings are closer to the neofunctionalist agenda (interlocking policy actors, pluralistic lobbying, supranational institutions) there is a major challenge to the linear progression of integration (which has nevertheless been reviewed even by neofunctionalists: Sandholtz, 1993) as well as to the prediction of a diminishing national administrations role.

Moreover, all the 'locked in' policy actors are not guided only by calculations and preferences, but are also becoming part of a wider environment that is incorporated into their policy choices. Nonetheless, systemic parameters like the influence of the global environment on the EU and *vice versa* cannot be isolated, even when the setting and shaping of sectoral common policies are considered. As already discussed, EU policy changes do not take place in a vacuum but as economic interdependence and internationalisation continue to increase, whilst some EU policy decisions (i.e. safe seas policy) are conditioned by the fact that the outside world conceives the EU 'more as an international regime than a federation'. Thus, this author would agree with Hurrell and Menon (1996), who suggest that in methodological terms the researcher of EU policies should cut across the supposed divide between International Relations and Comparative Politics and cast his/her net widely, both because of the continuation of the centrality of member states, and the fact that EU policies cannot in general be studied without reference to international factors (also: Sbragia, 1992).

Then, based on the variety of the EU policy-making patterns and 'bureaucratic games' (Peters, 1992) played, scholars have suggested that different frameworks may explain different stages of the policy process. For instance, Peterson (1995) suggests that 'history-making' decisions can be best analysed by macro-level theories, 'policy-setting' by neoinstitutionalism, and 'policy-shaping' by policy network approach. However, the CMTP analysis suggests a continuous feedback, rather than a clear cut between these stages, leading to the conclusion that this dichotomy seems to be, at the very least in some cases, inappropriate. On the other hand, employing different frameworks to different issue areas might be more essential. Apart from the fact that 'history making' decisions have their own logic and procedures, institutional profiles vary from one area of policy to another (Bulmer, 1994b) and a range of organisation formats and reciprocal influences between EU institutions and organised interests exist (cf. Greenwood and Ronit, 1994). Hence, in other sectors, or policy issues, distinctive policy characteristics arise, the multi-level governance differently configured (at least formally), and the consistent Euro-federation interests representation strategy observed in this study give its place to the mobilisation of an extensive network of actors. Therefore, other research frameworks, e.g. 'policy networks' analysis, might be more useful and different conceptualisations might ultimately arise. As it becomes widely accepted, the complexity of the EU means that we must live with multiple models and concepts in order to at least accurately describe its policy process (cf. Hix, 1996; Richardson, 1996).

In this context, the preceding analysis suggests that to explain the dynamism of particular policy sectors, much might be gained by the essence of the neoinstitutionalist set of assumptions, that *EU institutions matter*, and the exploration of which of them, and how, they do so. Of course, this framework can be helpful only if research avoids the danger of entering an ahistorical discussion, which would suggest that everything could be explained by the institutional framework and ignore the role of other policy actors. Moreover, as Cini (1996, p. 9) points out, EU research should also overcome the 'anthropomorphism' (which endows non-human entities with human characteristics) of the neoinstitutionalist account that focuses on the cohesive rather than the fragmentary element of the institutions. As this volume discussed, fragmentation and multi-level politics are core elements of the functioning of the institutions and the policy-making process of the EU entity, and its consequences may have much to say about policy developments. These disadvantages seriously considered, then the neoinstitutionalist perspective can be operetionalised as a sort of umbrella under which other theoretical and conceptual models will be applied, i.e. the useful elements of traditional theories and 'economic interdependence', or other comparative politics paradigms. Whilst in many respects this has been a point acknowledged when the level of the analysis is trans-sectoral or refers to the EU's distinctive configuration (Peterson, 1995), the distinctive role of the EU institutions in the progress of the CMTP developments examined works in favour of Bulmer's (1994b) argument that the neoinstitutionalist 'realism' can also be helpful when this level of analysis is policy- or issue-specific.

Epilogue

On a final note, the present volume discussed the factors that induce, determine, or interfere with the progress of the Common Maritime Transport Policy in the 1990s. Confirming the stimulus that the contextual economic internationalisation and the ineffectual policy responses of the national, international, and self-regulatory, non-EU policy making levels have provided for discussing EU policy developments, it concluded that a key element in the progress of the CMTP lies in the distinctive institutional dynamism of the EU. Through a reconstruction and analysis of the interactions between policy actors regarding the development of a common policy on maritime safety and shortsea shipping, it has detailed the ways that institutional parameters of the new system of governance, with its own dynamic and rules, have influenced the policy making process.

The conclusions can provide a useful background to all those who will seek to shed light on the making of this, or other EU policies. They might also be helpful at a practical level. Policy makers and interests representatives might use this analysis for understanding the policy arena within which they act. Beyond these, however, by establishing the decisive role of the EU decision-making institutions the research conclusions upgrade the importance of addressing the problems of transparency, accountability, and popular consent, that both academics (cf. Butt Philip, 1996), and politicians increasingly associate with a policy making process which impinges on the lives of millions of citizens.

Notes

1 Conceptualising US politics and policy-making, Kingdon (1984, p.188) suggests that 'policy windows' are created as three 'streams' are coupled: a given problem is recognised in the 'problem' stream, feasible policies are proposed in the 'policy' stream, and changes for the adoption of a policy in the 'political' stream are favourable.

2 Defined in Chapter 6 as the tendency of those standing at the edges of the Council to realise their no-win position and reluctantly abandon it sooner rather than later in order to have a more substantial contribution to the content of the agreed policy.

3 Notably, in the light of the 1989 developments Cafruny (1991) enriched his original thesis suggesting that to understand the CMTP we should not ignore the role of the EU institutions. The scholar's more recent writings on European integration are further distanced from the 'traditional' intergovernmental argument (Cafruny and Rosenthal,

1993; Cafruny and Lankowski, 1997).

4   The statement of an experienced lobbyist mirrors the general attitude in 'Brussels': 'before Mr. Kinnock it is fair to say that we had relatively weak Commissioners in Transport. Mr Kinnock came into the post having an idea and an intention of being a Transport Commissioner, so he has been able to give direction to the work. An interesting point is that even Commissioner Van Miert is recognised as a very powerful Competition Commissioner but when he was a Transport Commissioner this was not the case. He may simply have grown up in stature and with his experience' (Baasch, 1996). Notably, a Council official provoked the thought that even the personality of the Commissioner might be important (Vermote, 1996).

5   Trade unions argue that Euros did not have a particular advantage unless it was going to enhance European employment (Tselentis, 1996; also Cafruny, 1991). Shipowners, who never reached a common stance on Euros, argue that their interest was in the potential incentives to the industry rather than a European flag (Peppa, 1996). To quote an industry representative: 'I am not sure it was a completely united shipowners front... there were different groupings under the discussions of Euros coming from different viewpoints, all tried to fit these into a single policy area. But how one single policy would accommodate all these points was always debatable and in the event it could not. There was not sufficient support from any of the bodies coming together' (Southorn, 1996).

Bibliography

Abbati, D.E. (1986). *Transport and European Integration.* Luxembourg: Official Publications of the EC.

Ademuni, O. (1988). *Shipping in International Trade Relations.* Aldershot: Avebury.

Allum, P. (1995). *State and Society in Western Europe.* London: Polity.

Almond, G. (1988). The return to the state. In: *American Political Science Review*, Vol. 82, No. 3, pp. 853-874.

Amin, A. (1994) (ed.). *Post-Fordism: A Reader.* Oxford: Blackwell.

Anastasopoulos, G.N. (1994). *Horizontal Production (or Transport in Greece and Europe)* (in Greek). Athens: Euro-Community Publications.

Andersen, S. and Eliasen, K.A. (1993) (eds). *Making Policy in Europe: The Europeification of National Policy making.* London: Sage.

Andersen, S. and Eliasen, K.A. (1995). EU: Lobbying: The new research agenda. In: *European Journal of Political Research.* Vol. 27, No. 4, pp. 427-44.

Argirofo, E. (1972). Flags of Convenience and Substandard Vessels. In: *International Labour Review*, Vol. 110, No. 11, pp. 437-453.

Armstrong, J.D. (1982). *The rise of the International Organisations: A Short History.* London: Macmillan.

Aspinwall, M. (1995a). *Moveable Feast: Pressure Group Conflict and The European Community Shipping Policy.* Aldershot: Avebury.

Aspinwall, M. (1995b). International Integration or Internal Politics? Anatomy of a Single Market Measure. In: *Journal of Common Market Studies*, Vol. 33, No. 4, pp. 475-499.

Aspinwall, M. (1996). The Unholy Social Trinity: Modelling Social Dumping under Conditions of Capital Mobility and Free Trade. In: *West European Politics*, Vol. 19, No. 1, pp. 125-150.

Baasch, H. (1996). Secretary General, European Shippers Council, *personal interview.* Brussels, 28 May.

Bantias, D. (1996). Permanent Representation of Greece to the EU – Maritime Transport, *personal interview.* Brussels, 26 June.

Baum, H. (1993). Government and Transport Markets. In: Polak, J.B. and Heertje, A. (1993), pp. 52-80.

Bayliss, B.T. (1979). Transport Policies in the European Communities. In: *Journal of Transport Economics and Politics*, Vol. 13, No. 1, pp. 28-43.

Blum, U. (1985). The development and the effects of transportation investments in W. Germany: 1960-80. In: ECMT (1986), pp. 37-66.

Böhme, H. (1984). The Changing framework of Shipping: Trends in trade, technology and policies. In: *Marine Policy*, Vol. 8, No. 3, pp. 229-238.

Böhme, H. (1989). The Economic consequences of restraints on transaction in the International Market for Shipping Services. In: Yannopoulos, G.N. (1989), pp. 14-39.

Bradley, K.St.C. (1992). Comitology and the Law: Through a glass darkly. In: *Common Market Law Review*, Vol. 29, pp. 693-721.

Branch, A.E. (1988). *Economics of Shipping Practices and Management.* London: Chapman and Hall.

Bredimas, A. and Tzoannos, J.G. (1981). In Search of Common Shipping Policy for the European Community. In: *Journal of Common Market Studies*, Vol. 20, No. 2, pp. 95-114.

Bredima-Savopoulou, A. (1990). *The Common Shipping Policy of the EC*. Amsterdam: Elsevier.

Bromhead, P.A. (1979). Transport Policy. In: Coffey, D. (ed.), *Economic Policies of the Common Market*, pp. 122-145, London: Macmillan.

Brooks, M.R. and Button, K.J. (1992). Shipping within the framework of a Single European Market. In: *Transport Reviews*, Vol. 12, No. 3, pp. 237-251.

Bull, H., Kingsbury, B. and Robert, A. (1990) (eds). *Hugo Grotius on International Relations*. Oxford: Clarendon.

Bulmer, S. (1983). Domestic Politics and European Community Policy-Making. In: *Journal of Common Market Studies*, Vol. 21, No. 4, pp. 349-363.

Bulmer, S. (1994a). The Governance of the EU: a New Institutionalist Approach. In: *Journal of Public Policy*, Vol. 13, No. 4, pp. 351-380.

Bulmer, S. (1994b). Institutions and Policy change in the EC. In: *Public Administration*, Vol. 72, No. 3, pp. 423-444.

Bulmer, S. (1998). New institutionalism and the governance of the Single European Market. In: *Journal of European Public Policy*, Vol. 5 No. 3, pp. 365-86.

Burke, R. (1978). Introductory Address. In: *Transcripts of the Seatrade Conference "Towards a Shipping Policy for the EEC"*, Brussels, September 1978, pp. 9-36. Colchester: Seatrade.

Burley, A.M. and Mattli, W. (1993). Europe Before the Court: A political theory of Legal Integration. In: *International Organisation*, Vol. 47, No. 1, pp. 1-40.

Butt Philip, A. (1983). Pressure Groups and Policy-Making in the European Community. In: Lodge, J. (1983), pp. 21-26.

Butt Philip, A. (1985). *Pressure Groups in the European Community*, University Association for Contemporary European Papers (UACES), Occasional Papers No. 2.

Butt Philip, A. (1991) (ed.). *A Directory of Pressure Groups in the EC*. London: Longman.

Butt Philip, A. (1994). European Immigration Policy: Phantom, Fact or Fantasy? In: *West European Politics*, Vol. 17, No. 2, pp. 168-190.

Butt Philip, A. (1996). *Accountability and the European Union*. London: John Stuart Mill Institute.

Butt Philip, A. and Porter, M.H.A. (1995). *Business, Border Controls and the Single European Market: Free Movement of Goods in Europe?* London: Royal Institute of International Affairs.

Button, K.J. (1984). *Road Haulage Licensing, and EEC Transport Policy*. Aldershot: Gower.

Button, K.J. (1993). *Transport Economics* (2 edn). Aldershot: Edward Elgar.

Cafruny, A.W. (1987). *Ruling the waves: The Political Economy of International Shipping*. Berkeley: University of California Press.

Cafruny, A.W. (1991). Toward a Maritime Policy. In: Hurwitz, L. and Lequesne, C. (eds), *The State of the European Communities, vol. 1, policies, institutions and debates in the transition years*, pp. 285-299, Colorado: Lynne Rienner.

Cafruny, A.W. and Lankowski, C. (1997). Europe's Ambiguous Unity. In: idem, *Europe's Ambiguous Unity Conflict and Consensus in the Post-Maastricht era*, pp. 1-21. Colorado: Lynne Rienner.

Cafruny, A.W. and Rosenthal, G.G. (1993). The State of the European Community: Theory and Research in the Post-Maastricht Era. In: idem (eds), *The State of the European Community, vol. 2, the Maastricht debates and beyond*, pp. 1-18. Colorado: Lynne Rienner.

Calingeart, M. (1993). Government Business Relationship in the European Community. In: *California Management Review*, No. 35, pp. 118-133.

Caporaso, J.A. (1996). The European Union and Forms of State: Westphalian, Regulatory or Post-Modern. In: *Journal of Common Market Studies*, Vol. 34, No. 41 pp. 29-52.

Caporaso, J.A. (1998). Regional Integration Theory: Understanding our Past and Anticipating our Future. In: *Journal of European Public Policy*, Vol. 5, No. 1, pp. 12-16.

Caporaso, J.A. and Keller, J. (1995). The European Union and Regional Integration Theory. In: Mazey, S. and Rhodes, C. (eds), *The State of the European Union, volume 3, Building a European Policy*. pp. 29-62, Boulder: Longman.

Carlisle, R.P. (1981). *Sovereignty to Sale*. Annapolis: Naval Institute Press.

Caspers, F.N. and Ter Brugge, R. (1992). Logistic Requirement and Shortsea shipping. In: Winjnolst, N. *et al* (1993), pp. 40-51.

Chadwick, N. and Gleave, S.D. (1996). Strategic Environmental Assessment of Transport Infrastructure: The State of the Art. In: the *Proceedings of the 24th European Transport Forum, Seminar A: Pan-European Transport Issues*, London: PTRC.

Chlomoudis, C.I. and Pallis, A.A. (1996). Investment Policies in Ports' Infrastructure in the Perspective of the European Shortsea Shipping Networks: The Case of Greece. In: Peeters, C. and Wergeland, T. (1997), pp. 315-335.

Chlomoudis, C.I. and Pallis, A.A. (1997). Investments in Transport Infrastructure in Greece: Have the EU Initiatives Promoted their Balanced and Rational Distribution? In: *World Transport Policy and Practice*, Vol. 3, No. 4, p. 23-29.

Christiansen, T. (1996). A maturing bureaucracy? The role of the Commission in the policy process. In: Richardson, J.J. (1996a), pp. 77-95.

Cini, M. (1996). *The European Commission: Leadership, organisation and culture in the EU administration*. Manchester: Manchester University Press.

Clinton-Davis, Lord (1994). The UK, Europe and the global maritime trading system. In: *Marine Policy*, Vol. 18, No. 6, pp. 472-475.

Coombes, D. (1970). *Politics and Bureaucracy in the European Community*. London: Allen and Unwin.

Corbey, D. (1995). Dialectical functionalism: Stagnation as a booster of European Integration. In: *International Organisation*, Vol. 49, No 2, pp. 253-284.

Couper, A.D. (1977). Shipping Policies of the EEC. In: *Maritime Policy and Management*, Vol. 4, No. 2, pp. 129-139.

Couper, J. Browne, M. and Peters, M. (1991). *European logistics-market, management and Strategy*. Oxford: Blackwell.

Cram, L. (1994). The European Commission as a Multi-Organisation: Social Policy and IT policy in the EU. In: *Journal of the European Public Policy*, Vol. 1, No. 2, pp. 195-217.

Cram, L. (1996). Integration theory and the study of the European Policy process. In: Richardson, J.J. (1996a), pp. 40-60.

Crzanowski, I.H. (1985). *Introduction to Shipping Economics*. London: Fairplay Publications.

Dahl, R.A. (1961). *Modern Political Analysis*. New York: Prentice Hall.

Dahredorf, R. (1971). A New Goal for Europe. In: Hodge, M. (1972) (ed.), *European Integration*, pp. 265-284, Middlesex: Penguin.

Davies, M. (1992). *Belief in the Sea: State Encouragement of British Merchant Shipping and Shipbuilding*. London: Lloyd's of London Press.

De Dieu, J. (1996). Principal Administrator, Maritime Safety Unit Commission of the EU, Directorate General of Transport, *personal interview*. Brussels, 26 June.

De Villele, H. (1996). Secretary General, Committee of Transport Workers Union in the EC, *personal interview*. Brussels, 28 May.

De Weale, A. (1993). Epilogue. In: Polak, J. and Heertje, A. (1993), pp. 286-292.

Despicht, N. (1969). *The Transport Policy of the European Communities*. London: Chatham House.

Docksey, C. and Williams, K. (1994). The Commission and the Execution of the Community Policy. In: Edwards, G. and Spence, D. (1994), pp. 113-145.

Dowding, K. (2000). Institutional Research on the European Union: A Critical Review. In: *European Union Politics*, Vol. 1, No. 1, pp. 125-144.

Dunlavy, C.A. (1992). Political structure, state policy, and industrial change: Early railroad policy in the United States and Prussia. In: Steinmo *et al* (1992), pp. 155-187.

Economou, C. (1996). Executive Adviser, European Community Shipowners Association, *personal interview*, Brussels, 28 May.

Edwards, G. (1996). National Sovereignity vs. integration? The Council of Ministers. In: Richardson, J.J. (1996a), pp. 127-147.

Edwards, G. and Spence, D. (1994). *The European Commission*: London: Cartermill.

Erdmenger, J. (1983). *The European Community Transport Policy: Towards a Common Transport Policy*. Aldershot: Gower.

Erdmenger, J. and Stasinopoulos, D. (1988). The shipping policy of the European Community. In: *Journal of Transport Economics and Policy*, Vol. 22, Issue 3, pp 335-360.

Etzioni, A. (1965). *Political Unification. A Cooperative Study of Leaders and Forces*. New York: Holt, Rinehart and Winston.

Evans, P.B., Rueschemeyer, D. and Skocpol, T. (1985) (eds). *Bringing the State Back In*. Cambridge: Cambridge University Press.

Everard, M. (1995). *Coastal and Short Sea Shipping: An alternative to Road*. Reginald Grout Shipping Lecture, 11 April 1995, London.

Farthing, B. (1993). *International Shipping: An Introduction to the Policies, Politics and Institutions of the Maritime World* (2nd edn). London: Lloyd's of London Press.

Ferreira Da Rocha, J. (1996). Administrator, MIF Shortsea Shipping Panel Commission of the EU, Directorate General of Transport, *personal interview*. Brussels, 26 June.

Frankel, E.G. (1984). International Organisations in Marine Affairs. Shipping: Redefining functions. In: *Marine Policy*, Vol. 8, No. 2, pp. 165-170.

Frankel, E.G. (1987). *World Shipping Industry*. London: Groom Helm.

Garrett, G. (1992). International Cooperation and Institutional Choice. The EC's Internal market. In: *International Organisation*, Vol. 49, No. 1, pp. 17-81.

Garrett, G. and Tsebelis, G. (1996). An institutional critique of intergovernmentalism. In: *International Organisation*, Vol. 50, No. 2, pp. 269-299.

George, S. (1991). *Politics and Policy in the European Community* (2nd edn). Oxford: Clarendon.

Gönenç, R. (1994). A New approach to Industrial Policy. In: *OECD Observer*, No. 187, pp. 16-19, Paris: OECD.

Gorges, M.J. (1993). Interest Intermediation in the EC After Maastricht. In: Cafruny, A.W. and Rosenthal, G.G. (1993), pp. 73-89.

Gorges, M.J. (1997). Interest Groups, European Integration, and the New Institutionalism. A Paper delivered at the *5th Conference of the European Community Studies Association*, May 1997, Seattle, US.

Goss, R.O. (1968). *Studies in Maritime Economics*. London: Cambridge University Press.

Goss, R.O. (1977). *Advances in Maritime Economics*. London: Cambridge University Press.

Goss, R.O. (1989). Sense and Shipping Policies. In: Yannopoulos, G.N. (1989), pp. 61-87.

Goss, R.O. (1994). *Safety in Sea Transport*. In: *Journal of Transport Economics and Policy*, Vol. 28, No. 1, pp. 99-110.

Goss, R.O. and Marlow, P.B. (1992). Internationalism, Protectionism and Interventionism in Shipping. In: Gwilliam, K.M. (1992), pp. 45-67.

Goss, R.O., Nicholls, C. and Pettit, S.J. (1991). Seamen's Accidental Deaths and Injuries Worldwide: a Methodology and some estimates. In: *Journal of the Royal Institute of Navigation*, Vol. 44, No, 2, pp. 271-276.

Goulielmos, A. (1995). Secretary General, Greek Ministry of Mercantile Marine, *personal interview*. Piraeus, 21 July.

Gourevitch, P.A. (1986). *Politics in Hard Times*. Ithaca New York: Cornell University Press.

Grande, E. (1996). The state and interest groups in a framework of multi-level decision-making: the case of the European Union. In: *Journal of European Public Policy*, Vol. 3, No. 3, pp. 318-338.

Grant, W. (1993). Pressure Groups and the European Community: An overview. In Mazey, S. and Richardson, J.J. (1993a), pp. 27-46.

Greenwood, J. (1995). *European Casebook on Business Alliances*. London: Prentice Hall.

Greenwood, J. and Aspinwall, M. (1998) (eds). *Collective action in the European Union. Interests and the new politics of associability*. London: Routledge.

Greenwood, J. and Cram, L. (1996). European Level Business Collective Action: The Study Agenda Ahead. In: *Journal of Common Market Studies*, Vol. 34, No. 3, pp. 143-156.

Greenwood, J. and Ronit, K. (1994). Interest Groups in the European Community: Newly Emerging Dynamics and Forms. In: *West European Politics*, Vol. 17, No. 1, pp. 31-52.

Greenwood, J., Grote, J.R., and Ronit, K. (1992) (eds). *Organised interests and the European Community*. London: Sage.

Grilley, J. and Dean, C.J. (1992). Shortsea Shipping and the World Cargo carrying fleet: A Statistical Summary. In: Winjnolst, N. *et al* (1993a), pp. 1-21.

Gubbins, E.J. (1986). *The Shipping Industry: The Technology and Economics of Specialisation*. London: Gordon and Breach.

Gwilliam, K.M. (1979). Transport Infrastructure, Investment and Regional Development. In: Bowers, J.K. (1979) (ed.), *Inflation Development and Integration*, pp. 244-262, Leeds: Leeds University Press.

Gwilliam, K.M. (1980). Realism and the Common Transport Policy of the EEC. In: van der Kamp, J.B. and Polak, J.B. (1980), pp. 38-59.

Gwilliam, K.M. (1990). The Common Transport Policy. In: El-Agraa, A.M. (ed.), *The Economics of the European Community* (3rd edn), pp. 230-242. London: Harvester Wheatsheaf.

Haas, E.B. (1958). *The Uniting of Europe: Political Social and Economic Forces, 1950-1957*. London: Stevens.

Haas, E.B. (1976). *The Obsolescence of Regional Integration theory*. Berkley: Institute of International Studies.

Hall, P.A. (1986). *Governing the Economy: The Politics of State Intervention in Britain and France*. Cambridge: Polity.

Hall, P.A. (1989). *The Political Powers of Economic Ideas*. New Jersey: Princeton University Press.

Hall, P.A. (1992). The movement from Keynesianism to monetarism: Institutional analysis and British economic policy in the 1970s. In: Steinmo *et al* (1992), pp. 114-154.

Hall, P.A. and Taylor, R.C.R. (1996). Political Science and the Three New Institutionalisms. In: *Political Sciences*, Vol. XLIV, pp. 936-957.

Hammond-Suddards (1994). *The European Parliament comes of Age: The Anatomy of the Post-Maastricht European Parliament*. Brussels.

Harrison, R. (1974). *Europe in Question*. London: Allen and Unwin.

Hart, P. (1993). State aid and the Shipping Industry: A European Community analysis. In: idem *et al* (1993), pp 42-81.

Hart, P., Ledger, G., Smith, B. and Roe, M. (1993). *Shipping Policy in the EC*. Aldershot: Avebury.

Hart, T. (1994). Transport Choices and Sustainability: A review of changing Trends and Policies. In: *Urban Studies*, Vol. 31, Nos. 4/5, pp. 705-727.

Hatsakos, S. (1996). Director of the European Bureau, Piraeus Port Authority, *personal interview*. Piraeus, 30 August.

Hayes-Renshaw, F. and Wallace, H. (1997). *The Council of Ministers*. London: Macmillan

Hayes-Renshaw, F. Lequesne, C. and Lopez, P.M. (1989). The Permanent representations of the member states to the European Communities. In: *Journal of Common Market Studies*, Vol. 28, No. 2, pp. 119-137.

Hayman, C. (1978). EEC Shipping Policy: In search of a common ground. In: Seatrade (1978). *EEC Shipping 1978*. Colchester: Seatrade.

Healey, N.M. (1995). From the Rome Treaty to Maastricht: The Theory and Practice of European Integration. In: idem (ed.), *The Economics of The New Europe: From Community to Union*, pp. 1-41. London: Routledge.

Héretier, A. (1996). The accommodation of diversity in European policy making and outcomes: regulatory policy as a patchwork. In: *Journal of European Public Policy*, Vol. 3, No. 2, 149-67.

Herman, A. (1983). *Shipping Conferences*. London: Lloyd's of London Press.

Hindell, K. (1996). Strengthening the ship regulating regime. In: *Maritime Policy and Management*, Vol. 23, No. 4, 371-80.

Hix, S. (1994). The Study of the European Community: The Challenge to Comparative Politics. In: *West European Politics*, Vol. 17, No. 1, pp. 1-30.

Hix, S. (1996). CP, IR, and the EU! A Rejoinder to Hurrell and Menon. In: *West European Politics*, Vol. 19, No. 4, pp. 802-804.

Hix, S. (1999). *The Political system of the European Union*. Basingstoke: Macmillan.

Hoffmann, S. (1964). The European Process at Atlantic Crosspurposes. In: *Journal of Common Market*, Vol. 3, pp. 85-101.

Hoffmann, S. (1966). Obstinate or Obsolete? The fate of the Nation State and the Case of Western Europe. In: *Daedalus*, Vol. 95, pp. 892-908.

Hoffmann, S. (1982). Reflections of the Nation State in Western Europe Today. In: *Journal of Common Market*, Vol. 21, No. 1, pp. 21-37.

Hoffmann, S. (1989). The European Community and 1992. In: *Foreign Affairs*, No. 68, pp. 27-47.

Hooghe L. (1996). *Cohesion Policy and European Integration: Building Multilevel Governance*. Oxford: Oxford University Press.

Hooghe, L. and Marks, G. (1997). Contending Models of Governance in the European Union. In: Cafruny, A.W. and Lankowski, C. (1997), pp. 21-44.

Hurrell, A. and Menon, A. (1996). Politics Like Any Other? Comparative Politics, International Relations and the Study of the EU. In: *West European Politics*, Vol. 19, No. 2, pp. 386-402.

Ioakimidis, P.K. (1993). *European Political Union, Theory, Negotiation, Institutions, and Politics. The Maastricht Treaty and Greece* (in Greek). Athens: Themelio.

Jacobs, F., Gorbett, R. and Shackleton, M. (1995). *European Parliament* (3rd edn). London: Cartermill.

Jeffery, D.J. (1996). Chief Executive, Port of London Authority and Vice President of ESPO, *personal interview*. London, 1 May.

Jessop, B. (1993). Post-Fordism and the State. In: Amin A. (1993), p. 251-279.

Jones, M. (1996). Transport Policy Issues Division, Permanent Representation of the UK to the EU, *personal interview*. Brussels, 29 May.

Jonston, G. (1996). Executive Director, The UK Major Ports Group and Member of the MIF Shortsea Panel, *personal interview*. London, 7 May.

Jordan, G. (1990). Policy community Realism *versus* 'New' Institutionalist Ambiguity. In: *Political Studies*, Vol. 38, No. 1, pp. 34-48.

Judge, D. Earnshaw, D. and Cowan, N. (1994). Ripples or Waves: The European Parliament in the European Community Policy Process. In: *Journal of European Public Policy*, Vol. 1, No. 1, pp. 27-52.

Kappel, R. (1988). *The Norwegian International Ship Register; A new approach of a traditional shipping nation*. Bremen: Institute of Shipping Economics and Logistics.

Keohane, R.O. (1984). *After Hegemony: Cooperation and Discord in the World Political Economy*. New Jersey: Princeton University Press.

Keohane, R.O. (1986). *Neorealism and Its Critics*. Columbia University Press.

Keohane, R.O. and Hoffmann, S. (1991a). Institutional Change in Europe in the 1980s. In: idem (1991b), pp. 1-39.

Keohane, R.O. and Hoffmann, S. (1991b) (eds). The New European Community: Decision making and Institutional Change. Boulder: Westview.

Keohane, R.O. and Nye, J.S. (1972) (eds). *Transnational Relations and World Politics*. Cambridge Massachusetts: Harvard University Press.

Keohane, R.O. and Nye, J.S. (1977). *Power and Interdependence*. Boston: Little Brown.

Kessides, C. (1993). The contributions of Infrastructure to Economic Development. *World Bank Discussion Papers*, No. 213, Washington DC: World Bank.

Kingdon, J.W. (1984). *Agendas Alternatives and Public Policies*. New York: HarperCollins.

Kirchner, E.J. (1992). *Decision-making in the EC: The Council Presidency and European Integration*. Manchester: Manchester University Press.

Knudsen, O. (1973). *The Politics of International Shipping*. Toronto: Lexington Book.

Koelble, T.A. (1995). The New Institutionalism in Political Science and Sociology. In: *Comparative Politics*, Vol. 27, No. 2, pp. 231-243.

Krommenacker, R.J. (1989). Maritime Transport Services in the Uruguay Round. In: Yannopoulos, G.N. (1989), pp. 188-203.

Kuypers, G. (1980). Transport policy and politics. In: van der Kamp, J.B. and Polak, J.B. (1980), pp. 145-159.

La Saponara, F. (1993). Shortsea Shipping in Europe and Maritime Market Changes in the Nineties. In: ECMT (1993), pp. 9-58.

Laino, S. (1996). UK Association of Private Terminal Ports, *personal interview*. London, 20 May.

Laursen, F. (1982). *Superpower at Sea*. The Hague: Martinus Nihjoff.

Lawrence, S.A. (1972). *Sea Transport: The Years ahead*. Toronto: Lexington Book.

Ledger, G. and Roe, M. (1992). The decline of the UK merchant fleet: an assessment of government policies in recent years. In: *Journal of Maritime Policy and Management*, Vol. 19, No. 3, pp. 239-251.

Lee, N. and Hughes, J. (1995). *Strategic Environmental Assessment: Legislation and Procedures in the Community*. University of Manchester: EIA Centre.

Lindberg, L.N. (1963). *The Political Dynamics of European Economic Integration*. California: Stanford University Press.

Lindberg, L.N. and Scheingold, S. (1970). *Europe's Would-be Polity*. Practice Hall.

Lindblom, C.E. (1968). *The Policy Making Process*. New Jersey: Prentice Hall.

Lindblom, C.E. (1977). *Politics and Markets*. New York: Basic Books.

Lintner, V. and Mazey, S. (1991). *The European Community: Economic and Political Aspects*. London: McGraw-Hill.

Lodge, J. (1989) (ed.). *The European Community and the Challenge of the future*. London: Pinter.

Machpul, F. (1977). *A History of Thought on Economic Integration*. London: Macmillan.

Majone, G. (1993). The European Community: Between Social Policy and Social Regulation. In: *Journal of Common Market Studies*, Vol. 31, No. 2, 153-169.

Mann, M. (1996). Head of Economics, Aviation, Maritime and International Unit, Department of Transport, *personal interview*. London, 25 July.

March, J.G. and Olsen, J.P. (1984). The New Institutionalism. In: *American Political Science Review*, Vol. 7, pp. 734-749.

March, J.G. and Olsen, J.P. (1989). *Rediscovering Institutions: The Organisational Basis of Politics*, New York: Free Press.

Marks, G. (1993). Structural Policy After Maastricht. In: Cafruny A. and Rosenthal, G. (eds) (1993), pp. 391-410.

Marks, G., Hooghe, L. and Blank, K. (1996). European Integration from the 1980s: State-Centric v. Multi-level Governance. In: *Journal of Common Market Studies*, Vol. 34, No. 3, pp. 341-378.

Mavrommati, K. (1996). Maritime Policy Committee Hellenic Chamber of Shipping, *personal interview*. Piraeus, 20 July.

Mazey, S. and Richardson, J.J. (1993) (eds). *Lobbying in the European Community*, Oxford: Oxford University Press.

Mazey, S. and Richardson, J.J. (1994). The Commission and the Lobby. In Edwards, G. and Spence, D. (1994), pp. 169-201.

Mazey, S. and Richardson, J.J. (1996). The logic of Organisation: Interest Groups. In: Richardson, J.J. (1996a), pp. 200-215.

McKinnon, A. (1989). *Physical distribution systems*. London: Routledge.

McLaughlin, A.M. and Greenwood, J. (1995). The Management of Interests Representation in the European Union. In: *Journal of Common Market Studies*, Vol. 33, No. 1, pp. 143-156.

McLaughlin, A.M., Jordan, G. and Maloney, W.A. (1993). Corporate Lobbying in the European Community. In: *Journal of Common Market Studies*, Vol. 31, No. 2, pp. 191-212.

Meady, J. (1955). *The Theory of International Economic Policy*. London: Oxford University Press.

Menindrou, M. (1994). European Community fraud and the politics of Institutional development. In: *European Journal of Political Research*, Vol. 26, No. 1, pp. 81-101.

Mény, Y., Muller, P. and Quermonne, J. (1996). *Adjusting to Europe The Impact of the European Union on national institutions and policies*. London: Routledge.

Milward, A.S. (1992). The European Rescue of the Nation-State. London: Routledge.

Molle, W. (2001). *The Economics of European Integration: theory, practice, policy* (4 edn), Aldershot: Ashgate.

Morales, A. and Theander, M. (1996). Head and Administrator, Ports Unit Commission of the EU, Directorate General of Transport, *personal interview*. Brussels, 26 June.

Moravcsik, A. (1991). Negotiating the Single European Act: National Interests and Conventional Statecraft in the European Community. In: *International Organisation*, Vol. 45, No. 1, pp. 19-56.

Moravcsik, A. (1992). *National Preference Formation and Interstate Bargaining in the European Community, 1955-89*. Massachusetts: Harvard University Press.

Moravcsik, A. (1993). Preferences and Power in the European Community: A Liberal Intergovernmentalism Approach. In: *Journal of Common Market Studies*, Vol. 31, No. 4, pp. 473-524.

Moravcsik, A. (1995). Liberal Intergovernmentalism and Integration: A Rejoinder. In: *Journal of Common Market Studies*, Vol. 33, No. 4, pp. 611-628.

Moravcsik, A. (1998). *The Choice for Europe: Social Purpose and Sate Power From Messina to Maastricht*. New York: Cornell University Press.

Morgethau (1948, 1966). *Politics among Nations: the Struggle for Power and Peace*. New York: Knopf.

Muheim, J.F. (1978). EEC Shipping Policy and the European Shipper. In: *Transcripts of the Seatrade Conference "Towards a Shipping Policy for the EEC"*, *Brussels, September 1978*, pp. 37-47. Colchester: Seatrade.

Mutimer, D. (1994). Theories of Political Integration. In: Michelmann, H.J. and Soldatos, P. (eds), *European Integration: Theories and Approaches*, pp. 13-42, Boston: University Press of America.

Nielsen, J.U.M., Heinrich, H. and Hansen, J.D. (1992). *Economic Analysis of the EC* (2nd edn). Berkshire: McGraw-Hill.

Norgaard, A.S. (1996). Rediscovering reasonable rationality in institutional analysis. In: *European Journal of Political Research*, Vol. 29, No. 1, pp. 31-57.

Northrup, H.R. and Scrace, P.B. (1996). The International Transport Workers' Federation Flag of Convenience Campaign. In: *Transportation Law Journal*, Vol. 23, Part 3, pp. 369-423.

O'Neil, M. (1996). *The Politics of European Integration*. London: Routledge.

Orrell, B. (1996). Secretary General, National Union of Marine and Shipping Transport Workers and President of the CTWUEC Maritime Section, personal interview. London, 16 July.

Page, E.C. (1995). Administrating Europe. In: Hayward, J. and Page, E.C. (eds), *Governing the New Europe*, pp. 257-286, Cambridge: Polity Press.

Pallis, A.A. (1997). Towards a Common Ports Policy? EU-Proposals and the Industry's Perceptions. In: *Maritime Policy and Management*, Vol. 24, No. 4, 365-380.

Pallis A.A. and Chlomoudis, C.I. (2001). *Towards a European Port Policy: The Port industry in a sustainable mobility prospective* (in Greek). Athens: Hellenic Letters.

Papanikolaou, A. and Vassalos, D. (2001). Enhanced Safety Requirements for European Ro-Ro Passenger Ships: The Stockholm Agreement: Past, Present and Future. In: *Proceeding of the Second International Conference on Safety of Maritime Transport*, June, Chios, Greece.

Peeters, C. and Wergeland, T. (1997) (eds). *European Shortsea Shipping Proceedings from the 3rd European Research Roundtable on Shortsea Shipping*. The Netherlands: Delft University Press.

Peeters, C., Verdee, A., Declercq, E., and Winjnolst, N. (1995). *Analysis of the Competitive Position of Short Sea Shipping*. Delft: Delft University Press.

Pelkmans, J. (1984). *Market Integration in the European Community*. The Hague: Martinus Nijhoff.

Pentheroudakis, N. (1995). President, Hellenic Shipbrokers Association, personal interview. Piraeus, 11 July.

Peppa, K. (1996). Union of Greek Shipowners, *personal interview*. Piraeus, 11 July.

Pesquera, M.A. and De La Hoz, L. (1992). EDI Key for shortsea shipping development: the Arcantel platform. In: Winjnolst, N. *et al* (1993b), pp. 193-210.

Peters, B.G. (1992). Bureaucratic Politics and the Institutions of the EC. In: Sbragia, A.M. (1992), pp. 75-122.

Peters, B.G. (1994). Agenda-Setting in the European Community. In: *Journal of European Public Policy*, Vol. 1, No. 1, pp. 9-26.

Peters, B.G. (1998). *Comparative Politics: Theory and Method*. London: Macmillan.

Peters, H.J. (1989). *Seatrade Logistics and Transport*. World Bank Policy Research Series, No. 6, Washington DC: World Bank.

Peters, H.J. (1993). *The Maritime Transport crisis*. World Bank Discussions Papers, No. 220, Washington DC: World Bank.

Peterson, J. (1995). Decision making in the European Union: towards a framework for analysis. In: *Journal of European Public Policy*, Vol. 2, No. 1, 69-93.

Peterson, J. and Bomberg, E. (1999). *Decision-Making in the European Union*. Basingstoke: Macmillan.

Pickering, J.F. and Matthews, D. (1997). *Industry, Regulation, and the Single European Market*. London: National Institute of Economic and Social Research.

Pierson, P. (1993). When effects become cause: Policy feedback and political change. In: World Politics, Vol. 45 No. 4, pp. 595-628.

Pierson, P. (1996). The Path to European Integration: An Historical Institutionalist Perspective. In: *Comparative Political Studies*, Vol. 29, pp. 123-163.

Pinder, J. (1991). *European Community: The Building of a Union*. London: Oxford University Press.

Polak, J.B. and Heertje, A. (1993) (eds). *European Transport Economics*. Oxford: Blackwell.

Pollack, M.A. (1997). Delegation, agency, and agenda setting in the European Community. In: *International Organisation*, Vol. 51, No. 1, pp. 99-134.

Porter, M.H.A. (1995). *Interest Groups Advocacy Coalition and the EC Environmental Policy Process: A Policy Network Analysis of the Packaging and Packaging Waste Directive*. Unpublished PhD Thesis registered at the University of Bath, UK.

Power, V. (1992). *The EC Shipping Law*. London: Lloyd's of London Press.

Putnam, R.O. (1988). Diplomacy and Domestic Politics: the Logic of Two-Level Games. In: *International Organisation*, Vol. 43, No. 2, pp. 427-460.

Rhodes, R.A.W. (1995). The Institutional Approach. In: Marsh, D. and Stoke, G. (eds), *Theory and Methods in Political Science*, pp. 42-57. London: Macmillan.

Rhodes, R.A.W. and March, D. (1992). New Direction in the Study of Policy Networks, In: *European Journal of Political Research*. Vol. 21, No. 1, pp. 181-205.

Richards, M. (1996). Secretary, British Shippers' Council, *personal interview*. Tunbridge Wells, 7 June.

Richardson, J.J. (1996a) (ed). *European Union: Power and Policy Making*. London: Routledge.

Richardson, J.J. (1996b). Policy-making in the EU. Interests, ideas and garbage cans of primeval soup. In: idem (1996a), pp. 3-23.

Risse-Kappen, T. (1995) (ed.). *Bringing transnational relations back in*. Cambridge: Cambridge University Press.

Risse-Kappen, T. (1996). Exploring the Nature of the Beast: International Relations Theory and Comparative Policy Analysis Meet the European Union. In: *Journal of Common Market Studies*, Vol. 34, No. 1, pp. 53-79.

Roe, M. (1996). Recent Aspect of the EU maritime transport policy. A Comment on the paper by Theo Kiriazidis and George Tzanidakis. In: *Journal of Maritime Policy and Management*, Vol. 23, No. 1, pp. 81-83.

Ronit, K. (1995). European Action of Organised Shipping: Global and National Constraints. In: Greenwood, J. (1995), pp. 184-194.

Ross, J.F.L. (1994). High-Speed Rail: Catalyst for European Integration?. In: *Journal of Common Market Studies*, Vol. 32, No. 2, pp. 191-214.

Rothery, B. (1993). *What Maastricht means for Business*. London: Gower.

Sabatier, P.A. (1988). An Advocacy Coalition Framework of Policy Change and the Role of Policy Oriented learning Therein. In: *Policy Sciences*, Vol. 21, No.2, pp. 129-168.

Sandholtz, W. (1993). Institutions and Collective Action: The New Telecommunications in Western Europe. In: *World Politics*, No. 43, pp. 242-270.

Sandholtz, W. (1996). Membership Matters: Limits of the Functional approach to European Institutions. In: *Journal of Common Market Studies*, Vol. 34, No. 3, pp. 403-429.

Sandholtz, W. and Zysman, J. (1989). 1992: Recasting the European Bargain. In: *World Politics*, Vol. 41, No. 1, pp. 95-128.

Sangster, T. (1996). Director General British International Freight Association, *personal interview*. Feltham Middlesex, 17 May.

Sarlis, P. (1996). Co-ordinator of the Committee for Transport and Tourism, European Parliament, *personal interview*. Brussels, 27 June.

Sbragia, A. (1992) (ed.). *Euro-Politics: Institutions and Policymaking in the 'New European Community*. Washington DC: The Brooking Institution.

Sbragia, A. (1996). From "Nation-State" to "Member-State": The Evolution of the European Community. In: Lützeler, P.M. (ed.) (1996), *Europe after Maastricht: American and European Perspectives*, pp. 69-87. Oxford: Berghahn.

Scharpf, F.W. (1994). Community and autonomy: multi-level policy-making in the European Union. In: *Journal of European Public Policy*, Vol. 1, No. 2, pp. 219-242.

Schmitter, P.C. (1970). A revised theory of Regional integration. In: *International Organisation*, Vol. 24, No. 4, pp. 836-868.

Schneider, V., Dang-Nguen, G. and Werle, R. (1994). Corporate Actor Networks in European Policy-Making: Harmonising Telecommunications Policy. In: *Journal of Common Market Studies*, Vol. 32, No. 4, pp. 473-498.

Seatrade (1996). *Conference Papers of the 1995 Tanker Industry Convention, London, UK*. Colchester: Seatrade.

Seidel, K. (1996). Executive Secretary Alliance of Maritime Regional Interests in Europe, *personal interview*. Brussels, 29 May.

Seidenfus, H.St. (1987). European ports in the context of the World economy and the European economy: Changes in sea transport. In: *International Journal of Transport Economy*, Vol. 14, No. 2, pp. 133-138.

Shier, E., Nabel, E. and Rifon, B. (1985). *Outlook for the Liberalisation of Maritime Transport*. London: Trade Policy Research Centre.

Skocpol, T. (1984). *Vision and method in Historical Sociology*. Cambridge: Cambridge University Press.

Sletmo, G.K. (1989). Shipping's fourth Wave: Ship management and Vernon's trade cycles. In: *Journal of Maritime Policy and Management*, Vol. 16, No. 4, pp. 293-303.

Sletmo, G.K. and Williams, E.W. (1981). *Liner Conferences in the Container Age: US policy at sea*. New York: Macmillan.

Slot, P.J. (1992). The EEC Shipping Policy. In: *Proceedings of the Law of the Sea 26th Annual Conference*, Genoa, Italy, pp. 489-525, Hawaii: University of Hawaii.

Smith, B. (1993). The European Community Ship Register. In: Hart, P. *et al* (1993), pp. 82-101.

Smith, S. (1995). *Voice of the People: The European Parliament in the 1990s*. London: The Royal Institute of International Affairs.

Southorn, A. (1996). International Policy, British Chamber of Shipping, *personal interview.* London, 1 May.

Spruyt, J. (1990). *Ship Management.* London: Lloyd's of London Press.

Steinmo, S., Thelen, K. and Longstreth, F. (1992) (eds). *Structuring politics. Historical institutionalism and comparative analysis.* New York: Cambridge University Press.

Steinvorth, W. (1996). Seafarers Section, International Transport Workers Federation, *personal interview.* London, 17 June.

Stokes, P. (1992). *Ship Finance.* London: Lloyd's of London Press.

Sturmey, G.K. (1975). *Shipping Economics: Collected Papers.* London: Macmillan.

Sturmey, S.G. (1962). *British Shipping and World Competition.* London: The Athlone Press.

Suykens, F. and Le Garrec, P. (1996). President and Secretary General, European Sea Ports Organisation, personal interview, Brussels 29 May.

Swann, D. (1988). *The Economics of the Common Market* (6th ed.). London: Penguin.

Taylor, P. (1983). *The limits of European Integration.* London: Groom Helm.

Taylor, P. (1996). *The European Community in the 1990s.* Oxford: Oxford University Press.

Teasdale, A. (1993). The life and death of the Luxembourg Compromise. In: *Journal of Common Market Studies,* Vol. 31, No. 4, pp. 567-579.

Thelen, K., and Steinmo, S. (1992). Historical Institutionalism in comparative analysis. In: Steinmo, S. *et al* (1992), pp. 1-32.

Thomas, B.J. (1994). The privatisation of United Kingdom seaports. In: *Journal of Maritime Policy and Management,* Vol. 21, No. 2, pp 135-148.

Tinsley, D. (1991). *Short-Sea Shipping: A Review of the North European Coastal Bulk Trades.* London: Lloyd's of London Press.

Tsebelis, G. (1994). The Power of the European Parliament as a Conditional Agenda Setter. In: *American Political Science Review,* Vol. 88, pp. 128-142.

Tselentis, A. (1996). Director of International Relations, Panhellenic Seamen's Federation, *personal interview.* Piraeus, 2 August.

Tsoukalis, L. (1993). *The New European Economy.* London: Oxford University Press.

Tzoannos, I.G. (1989). The EEC Common Maritime Policy and the liberalisation of world Shipping Markets. In: Yannopoulos, G.N. (1989), pp. 40-59.

Tzoannos, I.G. (1990). *European Integration and Commercial Shipping* (in Greek). Athens: Institute of Economic and Industrial Research.

van de Perre, M. (1996). Asistant Manager, European Liaison Committee of Freight Forwarders, *personal interview.* Brussels, 31 May.

van der Kamp, J.B. and Polak, J.B. (1980) (eds). *Changes in the field of Transport Studies: Essays on the Progress of Theory in relation to Policy making.* Hague: Martinus Nijhoff.

van Gent, H.A. and Kuyvenhoven, R.A. (1980). Professor J.B.P. Tissot van Patot: his approach to the theories of transport policy and spatial transport Economics. In: van der Kamp J.B. and Polak, J.B. (1980), pp. 26-37.

van Schendelen, M.P.C.M. (1993) (ed.). *The Relevance of National Public and Private EC Lobbying.* Aldershot: Dartmouth.

van Schendelen, M.P.C.M. (1996). 'The Council Decides': Does the Council Decide? In: *Journal of Common Market Studies,* Vol. 34, No. 4, pp. 531-548.

Vanroye, K. (1996). MIF Shortsea Panel Commission of the EU, Directorate General of Transport, *personal interview.* Brussels, 30 May.

Verhoeven, P. (1996). Secretary General, Federation of European Private Port Operators, *personal interview*. Brussels, 29 May.

Vermote, L. (1996). Director, Council of Ministers, Directorate II (Transport), *personal interview*, Brussels, 26 September.

Vickerman, R.W. (1992). *The Single European market*. London: Harvester Wheatsheaf.

Vickerman, R.W. (1994a). Transport Infrastructure and Region Building in the European Community. In: *Journal of Common Market Studies*, Vol. 32, No. 1, pp. 1-24.

Viner, J. (1950). *The Customs Union Issue*. New York: Carnage Endowment for International Peace.

Wallace, H. and Wallace, W. (2000) (eds). *Policy Making in the European Union* (4d edn). Oxford: Oxford University Press.

Wallace, H., Wallace, W. and Webb, C. (1983) (eds). *Policy Making in the European Community* (2nd edn). Chichester: John Wiley.

Wallace, W. (1983). Less than a Federation, More than a Regime: The Community as a Political System. In: Wallace *et al* (1983), pp. 403-36.

Webb, C. (1983). Theoretical Perspectives and Problems. In: Wallace, H. *et al* (1983), pp. 1-42.

Weiler, J. (1982). Community Member states and European integration: Is the law relevant? In: *Journal of Common Market Studies*, Vol. 21, No. 1, pp. 39-56.

Wellens, K. and Borchardt, G. (1989). Soft Law in European Community Law. In: *European Law Review*, Vol. 14, No. 5, pp. 267-321.

Westlake, M. (1994). The Commission and the Parliament. In: Edwards, G. and Spence, D. (eds), pp. 225-248.

Westlake, M. (1995). *The Council of the European Union*. London: Cartermill.

Whitehead, D. (1996). Director, British Ports Association, *personal interview*. London, 7 May.

Whitelegg, J. (1988). *Transport Policy in the EEC*. London: Routledge.

Whitelegg, J. (1993). *Transport for a sustainable future: The case for Europe*. London: Belhaven.

Williamson, O.E. (1985). *The Economic Institutions of Capitalism*. New York: Free Press.

Wincott, D. (1995). Institutional Interaction and European Integration: Towards an Everyday Critique of Liberal Intergovernmentalism. In: *Journal of Common Market studies*, Vol. 33, No. 4, pp. 597-609.

Wincott, D. (1996). The Court of Justice and the European Policy process. In: Richardson, J.J. (1996a), pp. 170-186.

Windhoff-Héritier, A. (1991). Institutions Interests and Political Choices. In: Czada, R.M. and Windhoff-Héritier, A. (eds), *Political Choice: Institutions Rules and the Limits of Rationality*, pp. 27-52, Colorado: Westview.

Winjnolst, N., and Peeters, C. (1995) (eds). *European Shortsea Shipping, Proceedings from the Second European Research Roundtable Conference on Shortsea shipping*. London: Lloyd's of London Press.

Winjnolst, N., Peeters, C. and Liebman, P. (1993a) (eds). *European Shortsea Shipping*, Proceedings from the First European Research Roundtable Conference on Shortsea shipping. London: Lloyd's of London Press.

Winjnolst, N., Hoeven, H.B., Kleijwegt, C.J. and Sjöbris, A. (1993b). *Innovation in Shortsea Shipping*. Delft: Delft University Press.

Yannopoulos, G.N. (1988). The economics of flagging out. In: *Journal of Transport Economics and Policy*, Vol. 22, No. 2, pp. 197-207.

Yannopoulos, G.N. (1989) (ed.). *Shipping Policies for an Open World Economy.* Guildford: Biddles.

Zachcial, M. (1996). Land-sea Transport Flows in Europe. In: Peeters, C. and Wergeland, T. (1997), pp. 11-34.

Governmental Documents

Commission of the European Union

CEU (1961). Memorandum on the General Lines of a Common Transport Policy. Com (61)50. 10 April 1961.

CEU (1984). The European Community Transport Policy. Periodical 3/84.

CEU (1985a). Memorandum on the progress towards a Common Maritime Policy. Com (85)90, final. 14 March 1985.

CEU (1989a). A future for the Community Shipping Industry: measures to improve the operating conditions of Community shipping. Com (89)266, final. 3 August 1989.

CEU (1989b). Financial and fiscal measures concerning shipping operations with ships registered in the Community. SEC (89)921.

CEU (1990a). Implementation of the four Regulations in the field of maritime transport adopted by the Council on 22 December 1986. SEC (90)1594.

CEU (1990b). Report on the possibility of a group exception for shipping consortia agreements. Com (90)260, final. 18 June 1990.

CEU (1991a). New challenges for Maritime Industries. Com (91)335, final. 20 September 1991.

CEU (1991b). Amended proposal for a Council Regulation Applying the freedom to provide services to maritime transport within Member states. Com (91)54, final. 19 March 1991.

CEU (1992a). The Future Development of the Common Transport Policy. A global approach to the construction of a Community framework for sustainable mobility. Com (92)494, final. 10 April 1992.

CEU (1992b). Green Paper on the impact of transport on environment: A Community strategy for sustainable mobility. Com (92)46, final. 20 February 1992.

CEU (1992c). Communication and legislative proposals concerning the creation of a European combined transport network. Com (92)230, final. 11 June 1992.

CEU (1993a). A Common Policy for Safe Seas. Com (93)66, final. 24 February 1993.

CEU (1993b). Proposal for a Council Directive on the minimum level of training for maritime occupations. Com 93(217), final. 26 May 1993.

CEU (1993c). Proposal for a Council Regulation (EC) on the implementation of IMO Resolution A.747(18) on the application of tonnage measurement of ballast spaces in segregated ballast oil tankers. Com (93)468, final. 8 December 1993.

CEU (1993d). Towards the implementation of a comprehensive approach for the maritime industries: the first tangible results. Com (93)526, final. 4 November 1993.

CEU (1994). Amended proposal for a Council Directive on the minimum level of training for maritime occupations. Com (94)124, final. 21 April 1994.

CEU (1995a). The Development of Short Sea Shipping in Europe: Prospects and Challenges. Com(95)317, final. 5 July 1995.

CEU (1995b). Proposal for a Regulation on the safety management of Ro-Ro passenger vessels. Com 95(28), final. 13 February 1995.

CEU (1995c). Amended proposal for a Council Regulation on the Safety management of Ro-Ro passenger vessels. Com (95)286, final. 15 June 1995.

CEU (1995d). Opinion of the Commission on the amendments proposed by the European Parliament to the Council's common position on the proposal for a Council Regulation on the safety management of Ro-Ro passenger vessels. Com(95)667, final. 8 December 1995.

CEU (1995e). Report of the Commission to the Council on the Implementation of Regulation 3577/92 applying the principle of freedom to provide services to maritime transport within member states 1993-94. Com (95)383. 6 September 1995.

CEU (1996a). Maritime Strategy. Com(96)81, final. 13 March 1996.

CEU (1996b). Shaping Europe's Maritime Future: A Contribution to the Competitiveness of Europe's Maritime Future. Com (96)84, final. 13 March 1996.

CEU (1996c). Proposal for a Council Directive amending Directive 94/58/EC on the minimum level of training of seafarers. Com (96)470, final. 1 October 1996.

CEU (1996d). Proposal for a Council Directive on safety rules and standards for passenger ships. Com 96 (61), final. 5 March 1996.

CEU (1996e). Amended proposal for a Council directive on safety rules and standards for passenger ship. Com (96)536, final. 5 November 1996.

CEU (1998) Proposal for a Council Regulation (EC) amending Council Regulation No. 3577/92 applying the principle of freedom to provide services to maritime transport within Member States (maritime cabotage). Com (98)251, final. 9 July 1998.

CEU (2000a). Commission communication to Parliament and the Council on the safety of the seaborne oil trade. (2000)142, final. 21 March 2000.

CEU (2000b). Proposal for a regulation of the European Parliament and of the Council amending Regulation No. 3051/95 on the safety management of roll-on/roll-off passenger ferries. Com (2000)489, final. 19 December 2000.

CEU (2000c). Communication from the Commission to the European Parliament and the Council on a Second set of Community measures on maritime safety following the sinking of the oil tanker Erika. Com (2000)802 final. 6 December 2000.

CEU (2000d). Report on the implementation of Regulation 3577/92 applying the principle of freedom to provide services to maritime cabotage (1997-1998). Com (2000)99 final, 24 February 2000.

CEU-DG VII (1996a). *Structure and Organisation of Maritime Transport.*

CEU-DG VII (1996b). *Draft Report of a Study on the maritime professions in the EU.*

Core Group (1995). *"Core Group" on Maritime Transport Report on Proceedings.* Antwerp: Policy Research Corporation.

Committee of the Regions

CoR (1996). Opinion on the Communication from the Commission on the Development of Short Sea shipping in Europe: Prospects and Challenges. 17-18 January 1996.

Economic and Social Committee

Ecosoc (1980). Interest Groups and their Relations to the Economic and Social Committee.

Ecosoc (1985). Opinion on the Progress towards a Common Transport Policy: Maritime Transport. TRA/116.

Ecosoc (1989). Opinion on Positive measures for maritime transport. CES(89)1257.

Ecosoc (1993a). Opinion on the Commission Communication on the Future Development of the Common Transport Policy, CES(93)1006.

Ecosoc (1993b). Opinion on the Communication from the Commission on a common policy in safe seas, CES(93)1170.

Ecosoc (1993c). Opinion on the proposal for a Council Directive on the minimum level of training for maritime occupations, CES(93)1159.

Ecosoc (1994). Opinion on the proposal for a Council Regulation (EC) on the implementation of IMO Resolution A.747(18) on the application of tonnage measurement of ballast spaces in segregated ballast oil tankers. CES(94)746.

Ecosoc (1995). Opinion on the proposal for a Council Regulation on the Safety Management of Ro-Ro passenger vessels. CES (95)584.

Ecosoc (1996). Opinion on the Communication from the Commission on the Development of Short Sea shipping in Europe CES(96)93.

European Parliament

EP Doc. 5/77. Interim Report drawn up on behalf of the Committee on Regional Policy regional Planning and Transport n the Sea Transport Problems in the Community. Rapporteur: H. Seefeld.

EP Doc. A2-53/86. Report on the Regulatory Proposals included in the Commission's Memorandum on the progress towards a Common Maritime Policy. K. Stewart.

EP Doc. A2-95/86. Second Report on the Regulatory Proposals included in the Commission's Memorandum on the progress towards a Common Maritime Policy. K. Anastasopoulos.

EP Doc. A3-199/90. Report on the Commission's positive measures for maritime transport. P. Sarlis.

EP Doc. A3 111/93. Report on the European Maritime Industries. A. Donnelly.

EP Doc. A3-221/94. Report on the Proposal for a Council Regulation on the implementation of IMO Resolution A.747(18) on the application of tonnage measurement of ballast spaces in segregated ballast oil tankers. P. Sarlis.

EP Doc A3-68/94. Report of the Committee on Transport and Tourism on a common policy on safe seas. K. Stewart.

EP Doc A3-83/94. Report on the Proposal for a Council Directive on the minimum level of training for maritime occupations. P. Sarlis.

EP Doc A4-42/94. Recommendation for second reading on the common position of the of the Council on the proposal for a Council Directive on the minimum level of training for maritime occupations. P. Sarlis.

EP Doc. A4-41/94. Recommendation for second reading on the common position of the of the Council on the proposal for a Council Regulation on the implementation of IMO Resolution A.747(18) on the application of tonnage measurement of ballast spaces in segregated ballast oil tankers. P. Sarlis.

EP Doc. B 236/94. Resolution on the safety of ro-ro passenger ferries.

EP Doc. A4-115/95. Report on the Proposal for a Council Regulation on the Safety Management of Ro-Ro passenger vessels. K. Watts.

EP Doc. A4-288/95. Recommendation for second reading on the common position of the of the Council on the proposal for a Council Regulation on the Safety Management of ro-ro passenger vessels. K. Watts.

EP Doc A4 0167/96. Report on the Communication from the Commission on the Development of Short Sea shipping in Europe - Prospects and Challenges. N. Sindal.

Eurostat

Eurostat. *External trade by mode of transport.* Annual publication.
Eurostat. *Basic Statistics.* Annual publication.

Other Governmental Reports

Department of Transport Joint Working Group (1990). *British Shipping: challenges and opportunities*, London: HMSO.

ECMT (European Conference of Ministers of Transport) (1983). *Short Sea Shipping in the Economy of Inland Transport in Europe*. Report of the 60th Round Table on Transport Economics. Paris.

ECMT (1990). *Private and Public investment*. Report on the 81st Round Table on Transport Economics. Paris.

ECMT (1993). *Short Sea Shipping*. Report on the 89th Round Table on Transport Economics. Paris.

ECMT (1999), *Investments in transport infrastructure 1985-1995*. Paris.

ECMT. *Statistical Trends in Transport*. Annual publication. Paris.

House of Lords (1986). *European Maritime Transport Policy*. Select Committee on the European Communities, Session 1985-86. 9th Report, March.

OECD (1996). *Competitive Advantages Obtained by Some Shipowners as a Result of Non-observance of Applicable International Rules and Standards*. Paris.

OECD (2001). *Maritime Transport 2000*. Paris.

OECD. *Basic Indicators*, Annual publication. Paris.

Rochdale Report (1970). *Report of the Committee of Inquiry into Shipping* (named by its President Viscount Rochdale), CMND 4337, London: HMSO.

International Monetary Fund (1996). World Economic Outlook. Washington DC.

IMO Maritime Safety Committee. *Training and watchkeeping-Maritime education, training, and certification. Introduction in quality assurance principles*. Doc 62/INF 9, of 25.3.1993.

World Bank (1995). *World Development Report 1995*. Washington DC.

World Commission on Environment and Development (1987). *Our Common Future (The Bruntland Report)*. Oxford: Oxford University Press.

Non-Governmental Outputs

Interest Groups' Reports, Publications, and Official Statements

AMRIE (1995). *Progress Report Autumn 1995*. Brussels.

British Chamber of Shipping (1992). *Annual Report 1991*. London.

British Chamber of Shipping (1993). *Annual Report 1992-3*. London.

British Chamber of Shipping (1996). *Annual Report 1995*. London.

British Chamber of Shipping. *Shipping Factsheet*, quarterly publication. London.

Danish Shipowners Association, (1994). Danish Shipping 1994. Copenhagen.

ECSA (1993). *Shipping, safety and pollution prevention*. Brussels.

ECSA (1994). *Annual Report 1993*. Brussels.

ECSA (1995). *Annual Report 1994*. Brussels.

ECSA (1996). *Annual Report 1995*. Brussels.

ESPO (1995). *A Statement on European Sea Port Policy*. Brussels.

ESPO (1996). *Annual Report 1995*. Brussels.

FEPORT (1996). *Annual Report 1995*. Brussels.

Greek Shipping Cooperation Committee, (1995). *Annual Report 1993-4*. London.

Hellenic Chamber of Shipping. *Shipping Report*, quarterly publication. Piraeus.

ITF (1994a). *ITF Report: Activities 1990-1993*. London.

ITF (1994b). *European Transport policy: A trade union strategy*. London.

ITF (1996). *Flag of Convenience Campaign Clippings*. No 3, May 1996.

ITF. *Seafarers Bulletin*. London.

MIF (1993). Results of the Plenary Session, June 27th/28th Athens.

Union of Greek Shipowners (UGS) (1991). *Annual Report 1990*. Piraeus.

UGS (1994). *Annual Report 1993*. Piraeus.

UGS (1995). *Annual Report 1994*. Piraeus.

UGS (1996). *Annual Report 1995*. Piraeus.

Market Reports and Statistics

Fearnleys (2000). *Fearnleys Review 1999*. Oslo.

Group Transport 2000 Plus (1990). *Transport in a Fast Changing Europe*. A study prepared for the Commission of the EU. London.

Institute of London Underwriters (ILU) (1996). Casualty Statistics. London.

Institute of Shipping and Logistics (ISL) (1993). *Which role can Shortsea play in the accommodation of transport demand in the EU?* Bremen.

ISL. *Shipping Statistics and Market Review*, monthly publication. Bremen.

ISL. *Shipping Statistics Yearbook*. Bremen.

Lloyds' Register of Shipping. *Statistical Tables*. London.

MDS Transmodal. *European Container Freight Market: Containers by Sea*. Various editions. Chester, UK.